BATTLE
FOR THE
AMERICAN
MIND

ALSO BY PETE HEGSETH

*In the Arena: Good Citizens, a Great Republic, and
How One Speech Can Reinvigorate America*

American Crusade: Our Fight to Stay Free

Modern Warriors: Real Stories from Real Heroes

BATTLE FOR THE AMERICAN MIND

UPROOTING A CENTURY OF MISEDUCATION

PETE HEGSETH

WITH DAVID GOODWIN

BROADSIDE BOOKS
An Imprint of HarperCollinsPublishers

HarperCollins books may be purchased for educational, business, or sales promotional use. For information, please email the Special Markets Department at SPsales@harpercollins.com.

Broadside Books™ and the Broadside logo are trademarks of HarperCollins Publishers.

FIRST EDITION

Designed by Nancy Singer

Library of Congress Cataloging-in-Publication Data has been applied for.

ISBN 978-0-06-321504-7

22 23 24 25 26   LSC   10 9 8 7 6 5 4 3 2 1

To the parents who pioneered classical
Christian renewal, now forty years on

Only the educated are free.

—*Epictetus, Roman slave turned counselor to emperors*

CONTENTS

PREFACE

This work flows out of two very different journeys. Neither of these journeys originated in education, but then, this book is not just about education. It is about our freedom, our culture, and our families—and the quiet peril inflicted upon all three. Pete Hegseth's journey takes him through Ivy League colleges, Division 1 sports, military combat, and television news. My journey contrasts with Pete's experience—geographically and otherwise. I grew up in rural Idaho, went to state college, and spent my first decades in business and technology. Pete and I do share at least one experience: we were both educated in government schools, and both of us saw a problem. This prompted us to ask questions about some deep cultural fissures that have formed in our lifetimes. In the course of writing this book, the fissures have grown into a crevasse, and may threaten the future existence of America as a single nation.

More than a decade into my first career with tech company Hewlett-Packard, I had traveled and observed Europe and America, from Finland to Madrid, from New York to San Francisco. I did market research—specifically focus groups. From this experience, I noticed a curious disconnect between people's everyday lives and the stories they seemed to believe about life's big questions. I had friends who were atheists but lived noble family lives, sacrificing for a world created by random chance. Hmm . . . this perplexed me. I volunteered in church leadership, serving Christian college students, many of whom lived out beliefs that were inconsistent with the Bible we had studied together. They seemed shallow and unwilling or unable to connect the dots on big topics. Hmm . . . Christians and secularists seemed to live out the same story in their lives, more or less—myself included, in many ways. It was as if there were a powerful invisible force pulling both groups in the same direction.

When I first encountered classical Christian education in 1994, my wife, Stormy, and I joined a small group that eventually started The Ambrose School in Boise, Idaho. This was five years before our first child was born (she's now at a classical Christian college). Over the next two decades, I came to understand why people's stories did not correspond with their lifestyle—in both directions. In a word, it was called *paideia*. That invisible force I had noticed had a name. While I'm not an academic, I was a marketing analyst trained to size up anything's potential—whether it was a new product, a service, or an idea. In short order, I realized this word—*paideia*—was big. So big, that in 2003 I left my rising career in tech to help build a fledgling classical Christian school.

In this new career, I wanted to understand why classical Christian education mattered so much to so many people. Like me, many others had left lucrative professional careers to join the classical Christian school building project all over the country. As I talked to colleagues, it became clear that we had all seen the handwriting on the wall: Americans were increasingly diverging politically between "red" and "blue" states, but shared so much of everything else—from where they went to college, to what friends they had, to the goals they had in life, even to small things like the entertainment they enjoyed. This could not be stable. It could not last. So, I began a research project to find the answers.

After a guest lecture I attended on the Progressives, I took the elevator to the fourth floor of the library where I had been told to meet the archivist. I was searching for the source of a quote the lecturer had used. It included the word *plasticity*. Since I didn't have the exact citation, I asked to see every issue of *The New Republic* published between its founding in about 1914 and 1940. I expected a box of microfiche film. The archivist brought four stacks of magazines tied together with twine, and many more in cardboard boxes. They shed clouds of dust on the table.

This was going to take a while. But I had a plan that should shorten things a bit.

I planned to look at the table of contents for each issue on the topic of "education" and scan the articles with a portable scanner. I soon realized education appeared in nearly every issue—and often as a centerpiece. John Dewey, father of modern progressive education, wrote often. But the editorial board was almost as active and revealing about their intent. This was the first clue that the Progressives were far more interested in K–12 education than I thought. I later found out they essentially invented it, at least as we know it today.

The sun went down outside, unbeknownst to me. As I worked my way back to the elevators, a sign jutted out from a row of shelves simply labeled "education." All day, I had been just feet from this section. I was sure some academic must have already researched this topic, if only I could find it. I glanced at the clock and saw that I had fifteen minutes before closing. I walked into the aisle.

The section labeled "educational history" drew my attention. As I pulled book after book off the shelf, I looked at the authors' bios:

"Educational Doctorate," "U.S. Department of Education," "Professor of Education." Clearly, progressive educators were the ones writing about education's history. I took a few out. There wasn't much new in what I quickly fanned through. It seemed analogous to reading the story of the Bolshevik Revolution as told by Lenin. But I had been avoiding the thickest books on the shelf—three of them.

Finally, I opened the first of the three thick volumes of Lawrence Cremin's *American Education*. Cremin was an historian. One of the volumes had a seal on the dust cover that read "Pulitzer Prize." His bio said he was at Columbia University. This sounded promising. A quick internet search revealed that his revelations about the history of American education made progressive educators uneasy. Yet, rarely had I read such a well-sourced and thorough history of anything. Why was the educational establishment critical of Cremin's work?

Somewhere in the second volume, Cremin landed on the missing center around which all of those thinkers I had read thus far had orbited. You'll find the quote in Chapter 5 of this book. My research on the Progressives snapped into alignment. I had been looking for what the Progressives did; I wanted to know how they informed the "plasticity of the child." I had not imagined that they simply removed an ingredient. Nor did I imagine that any ingredient could possibly have been that significant.

Cremin used an unusual word—*paideia*. I went on to research this word and it opened a narrative that cast light into nearly every corner of our current situation. Research led me to scholarship on ancient Rome and Greece, America's founding, the changes to Christianity in the nineteenth century, and many more dusty library corners. I read another three-volume set by Harvard scholar Werner Jaeger, describing one single word—*paideia*. The reason for the discord in the lives of Americans and America's cultural decline came into view.

Early in 2020, I was introduced to Pete Hegseth. In my work for the Association of Classical Christian Schools, I'm often asked education-related questions by the media. Pete was the first member of the media to actually take up a shovel and dig for answers. He asked more and more questions. I sent him a few chapters of a draft manuscript I had written to provide him with in-depth answers. In the months that followed, Pete would call and say, "Do you really mean that . . . ?" It usually had something to do with the American founders, or some aha moment. At some point he said, "We have to get this story out. What can I do to help?" In the subsequent year, I consulted on a five-part documentary for FOX Nation called *The MisEducation of America*.

Our collaboration on this book project emerged because of our very different backgrounds. Pete lives among media and cultural leaders in New York and the eastern seaboard. But he also spends a lot of time in the heartland with *FOX & Friends*, talking to Americans who can sense something is off. My research, paired with his knack for communicating with Americans, launched this book project—to connect the twenty-four-hour news cycle with the deep and unexpected answers that our journeys uncovered.

Neither of us is an academic with a PhD. But we are Americans, working to preserve the right to share what we've learned. This book offers an explanation for our nation's biggest problems while it finds a path forward rooted in our smallest citizens. Perhaps it's better that way. Perhaps it takes flawed regular guys to find something that was right there in front of us, but no one seemed to see. I pray that God will use this work to heal America.

To keep things simple for the reader, Pete narrates this work in the first person, using his talents as a writer, investigator, and thinker. As the project unfolded, my historical and Christian research and insight was buttressed by Pete's own research on the course of politics and life in the twentieth and twenty-first centuries. The two voices come together as Pete investigates his growing list of questions and I feed him my research about Christianity, America's founding, history, and education, filling in the gaps with my years of experience in running and building schools. With his military background, he could see the "Battle for the American Mind" unfold. And with his experience in military counterinsurgency, he could see what needs to be done. Together, our goal is to connect this important, untold story with the reality on the ground in America today.

—*David Goodwin*

INTRODUCTION

This ambitious project is approached with humility and a full reckoning of human nature.

It is my brokenness that brings me to this book. Our brokenness. Nothing but the grace of our Lord and Savior Jesus Christ affords these two authors—Pete Hegseth (me) and David Goodwin—the sufficiency to undertake such an audacious task: writing a book that motivates others to reorient their lives around the education of their most precious gift—their children and grandchildren.

We, like everyone, are failed and fallen vessels. A fallen world, and our sinful nature, have taken their toll on our lives—in different ways, each. We do not approach this weighty topic positioning ourselves as ideal examples of parents or educators, but instead with an appeal to heaven to breathe timeless truths into this earthly work.

The insufficient quality of our own educations—in the classroom, and in life—is the inspiration for this work. Our humility about the past is what informs our hope for the future. If anything, we cannot think of two people *less* worthy to write this book. Our own winding paths inform the future we want for our kids—wiser choices, more intentional personal formation, and Christ at the center in the class-room. Not to mention the future we want for our country. We both stumbled our way to the mission of this book, and today hope that others will find their bearings sooner, saving our providential Republic in the process.

We are an unlikely duo. I live in the East Coast media world, of-ten embroiled in news of the day and incentivized by instant analysis. David lives in Idaho and has quietly and effectively immersed himself into the world of education. You might know me from your television set, but without David this book never happens. Think Indiana Jones (Harrison Ford) and his father (Sean Connery) on a quest to rediscover the holy grail—in this case, the holy grail of education.

Like Sean Connery and his dusty diary, David has dedicated his life to uncovering a lost art form of education, and then steeping him-self in the day-to-day application of that art. Like most of you, I am a parent trying—running like Indiana Jones!—to find and then provide the best possible education to my children. Not the most "elite" educa-tion, but the *best*. It turns out, we found both . . . but that's for future pages.

For both of us, this book has been a journey—both a long one, and a brief one. Since the day we first spoke, just a few short years ago, my nickname for David has been "my Sherpa." David has been on a long journey, uncovering long-lost truths—he knows the terrain, with sure feet and steady hands. My journey is more immediate, but we are eager to share our discoveries. I had questions, David had answers. Now, together, we are committed to sharing what we (re)discovered with all Americans.

This book is our journey, but we hope it becomes yours as well. *How did we get here? What have we lost? And is there still time?* Some chapters contain educational philosophy and Western history, others more practical application and current events. This change of gears is intentional; both are required to rediscover the lost art of *real* education.

Where does it lead? The answer will shock you, scare you, challenge you, and—we hope—motivate you. Join us in this search for the lost holy grail of American education.

PART I

THE 16,000-HOUR WAR

1

OUR COVID-(16)19 MOMENT

You drop your son off at high school, let's say at Leodis V. McDaniel High School, in Portland, Oregon. He walks through security, the bell rings, and he walks into his first period. The class says the pledge of allegiance. Throughout the day, as the bell rings, he moves between classes—seven periods in total. He studies modern literature, social studies, Spanish, and computer programming, among other subjects. In each class, the teacher has been there for many years—and emphasizes that the process of learning is most important, not obsessing over grades.

Sounds pretty standard, right? It's very similar to how I—Pete Hegseth—went to high school. Bells ringing, pledge of allegiance, seven class periods, social studies, experienced teachers, and the latest teaching techniques.

What if I told you that every aspect of what I described is a product of "progressive" education? The bell, the pledge, class periods, the subjects, the tenured teachers, the education philosophy, and the name—Leodis V. McDaniel High School (the school used to be named James

Madison High School, but was changed in the fall of 2021). Yes, even the pledge—except for the "under God" portion—is an invention of Progressives.

I am a product of progressive education, and so are you. We all are, and we didn't know it. We have been for the better part of one hundred years.

The experience I had, that you likely had, and that most Americans had—not just in high school, but also in middle school and elementary school—is the direct result of a progressive plan. A plot, really. The changes we see on the surface—in the hallways, classrooms, and textbooks—seem subtle, and often harmless. They look like high school in America. But they came from somewhere else . . . and for a reason.

But, you might say, didn't the outrage over critical race theory (CRT) being taught in Loudoun County, Virginia, schools change the course of a statewide election? Didn't voting parents remedy what was being taught? Not so fast. The Progressives will have the last laugh because whether or not they teach CRT in the public schools, the real damage was done more than a century ago. Progressives canceled a critical part of every school's curriculum back then, which led us to where we are today. Unless we undo that foundational damage, nothing we do in public schools will change our course toward tyranny and thought control. It might slow down a bit, but the course was set, and radical change is now needed.

Until I undertook this project with David Goodwin, I had no idea. I had a sense that public and private K–12 education was captured by the progressive Left—most likely a product of the radical 1960s—but had no idea of the extent to which they had created the entire pipeline of American education.

In fact, I've written two previous books on the fight for the future of America, titled *In the Arena* and *American Crusade*. Both books, especially *Crusade*, had an emphasis on the importance of education. But both missed the mark, badly. This book—this journey and resulting mission—is more important than both of those previous books combined. It's not even close.

THE 1619 VIRUS IN SCHOOLS

As a result of the virtual classrooms our children were forced into in 2020 and 2021 thanks to COVID-19, you likely have a growing sense: American education is *off the rails*. Finally, to the chagrin of many educators, parents have been *in* the classroom in ways they were never previously allowed. Lesson plans were posted online, classes recorded, discussions held in the open, and textbooks laid on the kitchen table—instead of remaining in classrooms.

The most evident revelation from this development was the theory our kids have been taught about race in the American classroom. Seemingly out of nowhere—and accelerated after the Black Lives Matter riots in the summer of 2020—concepts like white privilege and systemic racism and even a new founding date for America, the year 1619, were splashed across computer screens all over America. Critical race theory had fully arrived (often masked as "Diversity, Equity, and Inclusion"), along with a full-on attempt to redefine gender, infuse climate fatalism, and turn our children into activists. These types of revelations were powerful because they were not the result of media exposure, but instead a bottom-up, and often apolitical, recognition by parents that the very foundation of American education had taken a radical turn.

It was the "woke" versus the newly awake. You might call it the COVID-(16)19 effect.

A virus descended on our country at seemingly lightning speed, and with it, a slow-rolling educational takeover was revealed. The tip of the iceberg, you might say. Then, with parents finally questioning what was happening in their kids' classrooms, certain quarters of the news media, like FOX News, took notice in a substantial way. It wasn't just one parent's experience—it was everywhere. Not just in Portland and New York, but in Pennsylvania and Virginia. Local and national parents' organizations were formed, and state legislatures readied bills to ban critical race theory.

The problem is often not even individual schools or school boards; in fact, many parents, teachers, and administrators seem numb—or resigned—to the inevitability of these radical new concepts. School administrators amplified these radical new teaching theories with a sense of institutional entitlement, underestimating the reaction many parents would have. Even with the resulting (courageous) outrage at school board meetings from masked-up (and ignored) parents, very little seemed to change in the classroom. *This is the way it is. This is the future*, parents were told.

Get with the program! White people are inherently oppressive. Gender is completely fluid. Climate change will destroy the world. And America is the ultimate source of evil in the world. Up is down, left is right, good and evil are subjective—until an educator tells you who or what is good and evil, and then you must comply.

It snuck up on me as well. I thought I was well versed on the dire situation of American education. But I was far from the mark—embarrassingly so, especially when I go back and look at what I've previously written. In some cases, I missed the mark because the mark kept moving, but overall, I was just scratching the surface, playing patty-cake with the enemies of free thought. Like you, I continue to uncover more and more alarming revelations each day—in real time.

In my 2016 book, I exhorted readers to "get in the arena" with the fervor of "an evangelical preacher of America's civil religion—like Teddy Roosevelt." Unbeknownst to me, my emphasis on "civil religion" walked the reader directly into the snare of the progressive trap. The book was unabashedly conservative and pro-American, but the result was impotency. In 255 pages, I spend just a few paragraphs on education, insisting instead that a Teddy Roosevelt speech—himself a "Progressive"—should chart the course for our conduct.

In 2020, the cause of my second book was Americanism, a "holy war for the righteous cause of human freedom." The blame for problems in America, and rightfully so, was on Leftism . . . fed by worshipping concepts like multiculturalism, socialism, genderism, secularism, and other dangerous "isms." But, even in 2020, my chapter on racism included not a single mention of critical race theory or the now-ubiquitous terms *anti-racism* or *equity*. The Left moves faster than we can type! Marxism, where this all emanates from, received only a glancing mention. Howard Zinn, the godfather of modern anti-American "history," was not even mentioned. The book was about the evils of Leftism, and I missed the underbelly of their revolution.

This time, the book *did* contain an entire chapter on education—as the solution America needs to reverse our leftward lurch. But even then, I was prescribing "good intentions" to the formation of modern American education and my core solutions for confronting education were to "demand your school says the pledge of allegiance" and fighting for school choice—calling it "the most transformational tactic toward [education] equality." Reading this back—less than two years later—it all feels trite and shallow. In retrospect, I called on Americans to "crusade" in a way that almost ensured continued defeat. I thought I understood the Left, but again, had barely scratched the surface—especially in the most important place.

I did, however, spend a great deal of time talking about higher education—the campus craziness we are all familiar with. For decades we have known about the lunacy of college campuses, which are—to quote my last book—"indoctrination camps." In fact, in June 2021 a North Korean defector, Yeonmi Park—turned Columbia University graduate—went even further, saying of the state of Ivy League education, "Even North Korea is not this nuts." She continued with a dire warning, saying the United States' future "is as bleak as North Korea" unless our self-loathing education system is overhauled.

Think about that! A North Korean defector—who experienced the most brutal, repressive, and anti-American regime in the world until she was thirteen years old—believes our elite schools are even more nuts than North Korea. That should be a wake-up call. The condemnation of dissent may look different—North Korea prefers concentration camps, America prefers cancellation, marginalization, and labeling—but the reality is the same: America's elites are hell-bent on changing the landscape in America, one incoming freshman class at a time—and they are succeeding. In America today, private thoughts are not allowed to translate into public speech, provoking the question, *Are we really free? Are our kids?*

THE REAL BATTLEFIELD ISN'T COLLEGES; IT'S KINDERGARTENS

It's sad to say, but if I had a dollar for every parent I met across America in a *FOX & Friends* diner segment who told me that they sent a patriotic, faith-filled conservative off to college and soon had an America-hating socialist on their hands . . . I'd be a rich man. Save for a few exceptions—Hillsdale College, Liberty University, College of the Ozarks, to name a few—higher education is a wasteland. We know that, and this book does not need to make that case. However,

Christians and conservatives have been living under the false impression that colleges and universities are a self-contained ecosystem with little impact on the broader culture and K–12 education.

My former mentor at Princeton University—intellectual giant and constitutional scholar Professor Robert P. George—put it best, saying to me, "It used to be that liberal professors in higher education licked their chops at the prospect of challenging the conventional and conservative views of their incoming students. Today, it's the opposite. Conservative professors like me lick my chops at the opportunity to challenge incoming students who have *already* been indoctrinated by the 'woke' Leftist educational system. Especially in the past decade, the kids show up already indoctrinated."

Let me stop here to remind you: I'm no different than you. I'm learning these things right alongside you. Until last year, I had two kids in public schools. It was easy, familiar, and free. I still don't have all my kids enrolled in precisely the type of school we want. I have no idea where—or even *if*—I will suggest that my kids go to college. For many years, my fear was higher education—but, as has become clearer and clearer, the *real problem* is high school, middle school, and now elementary school.

The battlefield for the hearts and minds of our kids is the 16,000 hours they spend inside American classrooms from kindergarten to twelfth grade . . . it's the 16,000-hour war, for our kids and our country.

Through a seemingly unstoppable progressive pipeline—teachers union priorities, teachers colleges, Common Core prerogatives, and unchecked teachers and administrators—the woke, social justice agenda is showing up in the youngest of classrooms. Often the books and curricula are hidden from parents, or at least largely until now. In one Idaho school district alone, books like *A Is for Activist*, *Antiracist Baby*, and *Not My Idea: A Book about Whiteness* are being read to elementary students. Not only is A for Activist, but L is for L-G-B-T-Q , T is for Trans, X is for Malcom X, and Z is for Zapatista (I had to look that one up . . . but, of course, it's a socialist, militant group at war with the Mexican government). Anti-racist babies are taught to "confess when being racist" and that "whiteness is a bad deal. It always was."

At Creekside Intermediate School in Michigan, students read *Black Brother, Black Brother*, which highlights a black student who feels like he is "constantly swimming in whiteness." Cambridge, Massachusetts, public schools' "Early Childhood Curriculum" teaches black families to be "free from patriarchal practices" as part of the "disruption of Western nuclear family dynamics" and a return to the "collective village." Kindergarten students in Illinois and fourth and fifth graders in parts of Pennsylvania also read *Not My Idea: A Book about Whiteness*. The book pounds home the idea that being white is inherently evil and that being black means you are inherently oppressed. This is being taught to six-year-olds in America. These books—and so many more like them—are designed to divide students by race and gender; that is the goal, not just the result.

Stories for kids with good life lessons are no longer good enough; the pages must contain an agenda. Maybe your sixth or seventh grader will encounter the "gender unicorn" instead—a widely used Barney look-alike purple unicorn who explains concepts like gender identity, gender expression, and sexual attraction. But even before there was a gender unicorn, I had "sex education" in my middle school in the 1990s—a small conservative community—and my parents pulled me out, preferring to discuss intimate topics like that within our household. And it was pretty straightforward back then. Today, the gender unicorn, and ubiquitous concepts like it across the country, normalize the concepts of gender identity being completely separate from sex assigned at birth, and encourage kids to grapple with physical and emotional attraction—especially toward the same sex. It's not informational; there is only one right answer: biology doesn't matter. In elementary school. It's sheer indoctrination . . . for 16,000 hours.

THE INDOCTRINATION'S BIGGER THAN SCHOOLS

But it's not just schools. Do yourself a favor and visit your local Barnes & Noble bookstore. Check out the kids section, and notice what books are front and center. The last time I visited mine, of the forty children's books displayed, *at least* thirty were progressive, agenda-driven books. This bookstore was not in a "liberal" community—this was a conservative area. Books by or about Michelle Obama, Ruth Bader Ginsburg, and Kamala Harris were all front and center. There was *A Is for Activist* and multiple books about George Floyd and Black Lives Matter. Gender and sexuality were well represented, not to be outdone by at least five books about climate change and the environment. It is nearly impossible, without really digging, to find books that contain patriotic, Christian, or conservative themes.

For young people, it's no better on television and social media. As a parent of young children, I find that too often as they're watching Disney or Nickelodeon, I see commercials about Black Lives Matter, climate change, gender-bending heroism, or full-on infomercials about the historic life of Kamala Harris. Even Gonzo of Muppets fame was portrayed as a cross-dressing "Gonzo-rella." I know I should turn it all off, but we haven't completely yet. I still won't allow any of my kids on social media, but I know it's coming. What place do traditional values or patriotic celebration have on those platforms? Not much, if you can get past the mountains of self-reinforcing and vapid selfies. Instead these platforms use targeted temptation to lure young kids away from God, traditional values, and love of country.

The point is, we are culturally surrounded. The classroom, literature, movies, music, television, and social media are all full-blown avenues of attack for the Left. How do parents fight back? Well, considering my own winding personal path, one hour on Sunday morning and one hour on Wednesday night at church is not enough; not even close. And that was back in the 1990s and 2000s, before social media and smart phones. Your kids are not special, and neither are mine. The social pressure today (especially on social media) is enormous on American kids, with the only socially acceptable path being left-wing activism. Without careful cultivation, our kids have every reason to conform. Remember, A is for Activist.

In my book *American Crusade* I urged readers to "fight back with commonsense Americanism." But while I could see the problem—yet again—I missed the mark on the solution. What if, underneath the culture wars, I have been proposing nothing but a losing proposition? What if Americanism is not enough? What if free people, free markets, and strong militaries are not enough? It seems quite obvious they are not, because we keep losing. Why?

Andrew Breitbart famously said, and I agree, that "politics is downstream of culture." Meaning, politics is a lagging indicator. Things change in our politics *because* our culture has already changed. In this way, representative politics in America is a reflection of the culture we cultivate (or that is intentionally cultivated for us). My pastor, Chris Durkin, calls it the "cult of culture." Culture sets the tone. Culture determines what, as a society, we lionize and idolize. I am already convinced of this and have focused the bulk of my previous writing and advocacy on culture.

YES, CULTURE > POLITICS, BUT RELIGION > CULTURE

But then, one Sunday last year, Pastor Chris took it to the next level—saying, "Yes, politics is downstream of culture. But even deeper than that, culture is downstream of religion." His statement was not political, but instead a matter of fact. I remember driving home from church with my wife, Jenny, saying, "How could I have missed this?" Our current culture was not created in a vacuum, it is grounded in faith—faith, in something. For hundreds of years, including during our founding revolution and as we fought a civil war to end the sin of slavery, the single most important ingredient in our culture was our Judeo-Christian faith and tradition. We knew the Bible, we understood the Western tradition, and we appreciated America's special place on the historical continuum.

Collectively, we have lost all of that—or almost all of that. Empty church pews, combined with secular classrooms, have *intentionally* bred a sheer anti-American, anti-Western, and anti-Christian culture that is just now revealing itself. Not only do we not have our Christian faith, but we now don't even have faith in America. Fighting for the former, without fortifying the latter, is a losing proposition, because cultures, like classrooms and politics, always believe in *something*. What in the world do we believe in today? What is our religion?

That said, I am daily inspired by the goodness of average American citizens. The people I meet on the road, all across America, who understand what makes America exceptional. People of faith who are tough, hardworking, and fiercely protective of their God-given freedoms. There are enough "believers" out there to turn around our Republic, but the system is stacked against them. Against us. We know the "machine" is against us, but we haven't yet figured out how to rage against that machine.

I have often quoted Abraham Lincoln's warning that "the philosophy of the schoolroom in one generation becomes the philosophy of government in the next." The statement remains true, but it is incomplete. To put it more comprehensively, the strength of the church in one generation becomes the culture of its people in the next . . . followed by the philosophy of the schoolroom and the government. The schoolroom is a vital front in the battle for Christendom and Western civilization, but alone—it is not enough.

The crushing weight of our wayward culture is almost suffocating. America's instruments of media, Hollywood, corporate boardrooms, government bureaucracies, and even the new "woke" military have taken a turn toward an unrecognizable America, full of censorship, virtue signaling, cancel culture, political correctness, division, and loss of faith in our election system. The powers that be even deem our founding documents "harmful"—in fact, if you do an online search of the official National Archives for copies of the Declaration of Independence and Constitution, you are met with a warning—right at the top of each document—that says "Harmful Language Alert." I'm not kidding.

Most of us assume that the left-wing transformation of America's schools started in the 1960s, almost an accidental shift, born of the culture. The real answer goes far deeper.

AGITATION ISN'T THE ANSWER

Again, my previous suggested solutions have been woefully insufficient. In *American Crusade* I urged readers to "complain and agitate." I cited an example of complaining about the "Holiday Program" at one of my son's public elementary schools. As I'm sure had long been the standard, the holiday program made not a single mention of the "reason for the season"—no manger, no star, no angels, no menorah, and no Christmas (except for a few lines of "Feliz Navidad"—it's okay in Spanish, I guess). Instead, Rudolph and Frosty the Snowman and holiday shopping were front and center. Outraged, I sent the principal a detailed email, writing, in part, "it is okay to simply recognize holidays for what they are—religious, patriotic, or whatever."

The principal wrote back promptly, saying, "As a public institution, we are charged with respecting the rights and civil liberties of all individuals who have children in our school system—and because that encompasses a variety of different people, faiths and belief systems, it would be impossible for us to focus specifically on any one religion without the possibly [sic] of upsetting and/or offending someone else. I believe it is for that reason our lawmakers decided long ago that the separation of church and state is both fair and equitable for all Americans."

In his mind, it's "impossible." Someone might be offended. The wall of separation is impenetrable. It was exactly the type of response I anticipated; I can barely fault him, he was trained that way. Dumb it down, don't offend anyone, live to collect a paycheck another day. While sending that email may have been cathartic to me, it had no impact. Nothing changed the next year (except we took our kids out of the school). Short of that, complaining and agitating inside our public school system got me . . . nowhere. Like the Internal Revenue Service, the system is fixed. My email to the principal was like telling people who don't like the tax code to email the IRS and complain; it might feel good, but it will accomplish nothing.

As I undertook this project, I was reminded of a similar valiant attempt by my mother, Penny. My mother did *way more* than I did— and I wasn't even aware. In the 1990s, my mother and two other PTA moms took on my local school system regarding a new "values-free" curriculum that was being introduced into my elementary school. This particular curriculum was called "Quest" and focused on self-esteem and value-free behavioral teachings. The program was described as "components that are designed for universal, explicit, systematic and culturally relevant implementation"—sound familiar? *Value-free* and *culturally relevant.*

Alarm bells went off for my mother. How much time will this new curriculum take away from the basics: history, math, reading, science? What does this new concept of "value-free" mean? And will all parents receive information on this? Will they even care? Most important, at least for my mother, will parents have a voice, or even a choice, about whether to allow their child to participate?

At the PTA meeting where the program was introduced, my mother was the only parent to push back and question it. Much like the response I was given, the principal calmly told her that she could research it on her own. *You're on your own.* After the meeting, another mom approached her and voiced her concern. At that meeting, new agitating activists were born! From there, another mother joined the group, and they started meeting on a regular basis to research the program, ask more questions of the district, and plan ways to inform other parents of this new, secret curriculum. They even created a panel of experts to present to the community, which caused some consternation and concern with school district administrators and school board members.

What did they accomplish? Well, nothing. The curriculum went through, and 99 percent of public school kids at Forest Lake Elementary participated. However, my mother did win a victory for *her kids.* I was sent to "study hall" during the portion of the day in which the new curriculum was taught. Moreover, my parents exercised their right to choose *not* to send me and my brother to retreats that supported any value-free education. During those field trips—and I vividly remember this—my mother wrote her own curriculum. During one week, she took us to the Minnesota State Capitol, we spent a day at the Minnesota Historical Society, a day at the Science Museum, and a day researching US presidents—all while, as my mother puts it, "your friends talked about their feelings at a retreat center."

She told me, "As I reflect back, and think about what parents are facing today, the Quest curriculum probably was fairly benign, but it was the precursor to things to come, as far as the schools taking over the role of the parent in teaching the truths and values that should be taught and reinforced at home. Parents today need to continue to stay informed, involved, and active in asking questions, researching on their own, and fighting for their kids' rights." She is 100 percent correct, and I am beyond grateful for a mother who ferociously guarded our hearts and minds. I am a better man, and a better citizen, because of her efforts.

But, ultimately, what did she accomplish in school? What changed in the curriculum? And what makes us think that our righteous protests today at school boards will make things change—today, five years from now, or ten years from now? The answer, sadly, is *nothing*.

THE DEATH STAR

Recommending my "agitate" strategy and my mother's grassroots approach is like asking a few parents with pitchforks—no, Nerf guns—to charge a fortified machine-gun nest on the high ground. A huge, politically correct, risk-averse fortress with alligators in the moat. We honor the effort and salute the cause, but we will ultimately bury them all. Ill-equipped frontal assaults, especially on a case-by-case basis, are worse than defeat—they actually embolden the well-fortified systems.

They may work on occasion, and certainly in the lives of individual kids, but administrators generally brush them off, reinforcing their position and their power. The more we fail, the stronger they become. The solutions I previously talked about are not worth the paper they were printed on. It's time to regroup, rearm, and radically change our approach. Do we attack, or retreat? The answers will surprise and motivate.

Some are doing more, switching out their pitchforks for public office. It's not enough to yell at the school board when they erase names of holidays, change the gender designation on bathrooms, force our young, healthy kids into masks, and advance critical race theory curricula—you need to become the school board. Or a mayor or state legislator. The Right has long held the right principles, but the Left controls the positions. Changing that is part of the solution. That said, talk to those people—and you often hear familiar refrains: we try to change the classroom, but the *real power* is elsewhere. The teacher unions still control the classroom, the curriculum is still poisoned, and the gains that are made—*we got the pledge back!*—are almost always soon overwhelmed.

What if you thought you were charging a single machine-gun nest . . . but soon realized it was just one portion of a Death Star? In your school, in my school—in America's classrooms.

Or, to use another example, let's compare our schooling system to a modern cruise ship, weighing 115,000 tons—more than twice the weight of the RMS *Titanic*. When passengers enjoy a meal in one of the cruise ship's five restaurants, they take for granted the engineering that suspends thousands of tons of steel above a vast ocean. When something goes wrong and the ship capsizes, passengers start to think about what they had previously taken for granted. If you're like most Americans, you take education for granted and underestimate its power. And you took our American civilization for granted, until recently.

As we walk our children to school, we take for granted that "it's just the way things are." Few would call school "inconsequential," but most of us think it's just fine for kids. That is, unless we step back and consider the sheer size and scale of the institution: with 115,000 tons of power and 16,000 hours of influence, the unions are the cruise ship captains and our kids are the passengers.

To an outside observer, the sheer scale of "school" in America is head-turning. The largest transportation system in the world is not in New York or London—it actually takes children to American public schools in half a million yellow buses. The United States spends more on national defense than China, Russia, Saudi Arabia, India, France, United Kingdom, and Japan combined. Yet America spends even more on school than on defense—more than $700 billion annually on education alone. The largest union in the United States supports not steelworkers or the teamsters, but schoolteachers. Public schools in the United States are the largest state-owned monopoly in the world, outside of China. How and why did this education story become so massive in America? And why are more than 90 percent of students educated in progressive public schools? In a nation of capitalists, why is one of America's largest industries publicly controlled?

We're told that all of this "school" came with the modern need to do more cerebral work instead of manual labor. School is even credited with upholding our republican ideals, and equal opportunity. We're compelled by law to send our children to school. Most of us never think to question the "school" narrative, or it seems too unimportant to question. Or, in an institutional way, too important to question. Who tells this story? Could it be that this story protects a certain system of power? A system designed, today, to divide and destroy America?

Take, for example, fourth graders in central Minnesota. In July 2021, at a school board meeting of the Sartell–St. Stephen Independent

School District, fourth grader Haylee Yasgar took to the microphone and shared the following, "During distance learning I was asked to complete [an] 'equity survey.' My teacher said that I could not skip any questions even when I didn't understand them. One question asked us what gender we identify with. I was very confused along with a lot of other classmates. A boy in my class asked if his mom could explain the question to him, because even after the teacher explained it he couldn't understand it. My teacher said *he was not allowed to ask his mom and that we could not repeat any questions to parents* [emphasis mine]. I want the school board to know how uncomfortable and nervous this made me. My mom always tells me I can tell her anything . . . but she also tells me I can trust my teachers, too. Being asked to hide this from my mom made me feel very uncomfortable, like I was doing something wrong."

How long have "equity surveys" like this been going on? How many fourth graders are forced to choose a gender identity? Or consider their white privilege? And, even worse, for how long have teachers exercised their power to hide—coercively—what they are actually teaching to our youngest of kids? How many "Quest" programs—and much worse—have been launched without us ever knowing? How long have we taken our modern-cruise-ship-turned-Death-Star for granted?

That brings us back to COVID-(16)19. Through the lens of their kids' locked-down Zoom classrooms—while watching statues come down, the police being defunded, athletes taking a knee, race riots rage in our streets, and schools being renamed—many parents have belatedly, and finally, realized a tragic truth: the hard Left has completely captured the classroom as well. Marxist teachers colleges pump out ideological teachers, left-wing teachers unions reign supreme, PTAs are neutered, school boards scared fully "woke." Almost no school—public or private—seems safe. Conservatives and Christians are surrounded. The Death Star seems stronger than ever. Is there hope?

The answer is yes—but it's not what you think. In some ways, the answer is closer than we think . . . but also further away than it's ever been. Both the tactical and strategic situation is worse than you think because the enemy has the high ground. But we have an advantage, should we choose to rediscover it. My journey toward hope—grounded in an honest assessment of where we are in America's classrooms—started in the most unlikely of places.

2

"COMMANDING HEIGHTS"

Another week, another morning on the road with *FOX & Friends*, enjoying breakfast at a small diner in Carthage, North Carolina. It's early, but the restaurant—Pete's Restaurant, as it would happen—is packed with wonderful Americans eager to talk about the news of the day. On these mornings, I rarely get a moment to myself, which I don't mind. Introduction after introduction, conversation after conversation, picture after picture. But it's energizing. Each and every time, the working-class people of our great country revive my faith in the future. But this morning, that feeling is particularly poignant.

We're on a commercial break, and I glance over at a table across the restaurant. There are people sitting at the table on this particular morning, but I haven't met them yet. Instead, I envision a young family seated there from a year ago, with two little girls dressed for school. At that immediate moment, I cannot remember their names—but I starkly remember meeting them a year ago. It was an interaction that would change my life, even if I didn't know it at that moment. I remember smiling amid the crowd that day, thinking of the family that wasn't there.

The morning I'm thinking about—one year earlier—was February 5, 2020. I was in town getting reaction to President Trump's State of the Union address, delivered the night before. His speech, titled "The Great American Comeback," made the case for his reelection—and you might remember it as the speech where Rush Limbaugh was surprised with the Presidential Medal of Freedom. Speaking on the eve of his impeachment acquittal, President Trump was at the height of his reelection prospects. The speech barely mentioned education, and included nothing about curriculum or critical race theory. Only three sentences were dedicated to a coronavirus emanating from China.

Then COVID-(16)19 hit.

That February 2020 segment was one of the last *FOX & Friends* breakfast diners I would do before COVID-19 shut down the nation— and many of our schools—for more than a year. As I stare over at the table, it's now a year later. It's March 3, 2021. I'm back at Pete's Restaurant, but the world has been turned upside down. COVID lockdowns. Black Lives Matter riots. The 2020 election. January 6th. It seems everything has changed, and everything is under assault. I glance back over at the table . . . before remembering why I'm back in Carthage, North Carolina.

Three days earlier I was on the main stage in Orlando, Florida, for the Conservative Political Action Conference, or CPAC. My speech hit on a wide variety of topics—including faith, education, and Donald Trump—but it was the portion about my conversations with average people at *FOX & Friends* diner breakfast segments that, for some reason, caught the eye of my left-wing critics.

Unbeknownst to me at the time, my speech was not just broadcast live on FOX Nation—our online streaming service—but also on FOX News Channel. Millions of people saw it. As often happens, the leftist Twitter echo chamber—whose pathetic existence includes watching everything conservatives say and trying to make them look bad—picked up on a portion of my speech that praised the "commonsense wisdom" of the everyday Americans I speak with often.

From the stage, I simply shared what I hear when I'm at *FOX & Friends* diners across America. "I sit down with a schoolteacher, or a construction worker, or a small business owner, or a cook at a restaurant, or the waitress at the restaurant we're at . . . and they're not talking about esoteric things that the Ivy League talks about, or MSNBC talks about. They're talking about the Bible, and faith, and prayer, and their family, hard work, supporting the police, standing for the anthem, the First Amendment, the Second Amendment, the Tenth Amendment."

Almost immediately, the Left went into full mocking-meltdown mode. From Twitter to newspapers to CNN and MSNBC, the refrain was the same. *Newsweek*: "FOX and Friends Host Pete Hegseth Says the 10th Amendment Is Discussed by People in Diners." The *Independent*: "Pete Hegseth mocked for saying people in diners are discussing 10th amendment." *Political Flare*: "Fox Anchor Pete Hegseth Humiliates Himself at CPAC When He Claims Normal Americans Sit Around Talking About the 10th Amendment." Mocked! Humiliated! Of all the things I said, they pick up on this? I thought. It was stupid criticism, but it's what the Left does.

The reason was clear. The condemnation was so strong, because the gulf is so wide between what elite left-wing media talks about and what hardworking, God-fearing, taxpaying American citizens actually care about. If you never talk to working-class Americans, it's very easy to create a caricature of them as, well, ignorant "clingers," "deplorables," or "chumps." *They don't even know what the Tenth Amendment is!* To the Left, the values I hear almost every week in *FOX & Friends* diners are outdated, old-fashioned, and unimportant. Turns out, it's the other way around: the American Left has forsaken the principles of the First, Second, and Tenth Amendments. They have rejected faith, family, freedom, and our founding. The ignorance actually runs the other way. As Paul's letter to the Romans says in verse 1:22, "Claiming to be wise, they became fools."

Two days later, *FOX & Friends* played a four-minute flashback video of my diner segments—sharing the multitude of times the topics I outlined on the CPAC stage rolled off the lips of everyday Americans. The clips weren't difficult to find; it was like shooting fish in a barrel. The morning after we released that video, just to rub it in, I found myself back at Pete's Restaurant talking to diners who, as it turns out, are very well versed in the Tenth Amendment, states' rights, and federalism.

As I stood among the crowd in Carthage, North Carolina, in March 2021—thinking about February 2020 and the family I met—it all came full circle. What the experience reminded me of, yet again, is that despite the assault on our culture, the revisionist history in our classrooms, and the removal of God from our public square, huge swaths of America—not so-called elites but middle-class Americans— still remember the basic ingredients of our Republic. They have an inclination—a lingering instinct—toward long-forgotten principles; toward something our prevailing culture, our "cult of culture," has discarded. Despite a culture of foolishness, they seek timeless wisdom.

In the COVID-(16)19 moment, our country was imploding from within . . . but the reason was clearer than ever. We are missing something. Something huge. The lifeblood of Truth still pulses through the veins of some Americans, but the heartbeat feels faint. It is felt, but not seen. Our culture feels empty, without a core. Something is missing; *everything is missing.* The Left has stolen everything.

What do we see filling the void instead? Social justice, political correctness, "wokeness," "diversity, equity, and inclusion," Black Lives

Matter, gender fluidity—it's everywhere. On our smartphones, in our boardrooms, on our televisions, in the Pentagon, and certainly in our classrooms. Right underneath our noses—it seems—theories like "critical race theory" and "gender theory" have become predominant, no longer confined to Ivy League seminars. They are the new "religion" of mass culture. Mark Levin—radio and TV host and bestselling author—recently wrote a book titled *American Marxism*, which warns in its very first line, "The counterrevolution to the American Revolution is in full force. And it can no longer be dismissed or ignored. . . ." He's right.

HOW THE LEFT TOOK OVER

How did the Left get in such a dominant position? In many ways that is the main question of this book; unless we answer it, we have no chance of mounting an insurgency against the "counterrevolution to the American revolution." Subsequent chapters will reveal precisely how Leftists targeted the heart of Western civilization, removed it from our classrooms, and replaced it with their own worldview—the worldview we now see dominating our culture and our classrooms. It's not that the Left needed to control every piece of terrain in America; instead, they focused on key terrain—and the results, today, are sobering.

Avowed Marxist and "founding father" of the Soviet Union Vladimir Lenin gave voice to a key aspect of this strategy in 1922, when he used the term *commanding heights* in a speech. Following the Russian Revolution, the Soviet economy tanked; Lenin proposed a solution: limited capitalist activities were permitted at the local level, but all the main levers of the national economy would be controlled by the state. In short, Marxists didn't need to control every aspect of the economy; they just needed to maintain a grip on the big and influential industries like steel, manufacturing, and energy. It worked, and the Russian economy temporarily recovered.

This military analogy—the "commanding heights"—has captured the imagination of Marxists since, and it was famously dubbed "the road to serfdom" by free-market economists. Conservatives in America spent much of the twentieth century fending off Lenin's economic Marxism. Marx's entire theory was premised on economics and class warfare, and freedom lovers met the Soviet machine head-on—with free-market capitalism and sheer military might. In the end, that combination helped to eventually bring the Soviet Union to its knees.

Lenin was an economic Marxist. American progressives are cultural Marxists.

Underneath our noses, Progressives in America quietly labored to gain control over an even more powerful set of "commanding heights"—those that steer the hearts and minds of America's children. With American conservatives mostly preoccupied with defending economic freedom and military might, American Progressives knew that social control was far more powerful than economic control. As such, they set out to gain direct national control of the "commanding heights" of America's schools. A project set in motion more than one hundred years ago is today leveraged through 16,000 hours of government instruction.

Today, these cultural Marxists—the direct descendants of economic Marxists—control every strong point, every choke point, and every inch of high ground in the realm of American education, and by extension, American culture. That was the plan, and it worked. They are currently in mop-up mode, shooting their exposed opponents from their fortified high ground. These cultural Marxists are able to deflect any criticism, deny any accusation, and defeat any opponent—because we are fighting on terrain that they fully control. Again, they have the high ground, and they have their army. They seem almost untouchable. So untouchable that they are able, with a willing media, to deny their own existence.

THE PROBLEM IS PEDAGOGY, NOT JUST CURRICULUM

With the public rise of the COVID-(16)19 effect, the Left in America has mounted a sinister defense: *nothing to see here*. Rank-and-file Democrats like former Virginia governor Terry McAuliffe say criticisms of critical race theory are "conspiracy theories." So-called Squad member Ilhan Omar tweeted in June 2021, "Republicans love to create outrage over things that aren't actually happening. People should be asking them, what elementary, middle and high school is teaching Critical Race Theory and why they are spinning false narratives." Nikole Hannah-Jones, the chief author and proponent of the critical race theory–based 1619 Project, says her newly formed black liberation schools are "not teaching critical race theory." Even the chairman of the Joint Chiefs of Staff, Mark Milley, repeatedly dismissed claims that elements of critical race theory are being taught at West Point and throughout the military. He's focused on "white rage" instead.

More specific to the classroom, the two largest teachers unions in America—the American Federation of Teachers (AFT) and the National Education Association (NEA)—deny outright that critical race theory is being taught, even while the AFT invites Ibram X. Kendi— the author of *How to Be an Antiracist*—to be a featured speaker at their 2021 national conference. Moreover, while denying the teaching of racial and gender theories in classrooms, both unions have multimillion-dollar legal funds dedicated to defending teachers who run afoul of local or state laws that ban the teaching of critical race theory. Like corporate America, higher education, mass media, and our military, these unions call their efforts "diversity, equity, and inclusion" (DEI)—obfuscating their Marxist aims in cozy language. Note to self: when the Left denies something, they are usually just confirming it.

These unions and fellow-traveler Leftists have good reason to deny the existence of radical left-wing theories. The curriculum, and teachers, almost never come out and state that what they are teaching is "critical race theory." They don't have to. Instead, they hide behind coded language that is designed to confuse parents and hide the real goal. The preferred language of the Left is ever changing, which—as the authors of the fantastic book *Cynical Theories* point out—is because "they stem from a very particular view of the world—one that even speaks its own language in a way. Within the English-speaking world, they speak English, but they use everyday words differently than the rest of us."

A key part of the Left's CRT denial is the way in which they hide the difference between *curriculum* and *pedagogy*—a distinction that has recently risen to the forefront in public debates. *Pedagogy* refers to the methods, practices, and purposes of teaching; *curriculum* is what is specifically being taught. Curriculum is what kids are taught; pedagogy is how they're taught. Some today believe education is primarily an information and skill transfer, so they tend to talk only about what skills or information are taught—what content is in the curriculum. The hidden secret, used effectively by Progressives, is pedagogy—method of teaching. They deny CRT is in the curriculum, instead embedding their entire CRT methodology into their teaching pedagogy. The word *pedagogy* itself comes from the Greek root *paideia*, which has no direct English translation (a word you will hear for the rest of the book). But from it, we get the term *pedagogy*, which was the work a *paidagogos* did in ancient Greece—meaning a leader who walks with students and trains them in manners, academics, and virtue. Under the influence of today's progressive educational overlords, *pedagogy* has been reduced to mean "teaching," but as you'll see, this reduction far undersells what effect progressive education has had on America's children. This obscuring of school's true purpose by Progressives was the beginning of the end for America's culture. If you had to define *paideia* in a single word, it would be "enculturation," not teaching. Pedagogy is the act of formulating a culture in children. There's a clue here. What culture is the Left trying to form? And what word games are they playing to hide it?

The Left mostly denies their own (unpopular) theories outright, and then, when exposed, they hide behind words that they made up, defined, and are now wielding against unsuspecting Americans. Take, for example, so-called Squad member and Democratic-Socialist representative Alexandria Ocasio-Cortez. Here's part of what she said on CNN in the summer of 2021 about the teaching of critical race theory: "Why don't you want our schools to teach anti-racism? Why don't Republicans want their kids to know the tradition of anti-racism in the United States? Why are Republicans trying to ban books in this country? Ban speech? Fire certain professors? Attacking the core roots of history in this country? Why don't Republicans want us to learn how to not be racist? Why don't Republicans want kids to know how to not be racist?"

Why don't you want your kids to learn how not to be racist?! Why would we not want our schools teaching anti-racism?! She's not denying it. Instead, she is using the invented lexicon of the Left to advance racism masked as anti-racism. According to the modern Left, it's not enough to not be racist. You must be an anti-racist. And if you are against anti-racism, then . . . you guessed it . . . you are racist. They do the same with the term *equity*, which sounds almost identical to the word *equality*—a word we all love, and grew up on. Equality is the pursuit of equal opportunity; equity is the false promise of equal outcome. It's cultural Marxism and socialism . . . dressed up with words that sound irrefutable. As I mentioned earlier, the Left always moves the goalposts.

Only those trained in "proper critical methods" have the secret decoder ring to the Left's ever-shifting language. According to the authors of *Cynical Theories*, the Left's "very precise technical usage of [words] inevitably bewilders people, and, in their confusion, they may go along with things they wouldn't if they had a common frame of reference to help them understand what is actually meant by the word."

Equity or equality? Racism or anti-racism? Sex or gender? It's confusing. It confuses adults—*smart* adults. Imagine what it does to kids. It doesn't confuse kids, it is infused into kids. They start to instinctively speak the language of the Left. If they don't, they simply cannot navigate their coursework or the culture of their peers. "Diversity, equity, and inclusion" are the centerpiece of their curriculum. Teachers demand conformity to the woke lexicon, lest the student grades take a hit. As such, it becomes their "woke" language. They are indoctrinated.

The goal of that indoctrination? It's not about racism, or equality, or even gender. It's about deconstructing anything and everything that reflects not just the founding principles of America, but the foundations of our families and our faith. It's about control—of thought, and behavior. To the Left, our Western Judeo-Christian roots are the problem—they must be dismantled, one theory, one word, one classroom, and one mind at a time. And it's been a long-term project; a very long-term project.

The underlying assumption of the "woke" Left is that regular people are dumb—or, at best, will quietly acquiesce to their new status quo. When the progressive Left looks at students, today they see groups of people—by race, gender, or sexuality—but at the outset of their project, the masses of America's children were all future "workers." The "experts" and "professors" on the Left, from the very beginning of their progressive takeover, have assumed the *least* of average citizens— trying to shift the classroom from a place of virtuous living and liberated minds to a place where basic skills are bestowed upon future workers. The latest iteration of this trend is the push for STEM, or Science, Technology, Engineering, and Math education, to be at the forefront of our classrooms. America's classrooms have been centralized, technicalized, and scientized—with the aim of pumping out workers, not thinkers. I even, regrettably, wrote my Harvard graduate thesis on the topic of STEM schools. Foolish schools, foolish theses.

Evidence of this standard is everywhere. Take a run-of-the-mill June 2021 column in the *New York Times* by liberal Nicholas Kristof, titled "The Biggest Threat to America Is America Itself." The title itself is correct, but the shallow diagnosis is revealing. Kristof understandably bemoans low American graduation rates, math scores, and literacy rates—then asks, "How are those millions of Americans going to compete in a globalized economy?" He cites a "Social Progress Index" and "social outcomes, from education to health to the environment." He talks about competing with a "surging China" and a "rogue Russia," citing America's "underperformance at home."

Of course we want, and need, strong math scores and literacy rates—and should have them, considering how much we spend on government schools! That goes without saying. It also goes without saying that our public education system—especially in Democrat and union-controlled big cities—has been abysmal at delivering on these basics (the worst math and literacy rates in America for the past fifty years come exclusively from Democrat-run public school systems). What is more illuminating about the column, and the overall leftist view of our classrooms, is that they never talk about the ever-growing cultural, civic, patriotism, and faith gap in our country among young people. Apparently we are supposed to read and subtract our way out of conflicts with China and Russia. But what about a country that no longer believes in itself? What if you are creating workers who don't love their country for a future economy that doesn't exist? You get cultural serfs seeking new grievances and with limited economic prospects—you get division and chaos.

None of this is a thought for the modern Left. The "truth" of 1619 is baked in for them. It is unquestioned. It's already over. America is racist. America is inequitable. And America is sexist. Nicholas Kristof—like the legions of leftist elites he represents—already assumes that. As once famed, now disgraced, former New York governor Andrew Cuomo said in 2018, "We're not going to make America great again, it was never that great." Yes, it was part anti-Trump speak, but it was also a testament to how leftists currently think. The Left talks about literacy rates while not caring *what* our kids are reading and never proposing dynamic solutions (think, school choice) that would actually provide vulnerable American kids with a way up and out of the worst-performing schools. They propose fake solutions to their own problems—knowing full well that things will only get worse.

Once again, the powers that be in modern American education—mainly teachers unions at this point—control not just the politicians, but the teachers and the entire educational pipeline. Not just the classrooms and curriculum and teachers colleges, but also the PTAs and the school boards. That is why, for the Left, this COVID-(16)19 moment is unsurprising; they may not be willing to support it outright, and publicly, but they have been breeding it for years. When they started their project, they could not have known where it would lead—but they did know where it would *not* lead. Never toward the virtues that founded our country; always away from them. The place we are in today is the logical, if initially unforeseen, end state of the progressive educational takeover.

And it's working. Multiple polls in the past few years—from Gallup to Pew to Axios—have shown that for younger Americans, socialism is viewed roughly as favorably, and in some cases more favorably, than capitalism. How can you blame them? Their classrooms are inundated with whitewashed history about socialists and communists and full of anti-American views that paint our system, including our capitalist economic system, as predatory. Moreover, poll after poll shows that young people in the United States express far more skeptical views of America's global position than previous generations did; to a great many, other countries are better than the United States. A "Harvard Youth Poll" from December 2021 found that only 31 percent of young Americans (ages eighteen to twenty-nine) believe "America is the greatest country in the world." Fully half of young Americans believe that there are "other nations as great or greater than America." Worse, America's youngest generation has twice the number of avowed atheists—with young people rejecting religious faith in record numbers. You will soon meet some of the most powerful purveyors of this view . . . our kids have already met them, even if they don't know it.

All of this prompts, yet again, the obvious question: *how in the world did we get here?* Without knowing how we got here, we have no hope in rediscovering the ethos of a bygone country.

The public classrooms of twenty years ago—the ones I attended—looked much different than today. I don't need to tell you this. You already know this. Moreover, my classroom was much different than that of my parents. My grandparents' classroom—unrecognizable today. And, as you will soon see, even those midcentury classrooms were already captured by the newest testament of the Left. From my kids to my grandparents—a tiny blip in the timeline of human history—timeless truths and core educational tasks have not changed. Yet, in America's classrooms, everything changed.

When I was in grade school and high school, the overwhelming historical ethos of the classroom was the example of Martin Luther King Jr. We all knew that America had a past full of racial scars and other problems, but our modern responsibility was to fulfill the incomplete values of our founding. We were charged with creating a *more perfect* union—one where *all* children were "judged not by the color of their skin but by the content of their character." Like you, I was raised to ignore race as a factor in judging people. Call it color-blind or post-racial, but the idea was to raise children who look at who people are, not what they look like.

Enter critical race theory, or CRT. This is not a "latest fad," this is different. Critical race theory didn't pop up in a vacuum, but rather took decades of scholarship in the wilderness and quiet advancement to get to this point in time—yet another progressive plot this book will reveal. The *New York Times Magazine* elevated the 1619 Project and boldly proclaims that its aim is "to reframe the country's history by placing the consequences of slavery and the contributions of black Americans at the very center of our national narrative." Rather than making race irrelevant, the Left wants to put race at the center.

Some proponents of CRT even do both, out loud. Both advancing it, and denying it. Take Rich Milner, professor at Vanderbilt University, speaking in the summer of 2021 at the "Educators for Antiracism Virtual Conference." He said the quiet part out loud: "I want to suggest, as we think about this moment of the idea of this backlash against this and all of these movements against critical race theory, we have an opportunity as educators, right. To really not decrease our focus on race, but to increase a focus on race, because we realize as educators that this is exactly what we should be doing. . . . I'm not suggesting that teachers are teaching critical race theory. In fact, I can't name one teacher explicitly in K–12 schools teaching critical race theory. But I say we use it as a moment to amplify possibility for the inclusion of critical race theory. . . . So for those of you who are really interested in learning about how CRT can manifest in K–12 schools in ways that allow you to do the work in a transformative way, . . . we have to understand what CRT is and how it is supposed to be an analytic space for advancing practice."

Got it. We need to understand it, so we can (not) teach it, in K–12 schools. We need to increase our focus on race . . . in a transformative way. We were so close, and now we are so far. And modern Democrats, along with their cultural Marxists fellow travelers, want it that way— and they use their commanding heights to keep it that way.

THE UNIONS CONTROL EVERYTHING

On day one of his presidency, Joe Biden abolished the "1776 Commission"—a last-ditch effort created by President Donald Trump to reject the 1619 narrative and reinstall traditional American history. Biden, the husband of a longtime member of a teachers union, received record campaign donations from teachers unions. When he was elected, our federal bureaucracy opened the floodgates for unabashed education bureaucrats who had long since taken over the educational pipeline— but had mostly hidden their agenda. Teachers unions like AFT and NEA control who becomes a teacher, what teachers are taught, who gets accredited as teachers, what curriculum is taught, the school boards that oversee teachers, and which teachers get advancement. Teachers at teachers colleges teaching other teachers what they are allowed to teach—all controlled by Progressives. This is not an understatement: education unions in America *fully* control our classrooms.

Hillary Clinton would have been just as deferential to the left-wing education machine as Joe Biden is today. Hillary infamously wrote her 1969 thesis at Wellesley College about "community organizer" and known radical socialist Saul Alinsky. Alinsky famously wrote the book *Rules for Radicals: A Pragmatic Primer for Realistic Radicals*. His goal was to translate radical activism into raw political power. Hillary was pro–teachers unions, anti–school choice, and completely at the behest of the educational establishment. Hillary was a product of the 1960s, profoundly shaped by the cultural revolution of that era.

As it happens, so were teachers unions; in fact, the NEA used none other than Saul Alinsky as a consultant to train their own staff. A 1972 NEA training document, titled "Alinsky for Teacher Organizers," made the case that teachers should be used to organize, not just for changes in the classroom, but for social change. Think picket lines and teacher walkouts. As recently as 2009, the NEA website dubbed Alinsky "an inspiration to anyone contemplating action in their community! And to every organizer!" For more than sixty years, the NEA has been in cahoots with cultural Marxists—and growing in power. (It wasn't always that way; more on *how* that happened later.)

Unions wield the electoral power, and politicians open the door. It's a symbiotic relationship that goes back many decades, and started with the NEA's first-ever endorsement of a presidential candidate—Jimmy Carter in 1976 (in fact, at the 1976 Democratic National Convention, more delegates—180—belonged to the NEA than any other group of any kind). Carter rewarded the teachers unions by fulfilling his promise to them—to create a federal Department of Education, which he did in 1979.

It is not an understatement to say that the Department of Education would never have happened without the NEA and fellow teachers unions. A *Washington Post* article from 1980 asks the question point blank: "Is the department, then, a creature of the NEA? 'That's true,' says NEA executive director Terry Herndon. 'There'd be no department without the NEA.'"

So, there is no Department of Education without the NEA. There is no Common Core curriculum without the Department of Education. There is no Common Core without Democrat presidents. And there are no Democrat presidents without the NEA. The internal feedback loop, the complete capture of the system, has been in the works for decades. With each passing year the relationship manifests itself more and more in the classroom, as Democrats and unions use their power to push radical left-wing ideas into the minds of our kids—future voters, to boot.

COMMON CORE DROPS CLASSICAL CONTENT

Speaking of Alinsky, the previous Democrat president—Barack Obama—was no stranger to his worldview, especially during Obama's time community organizing in Chicago. If anything, Obama was the perfect manifestation of Alinsky's "rules"—don't look radical, or sound radical . . . but, underneath it all, be radical. Obama soothed America into electing him twice. In the meantime he was hell-bent on transforming education even further. Obama's signature educational initiative was the "Common Core State Standards," adopted in 2010. In short, Common Core federalized education standards and standardized testing, and in doing so, facilitated the federalization of curriculum and pedagogy in the classroom. It also completely overtook the traditional SAT college admissions test, which previously measured "reasoning" but now mirrors, you guessed it, Common Core (more on this in Chapter 8). When states accepted the new standards, they received millions of federal dollars. Most states did, and even though some states have since opted out, the impact on curriculum is long lasting.

Rebecca Friedrichs was an elementary school teacher for twenty-eight years in California and described to me the impact of Common Core this way: "When Common Core came into our schools, we teachers were told, you have to teach Common Core. And we said, what is it? *And they said, we don't know. It hasn't been written yet.* It was insane. But we started learning that what they wanted to do was remove the classics, the classical books that teach children morals and patriotism. They removed those and they were replacing them with ideological teachers who could just bring articles from the newspaper or articles from a random website."

You need to teach it, so you can find out what's in it! Once again, the secret to Common Core is what they removed. What replaced it is even worse. She continued: "So then the very next day . . . they say, oh, by the way, we've come up with these great websites where the lessons are already written for you. They're scripted, everything's there. All you have to do is go on the website, grab the lesson, and you can use it. So I took a look at some of these lessons; lessons on how the children should be against fossil fuels, there were lessons on how our founding fathers were nothing but slave owners and evil men. There are lessons on all kinds of anti-American, anti-family, anti-science, anti-truth . . . so Common Core is just like everything else these subversive unions do. It's convoluted, it's complex, it's confusing, and it's purposely created to undermine a great educational system."

Mary Grabar, a former professor and author of the book *Debunking Howard Zinn*, summed up the goal of Common Core this way:

"Common Core is a far left program [that] promotes the ideas that Howard Zinn wants to get out. And that the 1619 Project wants to get out. . . . Despite its name, it was falsely branded to be about a common curriculum. But it was [really] an attempt to undermine traditional learning. And it's still in place, and it was very, very harmful." Yet another pathway, created by the Left, predicated on rejecting "old" standards and replacing them with, well, whatever radical left-wing unions want.

Recognize that name, Howard Zinn? Around the time of the founding of the Department of Education, and throughout the 1980s, the radical activists of the 1960s became the tenured professors at our universities. Right at that moment, one book captured the minds of that tenured class: *A People's History of the United States*, by Howard Zinn. It is not hyperbole to state that no other book has had a greater impact on the minds of American youth for the past forty years. When not assigned in classrooms, it has been fully incorporated into the mass-produced textbooks in our classrooms. Zinn's view of history is enmeshed in American classrooms. The unions love it, endorse it, and teach it.

And what was Zinn's thinking? Zinn described himself as "something of an anarchist, something of a socialist. Maybe a democratic socialist," but his writing reads like communist propaganda. The best way to describe his *People's History* is that it is American history, written from the perspective of the Soviet Union. Zinn was openly anti-America, openly socialist, and always willing to bend history to make America look like an evil country. At first his views spread in universities, but they soon made it into Hollywood and pop culture, and today are in our K–12 classrooms.

Which, again, leads back to the unions. A ten-second Google search reveals that the NEA—the nation's largest labor union—openly works hand in hand with the "Zinn Education Project." The Zinn

Education Project's mission is to "promote and support the teaching of people's history in classrooms across the country," and they boast that "with more than 130,000 people registered, and growing by more than 10,000 new registrants every year, the Zinn Education Project has become a leading resource for teachers and teacher educators." Howard Zinn is no longer an antiestablishment historian . . . he is the establishment.

An NEA press release from June 2021 had the following headline: "On National Day of Action, Educators Join Together and Pledge to Teach the Truth." The NEA's top partner in this "day of action"? You guessed it . . . the Zinn Education Project, along with other left-wing groups, including "Black Lives Matter at School." The theme of this day of action, to bring us back full circle, is to fight *against* parents and politicians who are calling out critical race theory being taught in school. According to the NEA and Zinn Education Project, "As professionals, we—not politicians—know how best to support our students. What a good educator knows is we can't just avoid, suppress, or lie our way through our shared challenges. We will continue our commitment to our students so that they have the skills needed to better understand problems in our society and develop collective solutions to those problems."

The teachers unions (the political power), with the help of anti-Americans like the late Howard Zinn (the curriculum), will help students understand problems in our society and develop "collective solutions" to those problems. After decades of cavorting with socialists, the teachers unions are so used to saying things like this that they don't see the bastardization of their profession. Now it *is* their profession. Rather than teaching basic skills and knowledge to America's children, America's unions believe their job is to solve America's problems based on their social-justice, culturally Marxist view of the world. They no longer hide their agenda, because they don't have to. Who will rein them in? The politicians? Most don't care, and the ones who do don't know where to start. The bureaucracy? The government works for the unions. The courts? They stripped out the core of American education decades ago. The parents? Go ahead and try. It will feel good, but they will bury you, too.

NERF GUNS DON'T WORK

This brings me back to the analogy I used earlier: this fight feels like parents with Nerf guns versus teacher unions in fortified machine-gun nests. The Left controls the commanding heights—the unions, the teachers colleges, the bureaucracy, the textbooks, the standards, and education spending. And this is just the past few decades; the progressive takeover of the American mind—putting their 16,000 hours to good use—goes back much further. They stole the minds of our kids, and knew exactly what they needed to remove in order to make it happen. They could not have advanced their cultural Marxist agenda today without first removing the one thing standing in its way.

It feels hopeless. If we fight the system, it is. We will bury our own country. The hope lies elsewhere, embodied by that young family I met at Pete's Restaurant in rural North Carolina. I think of them often. They made a radical choice, an intentional one—that can save our country. They are actively rediscovering the one ingredient—the crown jewel—of our country and Western civilization that made us who we are.

They dropped their Nerf guns, and instead found the most powerful weapon of Western civilization. A weapon that was stolen from America's classrooms. They found a solution as big as the problem. What was it? Turn the page.

3

THE FORGOTTEN FORCE OF WESTERN CHRISTIAN EDUCATION

Imagine yourself walking over the rubble near dig sites in Egypt in 1921, looking for scraps of ancient treasure that might be in the tombs nearby. One year later, Howard Carter will find King Tutankhamun's tomb right under the rubble you're walking over. But, because you do not have that knowledge yet, it's all just sand and rubble—to you and to everyone else. You may even eat lunch sitting on a rubble stone just feet from one of the greatest treasures ever found.

In the past few decades, a treasure has been rediscovered under the rubble left by progressive experiments in modern schools. However, this is not a book about the educational rubble we see today in schools. This is a book that will expose a century-long strategy to redirect our culture away from Christianity and the West, away from the very ideals that invented and upheld our Republic. This was accomplished by targeting and removing a key ingredient in how children are raised—

an ingredient called the Western Christian Paideia (WCP). The loss of the WCP has led directly to the cultural collapse we are witnessing today.

How could a word virtually nobody's heard of—*paideia*—be both the key to civilization and the target of an entire political movement? Both taken for granted, and taken over? The answer is fascinating—and revealing. Paideia, simply defined, represents the deeply seated affections, thinking, viewpoints, and virtues embedded in children at a young age, or, more simply, *the rearing, molding, and education of a child*. Classical Christian education creates a paideia unique in all of human history—one that enables freedom. At risk of extending the *Star Wars* metaphor too far, paideia is the closest thing to a real-world cultural "Force" that envelops an entire civilization but is so deeply hidden, it's hard to see.

Just about 120 years ago, Progressives had big ideas to change the cultural and economic order while dissolving old reliances on Christianity. The fruits are now being seen, ripe on the vine—first in the Baby Boomers and now in the Gen X, Millennial, and Gen Z generations. The tree from which this poisoned progressive fruit is harvested has matured. It grows more plentiful and more bitter with each successive generation.

WHAT MAKES CULTURES DISTINCT? THEIR VISION OF THE GOOD LIFE

"An Irish priest, a Jewish rabbi, and a Southern Baptist met on a train . . ." Cultures make humor work because deep down, we understand the differences. Perhaps this is why our present politically correct sensitivities have killed comedy. When you boil cultures down to their essence, they rest on a common aspirational vision held by the members of the cultural group. This has been called "the vision of the good life." When you think of Italians, you may imagine large extended families, loyalty, and romantic youth. When you think of Germans, you may think of precision engineering, and direct and driven personalities. The Irish conjure a vision of music, dance, assertiveness, and friendship. Each culture's vision of the good life defines the very nature of a people.

A person's "vision of the good life" is driven by something called paideia. The "woke" culture we see today is a product of a progressive vision, infused into the modern American paideia. Paideia's power to influence culture comes, in part, as it forms the "vision of the good life" in children. This vision may not sound powerful, but it has proven to be the strongest cultural force throughout all of human history. The Western vision of "the good life" went virtually unchanged and unchallenged for centuries. It was tied to traditional families, church, communities, industriousness, and a virtuous population.

Today, our *modern vision* of the good life has been nearly universally transformed into the freedom of personal choice, control of your identity, being accepted for who you are, finding adventure, and creating your own path in life. For children of the Left, a slight supplemental variation includes finding meaning in particular causes, like climate change, gender identity, and so-called anti-racism. For children of the right—mostly Christian—they find some small portion of the good life in patriotism and personal faith. But both *modern* groups—the Left and the Right—roughly share the modern vision.

We don't think much about the roots of our assumptions today because we don't realize the depth and power of our "vision of the good life," especially over time. As our culture sinks deeper into an identity crisis, suicide rates climb, and families and churches shrink, our very survival requires a better way. The great plume of smoke we see rising from selfishness and hypersexuality in our culture emanates from a fire built to worship the creation rather than the Creator. We are trying to have the Kingdom, without the King. If we do not change the way we live now, our children will be sacrificed in this fire—not through the violence of a pagan ritual, but as they walk mesmerized toward a false vision of the good life that is absorbed from the vapid culture around them.

CHRISTIANITY SHAPED OUR WESTERN "VISION OF THE GOOD LIFE"

One deceptively difficult question lies at the headwater of any civilization: *what is man?* Our assumptions about man's nature transform everything that is downstream in the culture. As mentioned in the previous chapter, our assumptions are based in religion, even if that religion is atheistic humanism. Early civilizations assumed man was part of some sort of divine unity within the created world (animism, Hindu, Buddhism). Other civilizations saw a separation between humans and a pantheon of anthropomorphic or sometimes zoomorphic gods (common in the Middle Eastern, Indian, and Mediterranean religions). Of course, Islam (founded circa 600 AD), Zoroastrianism (circa 600 BC), and Israel (circa 1300 BC under Moses) all had a single, all-powerful God who created man for a purpose.

The ancient Greeks between 400 and 500 BC developed the idea that man has a special type of connection to the metaphysical, and thus can connect with the divine through a bridge called the "Logos," or ideas in the minds of men. The Greeks built a civilization on this assumption, and the Romans inadvertently popularized it through political conquest. In a small sliver of their empire, near a crossroads of trade, the Hebrew tradition held that man was made in the image of God, was fallen, and awaited a messiah. At the height of the

Greek-speaking, Roman imperial world, under the splendor of Herod's impressive new Jewish Temple, this crux of cultural "truths" was fused into a singularity—the person of Jesus Christ. He was the Logos to the Greeks, a king to the Romans, and the messiah for the Jews. Few of us consider the full picture of Christianity's ascent, through this nexus, to the world's largest religion as it is today. Man partakes in a divine nature, is fallen, and can be redeemed. This understanding built the Western Christian world.

The novelty of this fusion into "the West"—the merging of Athens and Jerusalem—is unmatched in any other culture. Its effects are far-reaching, so much so that nearly every experience we have today, from technology to culture to government, descends from it. Like any foundation, it holds up more of our civilization than we realize. It was perpetuated for almost two thousand years through a power we've forgotten about during the past century—a power discovered by the Greeks and called out in the Bible—called paideia. Paideia has the power to determine who we are and what we become—as individuals, as communities, and as a nation.

Until three or four generations ago, our paideia was highly coveted and was cultivated in our homes, schools, and churches. The concept was widely known to the educated class. The concept was embedded in daily life. Yet we have no translation for the word in English. Every Western generation from the time of Christ until the late 1800s knew of it. Then, about one hundred years ago, it was deliberately targeted to change the course of our nation. It was dismantled and buried by a group of determined Progressives.

For the first time in two thousand years of cultural history, these Progressives had a new understanding of humanity: we are simply the pinnacle of naturalistic evolution. We neither partake in a divine nature nor have we fallen, because there is no God. They called it "humanism," by which they meant an atheistic form of humanism. This new understanding of man may not have been popularly accepted right away, but its adherents wanted to build a society around this new idea of man. To do so, they needed to establish a new paideia.

When people hear the story contained in this book, most react with, "Why hasn't anybody told me this!" That was me, just a few short years ago.

INTRODUCTION TO THE WESTERN CHRISTIAN PAIDEIA (WCP)

Western civilization is in full retreat. And, as we saw in Afghanistan in 2021, retreats usually do not end well. It may seem as though we're still fighting the culture war through political means, but we lost the important strategic cultural ingredient generations ago—called the "Western Christian Paideia," or the WCP. The good news is that, though the WCP was dismantled and buried by the Progressives, it is not lost. It can be recovered. Let's break it down to its component parts.

Western

"Western" civilization has recently been associated with European colonialism and culture of the past four hundred years or so. In this book, *Western* refers to any civilization that descends from the convergence of Greece, Rome, and Hebrew cultures, dating back roughly 2,500 years to the golden age of Greece. It envelops nearly all historical Christendom, both in time and space, and much of the world— North Africa, the Middle East, Eastern Europe, Western Europe, North America, and Australia. Even Islam was influenced by classical Greece, Rome, and Judaism.

Christian

The term *Christian* is challenging because today we conceive of Christianity differently than our forefathers did. For us, Christianity is a personal religion. For most of the past two thousand years, it has been a kingdom. It was a certain kind of kingdom. It superseded the rulers of this world, but was transacted through the church. The church and the state were intertwined in civilization because both had separate, but related, roles to play. Western nations once recognized that the state resides under the eternal King. This distinction will become important as the story unfolds.

Karl Marx famously said, "Religion is the opium of the people." It turns out that, thanks to his many progressive disciples, removing that "drug" is precisely how Progressives turned the people "woke." The Progressives of the early twentieth century knew one central thing: they needed to open one all-important gate—like the gates of Mordor—through which they would be allowed to exploit an undefended vacuum. That is, they needed to remove the key ingredient of our civilization. They achieved this mission; it is our task to figure out how to slam this gate back shut.

Paideia

The term *paideia* (pie-day-ah, or παιδεια in Greek) presents yet another challenge. The ancient Greek word had a wide-ranging influence in history, and still does today. Yet, chances are, you've never heard of it. The very concept was buried by the Progressives a century ago. At its core, paideia motivates our decisions and behavior through our affections, cultivated in us at very young age. Because it influences each person in a culture, paideia forms a culture. How do we vote? Do we marry? Same sex? Large families? Small families? Do we do productive things? Start a revolution? A million actions lie on the surface, while paideia lies at a much deeper level. It is the blueprint of thought, affections, and narrative through which every one of us views everything. It is the building block of culture. It determines the future of a people. If you're struggling with the concept at this point, it will become more clear. It's hard to get a good look at your own face, and paideia is so deeply embedded in us, it's even harder to see.

The WCP, then, is a particular type of paideia that was intentionally created for a self-governing people. It is unique to the West, and America was founded based upon it. The WCP is a singularity in history. It was the innovation of a classical world dedicated to freedom and freedom-loving people. It was created specifically to sustain republics more than two thousand years ago. Our founding fathers leaned heavily on the WCP in their debates as they formed the American Republic. Citizens must be cultivated into it through what we now call classical Christian education, which has been largely missing for over a century. The WCP's loss over the past century was not an accident; its loss now endangers our nation.

Opening this book, you probably thought, as I did, that the problem in our schools is what is being taught. It's not. *The problem is what has been systematically, if quietly, removed.* Unless you understand the hidden backstory of this heist, you will almost certainly underestimate what once happened in America's schools. The Progressives are counting on the fact that we never remember.

PAIDEIA IS POWERFUL—AND CAN BE CONSCIOUSLY DESIGNED

The "common school" was the predecessor to today's public school. Prior to 1820, school in America had been the domain of the family and the church, which had been the center of perpetuating the WCP since the first century. While the WCP remained at the center of America's schools until about 1910, the call for a common, national school system was heard as soon as the Revolutionary War muskets fell silent. By the late 1800s, for a small group of early pre-progressives, "school" was not a sideshow. It was the main attraction because they knew what we have since forgotten—that paideia is a powerful tool, especially if you intend to transform the cultural landscape.

Why paideia? Paideia remains an unfamiliar word to us. But a brief explanation of its *power* explains why it was the primary target for Progressives—we'll unpack that more soon. Suffice it to say, its power had—until now—endured for millennia. During the golden age of Greece, three things were discovered about paideia:

First, every people, tribe, or nation depends on a paideia—instilled in future generations during childhood—to perpetuate their culture. Second, the quality of this paideia will be reflected in the greatness of the culture. As a rule, all cultures *naturally* and *unintentionally* culti-vate an unthinking, dogmatic, and narrow paideia. But some of these dogmas are better (more true) than others.

Finally, the Greeks realized that, while paideia is a natural part of growing up in any family and society, it might be possible to cultivate an *intentional* paideia—a paideia that supports a self-governing civili-zation. Their pre-Christian paideia was based on humanistic pursuit of the divine ideal. This was a world-changing idea: education of the young could create a culture that pursues higher purposes.

In fourth- and fifth-century BC Athens, the Academy (Plato's original school) was born of the question: What type of paideia is required for a people to govern themselves? To think for themselves? To enjoy the pursuit of divine Truth? To think freely rather than to merely accept the dogmas of their day? If they could accomplish these goals, they could establish a culture that grew greater and stronger with every generation. This culture would be exceptionally powerful. And exceptionally good. They experimented with cultivating the power of thought into children. In an irony, they were the original Progressives! But, unlike the American Progressives, the Greeks did not seek human ends; they sought to align humans with God (the Logos). The results were astounding and unparalleled in all of history. They built Western civilization with this idea. We'll soon see how Christianity later assumed this role as paideia cultivator.

You are likely still thinking, but what *is* paideia? A noun? A thing? An idea? Paideia is contained in that human part of the soul that makes us who we are. Why does a child born in Vietnam, but adopted as an infant into the United States, grow to be nearly indistinguishable from any other American in almost every way? Paideia is the reason. Paideia is common to a community. It does not reference individual differences brought about by temperament. It is associated with our youthful education because that is when we are shaped. Paideia is made up of ideas, presumptions, beliefs, affections, and ways of understanding that define us. Everyone's paideia is shaped during childhood—which is why the Left is so hyperfocused on things like universal pre-K. They can harness it to reflect their progressive plans, imprinted on the hearts of the impressionable.

Paideia, generally speaking, is ubiquitous, present in everyone in all cultures. Like DNA determines our physical attributes, paideia determines our cultural attributes. A cultivated paideia leads to a vision of what life should be and the virtues required to pursue it—"the vision of the good life." The Western Christian Paideia (WCP) is a unique form of paideia in that it was intentionally developed and cultivated beginning with the Greeks, and flows through all Western cultures. Like DNA, it intermixes with other cultures to vary slightly by region and era.

The Greeks had proven that education was a powerful influencer of paideia, and this made "school" a very attractive target for the pre-progressives as they contemplated a new order. And make no mistake about it, from the beginning, Progressives have sought to upend the American order. Recall that until the twentieth century, knowledge of Latin and Greek and the study of classic literature was universal in college. The entrance exams of colleges in the 1700s and 1800s were in Greek and Latin! So it should come as no surprise that these early Progressives had a working knowledge of paideia—a discovery fully unpacked in this book.

Up until about 1900, the power of paideia was camouflaged in lowly one-room schools and churches that were the intentional cultivators of Western Christian Paideia. Under the old form of classical Christian education, children gained wisdom by studying history and the classics. With the current American paideia in our schools, children look only to factual knowledge and only those facts that are new and recent. Old is outdated and irrelevant. With the WCP, children saw divine order in everything. Today, the current American paideia leads toward a twisted form of antihumanist anarchy, masquerading as progressive humanism. Under the WCP, children were practiced in the art of reason as they sought Truth. Today's American paideia consists of indoctrination from the secular cultural ideologues in power. The WCP set children on a lifelong search for greater meaning. The current American paideia has been reduced to a search for a vocational job. In the final analysis, the WCP created a strong-spirited citizen who was better together with others, in community. In our schools today, Americans have become weak-spirited citizens who serve only the state.

To break it down even more simply, here is a direct comparison of Western Christian Paideia (WCP) versus the American Progressive Paideia:

WCP: A lifelong search for greater meaning in life.
TODAY: Search for a job.

WCP: Seek wisdom.
TODAY: Seek facts.

WCP: Study history and classics.
TODAY: There's nothing worth knowing that wasn't just thought of.

WCP: Teach the application of reason.
TODAY: Preach the acceptance of indoctrination.

WCP: There is a divine order, revealed in Christ.
TODAY: There is humanist anarchy.

WCP: Strong-spirited citizens who are better together.
TODAY: Weak-spirited citizens who better serve the state.

AFGHANISTAN SHOWS THE CIVILIZATIONAL POWER OF A STRONG PAIDEIA

During the writing of this book, America's two-decade war in Afghanistan came to an inglorious end. After thousands of lives lost, and trillions of dollars spent, the Islamist Taliban are back in charge. It's a humbling, if illuminating, reality. Like most Americans, I was eager for "the folks who knocked these buildings down, to hear all of us soon," as President George W. Bush said atop the rubble of the World Trade Center in 2001. American military might quickly toppled the Taliban, and Al Qaeda scurried into Pakistan. What followed was a nineteen-year experiment in Afghanistan, during which I had a front-row seat.

Americans were proud to see the images of Afghans—including women—holding up their purple-stained fingers as they went to the polls to "elect" their new government. Democracy had arrived in Afghanistan! Girls were going to school, women were working in government jobs, and religious fanatics were relegated to the hinterlands of the country. Except, as I saw firsthand in 2011—and the world saw ten years later, in the summer of 2021—it was all a mirage. None of it was real; it was a house of cards, destined to collapse.

Why? Conventional answers abound: the Afghan Army was built in the image of the American Army, unable to operate effectively without air support. Or the Afghan government was irredeemably corrupt and beholden to Western aid. Or, my personal favorite, "the Americans have the watches, but we [the Taliban] have the time"—American political will was destined to break. (Osama bin Laden did predict as much.) All of these explanations touch on aspects of America's failure, but none explain the deeper reason. For two decades of work to collapse in two weeks, something more fundamental was at play.

When I served in Afghanistan, my job—as a counterinsurgency instructor—was to study the insurgency, meaning the Taliban. In short, we taught both Americans and Afghans that they needed to know the terrain, especially the human terrain. Who is our enemy? What motivates them? And how do they leverage and/or exploit the population? From there, we looked at the "root causes" of population grievances that our enemy was exploiting. Finally, our job was to find sustainable solutions that advanced the legitimacy of the Afghan Army, police, and government. Know the human terrain, identify root causes for problems, find sustainable solutions, and legitimize our allies. It sounded great, and I knew how to teach the hell out of it.

But, as it turns out, we always missed the mark on all aspects of what we taught. You know who did not miss the mark? The Taliban. They knew exactly who the people were, their root causes were clear, they were nothing if not sustainable, and they had legitimacy we could never manufacture. Why is that?

The answer to that question is, interestingly, central to the thesis of this book. The people of Afghanistan, for centuries and centuries—and despite invasion after invasion—have a learned, ingrained, cultivated sense of themselves—how they govern, whom they worship, and ultimately what they value. In short, they have a different "vision of the good life" than Americans do. This integration of culture, values, and education is called paideia. The paideia of Afghanistan is, quite clearly, much more closely aligned with the Taliban than with any sense of Western democracy or values.

That is why, when we point to raised "purple fingers," we are actually holding up a middle finger to the Afghan paideia. American-style democracy is not in the DNA of the Afghan paideia, and certainly cannot be imported by outsiders. If you and I had been born in Afghanistan and been confronted with such a drastically different view of the good life from the one we were taught in our youth, we would likely have had the same reaction. Americans are not special by default; we don't have some special sense of freedom imprinted on our souls by God. What makes America special is our own paideia—our Western Christian Paideia—which has taken centuries to cultivate. Ideas like religious freedom, freedom of speech, natural rights, and equal justice are the exception in human history, not the rule. They were gifted to us by previous generations.

So, when we attempt to replace core aspects of Afghan paideia with our own over just two decades (a blip in human history), it is doomed to fail. If anything, it only strengthens the Afghan paideia—fortifying their belief in the supremacy of their system. The condition of America's paideia—the Western Christian Paideia—depends not just on the past, but also on what happens now, and what will need to happen in the future. Without constant cultivation, America's paideia can change—or be lost altogether. We are not special, and we can lose it; in fact, watching another culture safeguard their (backward) paideia reminds me how defenseless we are in guarding our own. Not only could we not impose it in Afghanistan, but we are losing it at home.

THE PROGRESSIVE PLOT

If you're like me, you're inherently skeptical of conspiracy theories. Grand schemes pulled off, in the shadows, and executed to near perfection? Unlikely. In my efforts in conservative circles over the years, I've been accused of being involved in giant conspiracies that have massive and far-reaching impacts (*the Koch network!* and *FOX News!* come to mind). But our impact rarely, if ever, matched the accusations. And the level of coordination and conspiracy we are accused of usually comes down to fortuitous coincidence or honest, transparent, hard work.

The core problem with most conspiracy theories—from the Right or the Left—is that they assume *competency* on the part of the so-called conspirator(s). Efforts are often launched, but often not successful. Or the success of those efforts is the result of many groups and many people; the idea of all-powerful puppet masters is usually not reality. For a real conspiracy to happen, lots of people have to get a lot of things right, while predicting the future and keeping it all secret. Human beings, mere mortals, don't do that well.

But, in the case of the progressive takeover of our education system, the impact of the progressive planners *exceeds* the understanding of our accusations for one core reason: *their theory preceded the conspiracy*—or, in this case, a long-term movement. They have a coherent and powerful theory that, over time and with more institutional power, has catapulted them into a position to unleash a full-blown progressive plot against our country. And, once you look hard enough, it's not difficult to connect the dots.

Modern Progressives, who have long since institutionalized their theories into power at the K–12 level, are able to draw a nearly straight line to the origins of the academic theory upon which they now rely. They are open about it now—as future chapters will outline—but the intellectual underpinnings remain mostly hidden, shrouded in mystery.

The first thing they had to do was neutralize the Western Christian Paideia—and they knew the classroom was the place to do it.

SCHOOL IS MORE IMPORTANT THAN YOU THINK

What if education is something far bigger than just learning to read and vocational training? In Matthew 6, Jesus says to "seek first the kingdom of God and all these things will be added to you." He says this directly in response to those who are worried about their jobs—and money. Most parents see education as a path to a job. What if we were to build schools that took Jesus's teaching to heart? We used to.

Classical Christian education (CCE) was built for this purpose in the first century AD. Historically, classically trained Christians have built the best schools in the world to "seek first Christ's kingdom." The "who's who" of inventors, leaders, military generals, politicians, and businessmen in history were classically educated up until the past century—as were nearly all the missionaries, pastors, and theologians of prior centuries. The exclusive influence of classical education ended in the late 1800s both for K–12 and college.

Ross Douthat, columnist for the *New York Times*, laid out the situation in higher education well: "Between the 19th century and the 1950s, the American university was gradually transformed from an institution intended to transmit knowledge into an institution designed to serve technocracy. The religious premises fell away, the classical curriculums were displaced by specialized majors, the humanities ceded pride of place to technical disciplines, and the professor's role became more and more about research rather than instruction."[1]

Douthat articulates the problem in the university we have today. He echoes the conservative criticisms brought by great thinkers like C. S. Lewis, G. K. Chesterton, Dorothy Sayers, Robert Hutchins, and others. But, unlike the modern conventional wisdom brought forth by Douthat, these earlier critics realized that K–12 was the most important battlefield. Douthat, like so many today, is focused on the more obvious radicalization of the university, while the humble K–12 schoolroom simply remains a problematic sideshow. His critique strikes near the target, but like so many before him, Douthat fails to put his finger on the exact cause of the decline. *We all have.* The WCP's removal, as we shall see, from both colleges *and K–12 classrooms* has been carefully hidden. Make no mistake about it, the paideia of our youngest was the Progressives' ultimate prize.

PART II

THE *UNAUTHORIZED* HISTORY OF AMERICAN EDUCATION

4

THE STORY OF THE PROGRESSIVE HEIST

Over the past two generations, America's national vision of the good life has quietly changed. The new vision is the result of a clandestine war against Western civilization that has enveloped us for more than one hundred years. While we were busy staving off Marxist economics and "making the world safe for democracy," underneath our noses the Progressives slowly and quietly removed our key ingredient—the Western Christian Paideia—and replaced it with a paideia of their own making.

Here's how they did it: Like a burglar replacing a priceless artifact with a forgery on an alarmed pressure sensor, the Progressives needed to replace the engine of WCP with something else. Simply removing it, one hundred years ago, would have set off America's cultural alarm and caused an overwhelming backlash because the WCP had been fostered in schools, homes, churches, and communities for two thousand years. Had it been just removed, it would have been missed.

So, step one for the Progressives was to centralize the commanding heights of culture in a single, very powerful institution that could facilitate a clandestine removal of the WCP: the American public school.

America's schools have been a concern for conservatives for some time, but never on this scale. You may think you've heard this story before—"Public schools are 'liberal.'" You may think the problem is modern manifestations like the 1619 Project and gender pronouns. You may think it depends on where you live. "Our local schools here are still conservative," we tell ourselves. Or maybe that "good families can overcome the influence of progressive schools." These narratives have kept American families in progressive schools that were designed to undermine America's first principles.

Culture wars employ a different sort of armament. In Chapter 2, we learned about the "commanding heights" of cultural Marxism, each of which is almost exclusively contained within education: teachers colleges, teachers unions, accrediting agencies, state standards, standardized tests, and curriculum—all controlled by Progressives. In this chapter, we'll reveal the core of our enemy's initial strategy.

As with any forgery, the symptoms of this *new* paideia were noticed by experts. We were warned. Allan Bloom said that Americans were closing their minds (1987), and C. S. Lewis said that we were abolishing man by removing virtue from our schools (1944). Richard M. Weaver told us that these bad "ideas" would have consequences (1948), Rudolf Flesch warned that "Johnny can't read" (1966), and Mark Noll said that evangelicals had lost their minds (1994). Neil Postman told us we were amusing ourselves to death (1985). Dorothy Sayers told us that we were not teaching children to think (1948), and Francis Schaeffer said that we had "escaped from reason" (1968). In 2000, Jacques Barzun declared the culture war lost in his *New York Times* bestseller *From Dawn to Decadence*, recounting a five-hundred-year slide down to the present. Socioeconomic changes, poor theology, and progressive politics have all played a part. Each of these thinkers was orbiting around a bigger, central cause, but that central cause seemed elusive.

Before this torrent of midcentury warnings, America had already been quietly remade through its schools—advancing a new paideia. Advances in technology and prosperity throughout the 1900s masked the progressive transformation. While *progressive* is a broad term now associated with the Left in America, "the Progressives" were once a more concentrated and organized force. Their vision was not entirely economic. It was rooted in culture. In reality, their vision was for a new civilization that would replace Christianity and America's Western classical roots with a cultural form of Marxism.

How did we miss it? Conservatives, beginning in the mid-twentieth century, were transfixed by free-market economics. All the while, the real action was happening at the root of culture. Economics and politics follow culture—and culture follows faith. Civilization is now in crisis because cultural Marxism germinated for more than a century. The real story went virtually untold until now. It goes back to the roots of the country, when the seeds of progressivism were sown by Deist founders. It continues through Progressives making school mandatory, twentieth-century Christians splintering into groups that forgot their cultural heritage, and Progressives jumping into the vacuum with a new nationalist, godless paideia, trying vainly to fill the "God-shaped hole" in America's heart. Finally, they successfully hollowed out America's vision of education into nothing more than job training.

FROM "KINGDOM CHRISTIANITY" TO "HUMANISTIC UTOPIA"

From the time of the early church, classical Christian education was the defining force in Western culture and particularly America. Then, it all stopped. Why? How?

Up until about 1770, pretty much every European nation agreed on one point: Jesus Christ is the reigning King over this world. Indications of this belief saturate the pre-Enlightenment world. Read any governmental document from before 1700 and you'll probably see subjection to the "Reign of Christ" plainly stated in the text. "In the Year of our Lord" preceded nearly every date, regardless of the context—secular or religious. Nearly every European flag that dates from before 1700 has a Christian symbol on it to indicate the subjection of that state to the Kingdom of Christ (not simply "God"). Progressive textbooks cover only America, suspended without this Kingdom context. Perhaps they would rather keep history silent to prevent students from asking too many questions.

For most of history before 525 AD, people counted a historical date through a reference to a prominent reigning king at that time. We even see this in the Bible, as in Luke 3:1, "In the fifteenth year of the reign of Tiberius Caesar," to date Christ's ministry. Beginning in 525 AD, Western cultures replaced this dating practice with the birth of the eternally reigning King. This quickly became the universal annual count for every society. Until very recently, we referred to dates after Christ's birth as Anno Domini (AD)—the year of our Lord.

For well over one thousand years, Christianity was viewed as an actual kingdom within and above the kingdoms of this world. Kingdoms have citizens, and citizens have something called paideia, which is the instrument that creates and perpetuates culture. We have already seen that the paideia that permeated Western culture was the Western Christian Paideia (WCP). The loss of this cultural instrument, the WCP, is the beginning of our story.

By the time of America's founding, nearly every colonial child received some classical Christian education and practically every school and college had classical Christian roots. The classical Christian form of education had been in continuous and near-exclusive use for well over 1,500 years. It was the source of the WCP. Then things began to change.

DEISM FORESHADOWED PROGRESSIVISM

At America's founding, two powerful ideas charted an early, almost imperceivable course away from Western Christian culture. The first was Deism. Among many of the elites, Deism replaced "Jesus Christ" with a general, passive "God." You were probably told (in progressive textbooks) that "Deism" was simply a moderate form of generic Christianity held by some of our founding fathers, but this isn't the full story. Deism was ideological. Thomas Paine, like other Deistic founders, asserted that "a revolution in the system of government would be followed by a revolution in the system of religion," and that "man would return to the pure, unmixed and unadulterated belief in one God and no more."[2] In other words, to progress with this American vision, there could be no recognition of Christ in public institutions. The two kingdoms were no longer a pair.

Enlightenment leaders were turning back to the pre-Christian, Greek idea of education as based on divinely informed reason. As educational historian Lawrence Cremin points out, Deism "baldly [attacked] the most cherished teachings of contemporary Christianity: The divinity of Christ, the authenticity of Scripture, and the authority of the church."[3] Aside from these philosophical reasons, Deism had practical benefits. With Maryland mostly Roman Catholic, Pennsylvania Quaker, New England a blend of Puritan and Congregational, and most southern states Presbyterian, there was disunity in America's Christianity at a time when unity was vitally important to the nation.

To understand the second development, we must first understand the Christian viewpoint that had dominated the world for about thirteen centuries: God created. Man fell. Jesus came, died, was resurrected, and was enthroned over all the nations. We live in His Kingdom today. We also live in "the city of man," governed by men's institutions, but under the authority of Christ's Kingdom. The Christian "vision of the good life" was tied to our desire as Christian citizens to live "to the Glory of God and His Kingdom."

When Benjamin Franklin proposed the first seal of the United States, he wanted an image of Moses bringing down the sea upon Pharaoh. Thomas Jefferson pictured the Israelites wandering in the wilderness. You might think Franklin and Jefferson had Christian intentions, but they did not. They both saw America as a new order—a sort of redemptive force in itself that would become a new promised land. Their imagery conflated the kingdom-purpose of Christianity with America. In the end, the creators of America's seal prevailed with the Latin phrases *Annuit Coeptis* (He has favored our undertaking) and *Novus Ordo Seclorum* (A new order of the ages has begun). The seal's design had moved to a Roman-inspired eagle, with the Deistic symbol of the all-seeing eye on the reverse. We no longer needed a Christian kingdom, or a symbol of the cross, but a new order under a generic God, vested in a nation based on new ideas. America's destiny as a City on a Hill, inspired by John Winthrop's speech of many decades earlier—"A Model of Christian Charity"—was reimagined with America as the light of the nations, not Christ.

For the many Christians among America's founding fathers, such as Patrick Henry, John Jay, and Samuel Adams, Christianity still remained firmly ensconced in homes and culture. They saw America with a different purpose. Their view of limited government played more prominently than their view of America's destiny. This admixture of Deists and Christians established America on a firm foundation through our Declaration of Independence and Constitution. Both groups realized the danger of tyranny, especially on religious liberty, and thus sought to limit the powers of government. Both groups also revered scripture: for the Christians as God's revelation, and for the Deists as the most important piece of religious literature.

But, with all due reverence and gratitude for the founding generation, the diminished role of Christ's Kingdom in America's founding would unintentionally create structural vulnerabilities that Progressives eventually exploited. Cremin identifies how this beginning was eventually used by Progressives to turn America toward their ends: "At bottom, it was a conflict over the nature of man and his institutions. If God were indeed benevolent and man essentially rational . . . then reason and Scripture were man's truest guides to that slow but steady moral and civic improvement that would facilitate his progress toward perfection."[4]

This was the earliest flicker of "progressive" thought—the pursuit of utopian perfection. Later, this flicker would combine with Marxism and the "Social Gospel" to become progressivism. With a powerful national vision, sometimes now labeled "manifest destiny," old civic institutions needed to be transformed. And a new institution was needed—the common school.

PROGRESSIVES MAKE SCHOOL MANDATORY

With America's "new order" in view, Horace Mann, father of American education, embarked on his circuit-riding crusade between 1840 and 1860. Mann organized school districts and implemented a common curriculum in many states. He emphasized "nationalistic" purposes for school. Mann imported the ideas of mechanistic Prussian (German) education into the United States to gradually replace the older, classical tradition. You may recall that Germany, at the same time, was also incubating the Enlightenment and utopian philosophies of the likes of Immanuel Kant, Georg Wilhelm Friedrich Hegel, Karl Marx, and Friedrich Nietzsche, to name a few. John Dewey, who we'll soon see is the father of progressive schooling in America, wrote his PhD thesis on the philosophy of Kant. As you can imagine, this new form of German education was not rooted in classical Christianity; in fact, it was meant to replace it. To underscore how significant this connection was, we get the word *kindergarten* from Mann's German influence— German for "child's garden."

In support of Mann's effort, his home state of Massachusetts was the first state to require that all children attend school, in 1852. Mississippi became the last state to require education of every child, in 1918. These were called "compulsory education laws." Local school boards had control and schools were not yet seen as "secular" but rather a community activity with the Western Christian Paideia deeply embedded. So, naturally, the Bible remained freely taught within American communities and schools. *Yes, until the past century, the Holy Bible was freely taught in American schools.*

This new compulsory education movement had a profound side effect that few people, now or then, realized: states that require parents to send their child to school must create a state-based control apparatus for that education. Over this time period, state and local governments took on the role of schoolmaster, supplanting the church, the parents, and even the influence of the local community. The commanding heights of culture were slowly centralized. There were immediate positive effects of this government centralization: more kids were in school and economic prosperity flourished. And soon, Americans identified strongly with public education. As with any major change, however, there were significant consequences, ones that would not emerge for nearly a century—and were soon exploited by actors with other intentions.

TWENTIETH-CENTURY CHRISTIANITY SPLINTERS

In *The God Who Is There*, Francis Schaeffer wrote of the "Faith vs. Reason divide" that radically undermined the influence of the Christian church in the twentieth century. That divide influenced schooling in America. As the sun set on the 1800s, the nascent progressive movement caught a break when the Protestant church divided and yielded its traditional role in society. One side of this church divide joined the Progressives. The other side took a diminished view of education (and thus reason) and forgot the importance of paideia.

Prior to this divide, of course, there were denominations in Protestantism, and there were Roman Catholics, and other sects of Christianity. Despite doctrinal differences, all of these groups saw Christianity and life as intertwined. Society, politics, family, business, charity, medical care, education, orphans, widows, marriage . . . the list goes on . . . were all viewed as under subjection to the Kingdom of Christ and His ordinances. All shared a nearly identical vision of the good life, and everything was connected and made sense within the orbits of the Western Christian Paideia.

The earliest dawn of this new, fateful divide is symbolized by a chance meeting at an 1875 revival in Massachusetts. This revival brought together the father of modern fundamentalism, who would pioneer evangelicalism in America, and the father of the Social Gospel, who would influence the progressive mainline Protestants in America. Dwight L. Moody conducted revivals and started Bible institutes to train Christians for missionary work without the trappings of a seminary or university. Moody has been called the father of Christian fundamentalism. Washington Gladden promoted the idea that Christianity was more about the practice of social justice than worship. Gladden, a congregational minister in Massachusetts, became the father of the Social Gospel and liberalism in the church.

Gladden's progressive Christians believed they should balance the wealth scales, seek women's suffrage, advance prohibition, and pursue a host of other problems in society. Gladden's "Social Gospel" went on to become the rallying cry for social justice in the liberal church, leading to alliances with the Progressives in the first decades of the 1900s. Because the government had a clear interest in administering justice, enveloping Marxism into "justice" gave Progressives the government role they needed. The Social gospel soon left the Christian tradition behind in its pursuit of labor laws, temperance, women's rights, and other social activism.

On the other side of the divide, the "Fundamentalist Gospel" had more orthodox leanings. Gladden did not believe in the inerrancy of the Bible. Fundamentalists, recognizing the danger of his view, reacted by creating new eschatology called dispensationalism. In this view of end-times prophecy, the Kingdom was coming at some future time, so now was the time to evangelize. This view allowed for a very literal reading of the book of Revelation. But it also distanced Christian life from an integrated view of the world and the Kingdom—on earth now. The WCP depends on this integration. Prior generations of Christians believed Isaiah's prophecy "The government shall be upon His shoulders," foretelling Christ's birth; Daniel's prophecy that after the Persian, Greek, and Roman governments fell, Christ's Kingdom would rise in their place; and Christ's own words that the generation present when He was speaking would not pass away until His Kingdom came. These historical Christians took the whole of scripture to mean that Christianity was an existing Kingdom on earth. When fundamentalism emphasized evangelism and deemphasized the church as an existing kingdom, the idea of paideia to enculturate that kingdom was largely forgotten. For example, during the late nineteenth century, "Sunday school" was popularized by the Fundamentalists to replace the functions of the integrated paideia schools that were pervasive in America at the time—further isolating Christianity from its traditional worldview.

The divide, at first unknowingly, served the progressive battle plan well. Battles have decisive points at which they turn. And, in any battle, an often-successful strategy is to divide your opponent's force between two objectives. The Progressives caught a break when American Christianity divided itself.

Two dominant church movements emerged*—the evangelicals and the mainline Protestants. The evangelical church descended from fundamentalism. Evangelical churches made evangelism their first purpose and retreated from traditional roles in society and government. Because they treated "sin and salvation" as the extent of the Gospel message, they were occupied with revivals and insufficiently concerned with church responsibilities as they were turned over to the government—first in education, and then progressively in caring for widows, orphans, the sick, the elderly, and the poor, to name just a few. Mainline churches made social and governmental causes theirs, with little use for the gospel of salvation or the truth of scripture. This latter mainline Christian group would come to form one of three constituencies of the progressive movement.

---

* Roman Catholics retained a more integrated view, but they were a small minority at the time.

THE PROGRESSIVES ENVISION A UTOPIAN "NEW ORDER"

In the late 1800s, atheistic Marxism rose up against traditional powers in Europe. Wars and revolutions, including the Russian Revolution, World War I, and World War II, were fueled by this new ideology. At the same time, radical Marxists were getting little traction in America because of a more deeply set WCP. So, a soft-Marxist coalition of sorts formed: the Progressives. American Progressives in the late 1800s blended the idea of Marxist government with aspects from the Social Gospel and the belief in an American national destiny in order to make Marxism more palatable to Americans. The result was a movement of both economic and cultural Marxism.

Progressive politicians like Teddy Roosevelt saw potential in America's world leadership exporting democracy. (I wrote my first book, *In the Arena*, largely based on a 1910 speech by Teddy Roosevelt; the pull of this viewpoint remains powerful to this day.) Many progressive pastors and clergy saw government solutions to problems of economic and social justice. Marxist reformers and feminists sought a new social order based on equality (later to become "equity"). The odd alliance of Manifest Destiny proponents, Christian socialists, and cultural Marxists fueled the powerful progressive movement between 1900 and 1940.

Each of these constituent groups joined together to harness humanism and to achieve utopian ends. The progressive vision would be dubbed years later by President Lyndon Johnson the "Great Society." Progressives sought to unite America around this new vision of a new order—through a long-term fusion of politics, academia, pseudo-Christianity, culture, and the classroom.

THE PROGRESSIVE SCHOOL PROJECT BUILDS A GOD-FREE PAIDEIA

From the 1930s and before 1950, the Great Depression and World War II steered the nation toward a relatively conservative era. Then we all know what happened in the 1960s. So, many of us think the good ol' days before 1960 were marked by common Christian values. This is not true. The change began in the late 1800s. When we miss the true story, we fail to understand the world we are in today.

From 1865 to about 1925, America underwent one of the most dramatic social changes in its history—maybe in any nation's history, barring revolution. During this time, the cultural paideia we see in today's America—the American Progressive Paideia—was first imagined. To understand this movement, historical context is helpful.

After the end of the Civil War, an abundance of land in America's West and political forces in Europe drove immigration, particularly from Germany, Ireland, and Italy. America became even more religiously and culturally diverse. This diversity created factions in communities that had previously been united by the local church. A new point of unity was needed. Mann's common school was the obvious choice. Until the late 1800s, these schools were overwhelmingly Christian—nearly entirely Protestant—and they were built to sustain the WCP.

We tend to think of the period between 1880 and 1910 in America as a time dominated by western industrial expansion. And we think of the time between 1910 and 1930 as an era of financial wealth and excess (think the Roaring Twenties, robber barons, and the rise of Wall Street financing), with World War I inserted.

But despite—or perhaps because of—the success of industry and capitalism, these periods were also marked by radical activism. Anarchists like Emma Goldman, suffragists and feminists like Margaret Sanger, and socialists and labor movements led by men like Bill Haywood were arguably more active than protest movements of the twentieth century, or even the twenty-first. The protests were often violent and strongly ideological. Chicago's Haymarket Riot and the Colorado Labor Wars were just a few examples of large and violent protests. They often advocated for pure forms of Marxism. You may remember that President William McKinley was assassinated by an anarchist associated with Goldman during this time. Significant anarchist protests in the United States supported the communist revolution in Russia in 1917. Radical atheistic socialism was bigger than we now remember.

In contrast with these Marxist radicals, the Progressives represented a more moderate blend: a new order based on the social gospel, soft Marxism, and Manifest Destiny. Compared to the alternative, this left-wing movement seemed reasonable . . . and even patriotically American.

If you were to time-travel to the mid-1890s and observe America, you might make out the outlines of the earliest progressive players as they coalesced into a movement. Teddy Roosevelt's Rough Riders were determined to drive the Spanish out of Cuba, motivated by America's desire to promote Cuban independence. This became the precedent for American intervention in foreign wars. Christian temperance workers like Frances Willard were frenzied in their third-grade curricular work (more on this in a minute), and Social Gospel activists were working on legislative action across most states. Socialist ministers like Francis Bellamy were doing their part to transform America's schools with a new creed (called a "pledge"), to displace a Christian one.

In 1892, Bellamy, an early Progressive, authored the precursor to the pledge of allegiance, called the Bellamy Salute, which would come to be used in schools across the United States. Curiously, Bellamy's pledge included the Roman salute with outstretched arm—very similar to what would later be known as the Nazi salute. It was nearly identical to what would become our current pledge, except that it made no mention of God. Bellamy's salute had a purpose: to unite and elevate the American people with reference only to America, not to Christ. The WCP no longer bound America together; the new pledge was designed to supplant the creeds of Christianity. The public school classroom would become a shrine of sorts to progressive ideas.

The Bellamy Salute was intentionally part of that liturgy, as were American flags. By the early 1900s, there were portraits of John Dewey and Horace Mann in the classroom, alongside George Washington. In 1942, the original salute, with hands outstretched, was replaced for its obvious connection with the Nazi salute. In the 1950s, Bellamy's original pledge was amended to add "under God" by Congress amid fears of another form of Marxism—atheistic communism. Modern liberals don't share the same fears, and during the 2020 Democratic National Convention, more than one speaker returned the pledge closer to the Bellamy original by removing "under God."

The original 1892 Bellamy Salute:

I pledge allegiance to **my** Flag and the Republic for which it stands; one Nation indivisible, with Liberty and Justice for all.

The current pledge of allegiance:

I pledge allegiance to **the flag of the United States of America**, and to the Republic for which it stands; one Nation, **under God**, indivisible, with Liberty and Justice for all.

The Bellamy Salute served its purpose as nationalism slowly replaced Christianity over a period of decades. This form of nationalism, married to what has been called Manifest Destiny, became a sort of civil religion in its own right in America. Nationalism has its place—no doubt—but this form of American "democracy" was intentionally disordered. It was an early placement of "nation" above "Christ"—and executed intentionally.

In the cauldron of cultural change between 1865 and 1910, American public schools became a proven tool for social reformers and "proto-Progressives." In the 1870s, Frances Willard tapped into the power of the new universal school curriculum. She was the head of the Woman's Christian Temperance Union near the end of the nineteenth century and an advocate of Christian socialism, feminism, and women's suffrage.

Frustrated by nearly fifty years of political inaction on alcohol prohibition, Willard experimented with a fledgling tool at the time—the American common school system. In the 1870s, she employed an anti-alcohol curriculum among the nation's third graders. She used a newly instituted common curriculum across many states. Within a generation, prohibition was passed not just as a law, but as a constitutional amendment; this was not just a limit on alcohol, but a complete prohibition. This exceeded the wildest political aspirations of the prohibitionists.

Willard had proven that the new American school system could steer our country, albeit with a generational lag, anywhere the Progressives wanted it to go. She lived out Lincoln's adage that "the philosophy in the schoolroom in one generation, becomes the philosophy of government in the next." School as an instrument of progressive social power had been discovered; perhaps, in part, this experiment inspired John Dewey's turn toward education.

EDUCATION IN THE WCP IS REPLACED WITH VOCATIONAL TRAINING

In the late 1890s, John Dewey gave a series of lectures on "The School and Social Progress." The series was later published as a book, in which Dewey rejected schools that served parental purposes for their children in favor of school as a tool for social manipulation and progress. He argued for vocational training rather than a focus on the liberal arts, saying, "It is our present [classical Christian] education which is highly specialized, one sided and narrow. It is an education dominated almost entirely by the medieval conception of learning. It is something which appeals for the most part simply to the intellectual aspect of our natures, our desire to learn, to accumulate information and to get control of the symbols of learning; not to our impulses and tendencies to make, to do, to create, to produce."[5]

Dewey proceeded to argue that most students do not need a liberal education; that could be left to the elites. Dewey rejected the WCP's necessity, in favor of pragmatic education. For his revolutionary work in transforming American education, Dewey is widely regarded as the father of progressive American education—the father of the modern American school. His pragmatic approach to education set most students on a path of vocational training, untethered from the WCP. C. S. Lewis later wrote, in 1939, that "education is essentially for freemen and vocational training for slaves . . . If education is beaten by training, civilization dies." Lewis wrote this from the perspective of preserving WCP; Dewey's aim was to end it.

From 1900 to 1940, education as we know it today was created by Progressives for progressive ends. The Progressives' true purpose was insidious because once they removed the WCP, they controlled the trajectory of the school system—writing the history we've all learned. Rather than simply add progressive influence, Progressives sought to take a vital ingredient out of school and replace it with industrialized education. This vital ingredient had been there for a very long time—it had perpetuated Western culture for almost two thousand years. Like the diseases of scurvy or rickets, our situation today is not caused by some bacteria or pathogen that we become indoctrinated with through our schools, but rather the absence of an essential nutrient. The untold story is in how Progressives removed this nutrient and kept their actions hidden.

A DECLARATION OF WAR

By now, you probably realize this is a very different story than you learned about Progressives from your high school history textbook. You may have learned that their movement ended child labor or regulated the "robber barons." The Progressives write the textbooks, so they tend to emphasize their popular and positive achievements. And, as the saying goes, the victors tell the stories the way they want them to be told. Their war was clandestine, so it stayed out of their textbooks.

If the origins of today's vision of the good life were known, people might challenge the viewpoint. As it is, we've absorbed so much of the progressive view that its origins are masked as common knowledge. In 1909, progressive senator Robert La Follette, who we will see inspired Chief Justice Earl Warren, declared a war of sorts as he spoke for the movement on the opening page of his *La Follette's Weekly Magazine*, which became *The Progressive*: "The battle is just on. It is young yet. It will be the longest and hardest ever fought for Democracy. In other lands, the people have lost. Here we shall win."

And with that, we had a declaration of war, in black and white. If we hope to defeat America's longtime progressive opponents, we must fight back—not just harder, but wiser. We need to prepare children who, with an independence of mind, still revere divine order, lest they succumb to anarchy. We need to train children to apply reason to find Truth, sourced in God, not themselves. And to reject indoctrination. If we do this, the young will find higher meaning in a higher purpose. Their job will be but a part of who they are, not a life-defining purpose. We will return to an America recognized for its strong-spirited citizens who live in community, rather than eventually dying as weak servants of the state.

But, before we realize any of this, we need to understand our hidden past by continuing to unpack the next step Progressives undertook.

5

THE ELITIST ROOTS
OF PROGRESSIVISM

Each of our children will spend approximately 16,000 hours between the ages of five and eighteen in school. More than 4 million students will start kindergarten this year in America. Through eighth grade, about 34 million children will learn the basics of reading, writing, math, and other subjects. Then, between grades 9–12, about 18 million students will get ready for college. If all goes well, they will find that special college and take about 130 credits over four years to get a bachelor's degree that will get them their first job, and off they go. At age twenty-one, the educational assembly line has done its work.

The outright removal of the WCP left a gaping hole in America's culture in the early 1900s. With the new public education system developed and tested, the Progressives secured their commanding heights. On to step two: after narrowing parental options to the public school, Progressives built a close forgery to replace the WCP in school—the American Progressive Paideia (APP).

To form this new APP, they needed new symbols, a new creed,

new heroes, a set of virtues, and an allegiance that could supplant Christianity. We saw the Progressive Era rise in the late 1890s with the formulation of a creed, curricular manipulation in the common schools, and Dewey's call to create a public school system in the progressive image.

In this chapter we move from a big-picture vision of the progressive heist to examining the movement's deeper intentions. Was there really a purposeful plan to drive God and "creed" from schools? Yes. Progressive institutions and publications talked about it openly. Progressives preached of the "plasticity" of children's minds and the sacredness of democracy, and openly admitted that their plans to dilute educational quality were designed to keep elites in power, while, as Woodrow Wilson put it, "[we need an education for] another class of persons . . . perform[ing] specific difficult manual tasks."

By 1910, the progressive movement was executing its battle plan to take the commanding heights of the culture. But first they needed to completely remove the most stubborn obstacle to their progress—Christianity.

PROGRESSIVES CENTRALIZE THEIR CONTROL

Between 1890 and 1940, the progressive movement was far more influential and cohesive than most people realize today. It was held together in colleges, universities, and societies and through publications like *The New Republic* (first published in 1914) and *The Progressive* (first published in 1909), and later by many mainstream publications. We were told in public school that the Progressive Era ended by 1929, but that is not true; progressivism simply moved into the mainstream of the Democratic Party through Franklin D. Roosevelt. And it had influence on the Republican Party as well. By the 1930s the movement had found its dominant neo-Marxist voice through public declarations like the Humanist Manifesto, and through the writings and work of John Dewey, William James, Upton Sinclair, Margaret Sanger, Eleanor Roosevelt, and countless other self-proclaimed Progressives, and through the press.

With Christianity still embedded in "common schools" in the 1890s, moves were afoot to limit religious education. America's cultural Marxists sought direct government control of education.

Progressives had caught a break back in the 1870s when, in alliance with anti-Catholics, President Ulysses S. Grant and Senator James Blaine attempted to completely prohibit public funds for religious schools. Of course, neither Grant nor Blaine intended to cede control of education to progressive ideals. But they did succeed in concentrating the power of education in the public schools. The Blaine Amendment to the US Constitution was narrowly defeated by the US Senate in 1875 but was passed in thirty-six state constitutions thereafter. Americans at the time, unaware of the future danger, were not concerned, because the WCP, in its Protestant form, was deeply entrenched in the public schools.

All that remained in order to gain an educational monopoly was for Progressives to command the heights of public education and close private schools; this would give them control of all education in the United States. As Progressives neared complete control of public education by 1920, they launched an effort to close all private schools. In 1925, Oregon passed a law that outlawed private Christian schools. Other progressive states had similar laws in process, but the Oregon law was struck down by the US Supreme Court in *Pierce v. Society of Sisters* before it could be enacted. Private Christian schools were narrowly spared from extinction.

Direct legislative control ultimately proved unnecessary because the Progressives, led by Dewey, were establishing control of the commanding heights of the educational establishment. By 1915, the fledgling progressive movement had their "school tool" in place, with nearly every American child in public school. Now they needed to shape it. Dewey emerged as the chief educational architect. His regular contributions to *The New Republic* magazine revealed the progressive strategy.

The New Republic became the Progressives' leading publication. First published in 1914, it featured countless articles by John Dewey and his disciples calling for the overhaul and replacement of the classical school model in some way. Early on, a debate in the publication between the editorial board and proponents of a new progressive "model school" revealed their intention to undermine the WCP.

A PROGRESSIVE PROTOTYPE: THE GARY PLAN

When troops are massed in a particular location, history tells us to pay attention. Not since ancient Athens has any group ever put so much energy and time into experimenting with school as the Progressives. Within a decade of 1900, they created revolutionary school prototypes. They knew paideia was powerful, and that the schools controlled much of the paideia. And they knew classical schools were designed to form the WCP in students. These facts made classical education an impediment—or an all-out showstopper—on their plan. So they set about with a generational plan to shape the hearts of Americans with an American Progressive Paideia instead. To do this, they needed to insulate all children from Christianity.

To transform public schools, the Progressives needed a model school. By 1907, a new progressive model school was ready to launch. The plan emerged in Gary, Indiana, and was aptly called the "Gary

Plan." The Gary Plan, along with several other progressive model schools, would become the prototype for much of America's education in secondary schools. The Gary school system and plan were led by William Wirt, a disciple and former student of Dewey's. From Gary we get many school practices that we now think are normal, including the multi-period high school schedule and much of the modern curricular format. Gary's plan sought to replace the Christian gospel with the progressive gospel.

For our purposes, the most interesting part played by the Gary Plan was not the plan itself, but the debate it stirred among Progressives at the time, revealing their strategy. Christianity in schools was an unwanted competition for a progressive "vision of the good life." When the successful Gary Plan was first transplanted into the New York City public schools between 1908 and 1914, a debate arose—much of which unfolded in the pages of *The New Republic*—within the progressive camp about how best to extract Christianity from the educational system in America. The internal debate among Progressives reflects their true intention to remove Christianity, and the WCP, from school.

The vast majority of Americans at the time expected public schools to teach Christianity and the Bible. *Yes, Christianity and the Bible.* To overcome the Christian influence nationally, Progressives knew they had to move slowly, or else their takeover would fail. The Gary Plan, rather than including Christianity in its program, allowed for students to leave school for religious education during the school day. This was a compromise that kept religion near the school but not in it. But even this arrangement created conflict within the progressive camp.

In the debate over the plan's transfer to New York City, progressive hard-liners feared that "'creed consciousness' will be revived, and religious feeling, [which had been] banished . . . from our American school [in New York], will be brought back in perilous form."

The Gary Plan's progressive supporters, once again writing in *The New Republic* in November 1915 in an article titled "Religion in Public Schools," countered that "as long as the public school is in any sort of competition with the church school, religion will not be entirely divorced from the schools. . . ."[6]

In other words, they wanted to separate religion from school so they could create a new paideia without religion. If they removed Christianity outright, parents would flee to private schools. To prevent this, they first needed to separate the two. Then they could eliminate Christianity from the classroom when the time was right.

The defenders of this so-called pull-out period for religious education knew they could end Christian education if they played their cards right. Defending the pull-out period in the same *New Republic* article, they wrote that "the [church] school [will be] less necessary for those who wish religious instruction for their children. What the Gary Plan seems to do is not to bring religion into the schools, but for the first time to take it out of the schools."

This debate was occurring not in some obscure educational journal, but in the primary activist periodical of the Progressives. In other words, it wasn't a sideshow. The Progressives wanted—no, needed—Christ removed from the schools.

PROGRESSIVES WANTED TO CONTROL THE KIDS

The progressive argument against religion in education was clearly an attempt to create an American paideia devoid of Christ, God, or even reference to the divine. Two years after the Gary Plan had been brought to New York, in a telling exchange between the editors of *The New Republic* and a Catholic priest who ran a school and orphanage, the Progressives exposed their underlying motive. This time we see

Progressives conflating their agenda with "Democracy." Shortly we'll see how this word *democracy* was part of their plan.

The editors of *The New Republic* wrote,

> Twentieth-century democracy believes that the community has certain positive ends to achieve, and if they are to be achieved the community must control the education of the young. It believes that training in scientific habits of mind is fundamental to the progress of democracy. It believes that freedom and tolerance mean the development of independent powers of judgment in the young, not the freedom of older people to impose their dogmas on the young. Democracy claims no right to interfere with worship or opinion, but it does claim the right to develop in every child the capacity for testing its own convictions. *It insists that the plasticity of the child shall not be artificially and prematurely hardened into a philosophy of life, but that experimental naturalistic aptitudes shall constitute the true education.* (emphasis mine)[7]

In other words, parents should not be allowed to pass their WCP ("their dogmas") on to their children. This "plasticity" points to the underlying power of paideia to shape how children develop a "philosophy of life." Progressives understood paideia, and they coveted its power and control for their own purposes.

The Progressives realized that true classical Christian education did something much more powerful than just teach virtues—it cultivated a Western Christian Paideia with a foundation in divine Truth. At its very core, it reaches for an ideal higher than human institutions. This type of paideia was a feared and powerful tool because it was anchored, not in the "progress" of human institutions, but in an unchanging, divinely inspired set of assumptions. This anchorage to the past constrained the societal change so necessary for the progressive movement to achieve its ends. Progressives saw danger in allowing parents to influence their children's worldview, and thus perpetuate a Christian culture in America. We'll soon see again why classical Christian education was such a threat to Progressives.

NEW PROGRESSIVE GOSPEL: "DEMOCRACY"

For more than half a century, liberals and conservatives have been talking past each other because they use the same word with different meanings. From Trotsky, to Lenin, to Mao, to Castro—to socialist Bernie Sanders and Comrade Ocasio-Cortez—a common tool for manipulating paideia is to use words that people associate with positive virtues, but to change their meaning.

Conservative writer Rod Dreher explains, "[Progressives] are repeating the Marxist habit of falsifying language, hollowing out familiar words and replacing them with a new, highly ideological meaning. Propaganda not only changes the way we think about politics and contemporary life, . . . [Progressives] imbue other words and phrases—hierarchy, for example, or traditional family—with negative connotations."[8]

The Progressives began their takeover by redefining the word *democracy*. In this case, rather than turning a word negative, Progressives were clever. They took a positive word that people revered and poured into it an affection for progressive values. *The New Republic* editorial board wrote on July 29, 1916:

> The older theories of democracy were negative, built up to protest against kings, aristocracies, and oppression. Those theories were concerned chiefly in saying what government must not do.

But during the nineteenth century popular rule became increasingly a reality, and people came to feel that government is not an alien thing to be limited, but a social instrument to be used. Democracy has been evolving from a protest into a purpose. It is becoming a philosophy of life, no longer protestant but in its own way catholic. To be a democrat today is to be something more than a voter. It is to believe in a scale of human values, to have a morality and to think with certain assumptions. "Modern sociologists" are simply men engaged in stating the affirmative faith of democracy.[9]

By loading the language, democracy as a moral sociology project sounded as "American" as it gets. We still hear this use of *democracy* today from the modern Left. With this new gospel, the Progressives now needed to establish the "American Progressive Paideia" to replace the "Western Christian Paideia." Because they controlled the commanding heights of education, they also held the keys to America's culture. With social scientists as priests, "social studies" were created in K–12 schools, replacing the liberal arts. These "sciences" redefined how we study history and literature in school. Émile Durkheim and Max Weber are considered the fathers of the social sciences. Both were Darwinists and atheists. We know all public schools teach this now, but even most Christian schools, unaware of the progressive influence, have classes called "social studies" that present the prevailing view of these social scientists. They fail to teach history, literature, philosophy, and the human arts in the classical tradition.

In 1519, the Spanish conqueror Cortés famously burned his own ships off the coast of Mexico to remove any temptation to return to Cuba (a Spanish settlement). Around 1900, the Progressives effectively scuttled the very idea that we should look to the past for insights about anything—certainly for education. Progressives built a "history-phobic" value system into our social studies mind-set. Old is yesterday. Old is irrelevant. Old is outdated. Progressives sunk the very idea that we could or should look to the past for insights about how to live or learn. This is why few, if any, modern public or Christian schools study much history before America's founding.

The progressive logic is simple: society is evolving. As with biological evolution, society is improving over time. Older wisdom is as primitive as extinct fossils. During the Progressive Era, engines propelled us faster than horses. Telecommunication infrastructure seemed miraculous. Medicine healed. Our command of nature progressed, systems of global transportation were established, and great wealth resulted. This made it easy for the Progressives to support their position: ideas and events of the past were the works of backward, inferior intellects who weren't yet enlightened as we are. Our forefathers were "racist!" and "sexist!" after all. The further back in history you go, the more this is true, or so the Progressives claimed.

Like the wake behind a great ocean liner, we have no reason to dwell on our past, or its art or literature. These smooth and dissipate as we move ever forward. Progressives believe that by looking forward, "democracy" can become a tool for government progress, rather than government restraint.

THE SANCTIFICATION OF THE PROGRESSIVE PUBLIC SCHOOL

By 1910, Progressives successfully associated their idea of public school with the tradition of common schools, the flag, the pledge, democracy, and all things American. Soon every small town had a flag flying over the US post office *and* the school—and a flag in front of every classroom. One task remained.

As we've seen, many Christian leaders were Progressives. Countless ministers joined the crusade for social innovation through schools. Dallas Lore Sharp, a Methodist minister, professor, and Progressive, is a typical example, writing:

The American public school is as truly national as the American flag . . . we send our American children by the tens of thousands to [church and private], schools named with old names, not with the new name of our Nation, schools which look back into a dim dead past, not out upon a living present. And we expect these Old-World schools to make New-World minds! Do men gather figs of thistles?

He continues:

My child is first a national child. He belongs to the Nation even before he belongs to himself. His education is first national and after that personal. We parents can hardly see this. It is a particularly difficult point of view for the highly individualized, assertive Anglo-Saxon whose political weakness is his undeveloped sense of social solidarity.

Apparently, Christians who believe that fathers are charged with educating their children (Ephesians 6) are simply "undeveloped."

The true end of American education is the knowledge and practice of democracy—whatever other personal ends an education may serve. . . . Life and the getting of a living may have been the proper ends of our private education heretofore; such ends are no longer legitimate. Neither life nor the getting of a living, but living together—this must be the single public end of a common public education hereafter.[10]

By the time Woodrow Wilson was elected president in 1913, progressivism had become far more statist and Marxist than it had been in Teddy Roosevelt's day. Wilson's view of education reveals the departure from a universal classical education for free citizens: "We want one class of persons to have a liberal education, and we want another class of persons, a very much larger class of necessity in every society, to forgo the privilege of a liberal education and fit themselves to perform specific difficult manual tasks."[11]

Wilson declared "Flag Day" (June 14) in 1916. Some may be surprised that America's first truly progressive president started this patriotic day. In fact, it's consistent with the Progressives' takeover of "America" as their own; the flag was intentionally used to replace religious allegiance. This strategy would allow an unquestioned assumption of the American schoolroom in the 1920s.

Progressives, like Wilson, believed that most people just needed a vocational education—they had no use for a free-man's (classical) education. This view flowed from the Marxist concept of the proletariat, or worker class. "Most people" also amounts to a majority in elections. Could it be that Progressives found it helpful to advance their agenda when "most people" lack a classical education and are therefore more easily steered? The progressive view of "Democracy" was easier to manage when most people were not thinkers, but rather doers. The founding fathers' desire for education to support a classically liberal republic had met its pragmatic end.

With the public school firmly attached to America and the new progressive religion of democracy unquestioned, Christians followed without realizing what had happened. Early in the twentieth century,

Progressives revealed their true intent. They did not just want unity: they wanted to undermine the WCP in the hearts and souls of our children.

Progressives built a system to train the "plasticity of the child" toward their new vision. They saw that children got three things from a Western Christian Paideia—a vision of the good life that rendered the progressive vision inert, a collection of deeply held Christian virtues at odds with new progressive values, and a collection of intellectual virtues that made Americans freethinkers.

To understand the progressive fixation on education, we need to understand the two-thousand-year-old tradition they took out of schools. With a focus on vocation instead of wisdom, the souls of students were oriented toward servile tasks rather than the pursuit of divine Truth. So, assumptions shifted. What we now call "worldview" shifted. Virtues shifted. Thought shifted. The whole ship of society gradually reoriented to a set of new ideas—progressive ones. Progressive ideas could now be subtly assumed in the classroom. These were not "red flag" types of ideas, at least not at first. But they were meant to indoctrinate, not to free minds to think wisely. They were meant to orient our nation toward an idol of individual identity within the bounds of progressive social solidarity, not the enjoyment of God and His eternal world.

Without realizing it, today's American students absorb a deep affection for scientism (science is the only way to find truth), equity/equality (there is nothing better or worse, just different), individualism (identity politics), neo-Marxism (the government can and should solve all inequalities), along with a host of other modern and postmodern affections that lead to servitude (it's all about your job).

Where did these affections come from? To answer this question, we can follow the progressive leaders in education. John Dewey was the father of progressive education. Dewey wrote his major treatise on education in 1916, but his influence grew through 1940. In 1929, Dewey was also one of a handful of men who helped found the First Humanist Society of New York. Charles Potter was its president. Potter's obituary from the *New York Times* in 1962 quoted him: "By freeing religion of supernaturalism, it will release tremendous reserves of hitherto thwarted power. Man has waited too long for God to do what man ought to do himself and is fully capable of doing." Also, "The chief end of man is to improve himself, both as an individual and as a race." (You may note the contrast with the Christian catechism "The chief end of man is to glorify God and enjoy Him forever.")

The views of the Progressives and humanists of the first half of the twentieth century are summed up in one of Potter's most telling statements: "What can theistic Sunday School, meeting for an hour once a week, do to stem the tide of a five day program of humanistic teaching?"[12]

This may be the most powerful revelation of their intentions.

What were these humanists teaching? Why was it in competition with the church? Dewey and other progressive educators had a new vision for America, a new vision for school, and now a tool that could shape the most powerful force in a democracy, or any nation: they had control of the affections. We will explore this consolidation in the next chapter.

Progressives have returned us to what the ancient Greeks once called a "barbarian" paideia. In a sense, to be a "barbarian" is to be trapped in the narrow mind-set of your own servile culture, with little exposure to other ideas. A "barbarian" is not easy to reason with, but is easy to capture. Because most American students cannot think well or speak well, and have no knowledge of the ages, they have become subjects under the new progressive order. They are well down the "road to serfdom." It is much easier to "progress" (move in unity toward the progressive vision) with "an affirmative faith of democracy" when subjects are trained to think with certain assumptions, but are not taught to examine those assumptions.

In his Pulitzer Prize–winning magnum opus on American education, Lawrence Cremin summarizes the progressive intent: "If education was to be the principal engine of an intentionally progressive society, then the politics of education would have significance far beyond the control of schools. Or child saving institutions. Or communication organizations; in the end, it would hold the key to the achievement of the most fundamental political aspirations—in effect, the key to the American Paideia."[13]

Cremin completes his compelling case that, from its earliest beginnings, the Progressives were establishing a new paideia to replace the old Western Christian Paideia. He points out that they sought to replace Christ with "democracy" or "America" as the object of education. Specifically, they promoted a view of the good life in progressive America, with religion separate, compartmentalized, personal, and eventually nonexistent.

Despite Cremin's award-winning scholarship, and tenure in the famed (shall we say "notorious") Columbia Teachers College, his conclusion was attacked, ignored, and rejected by the educational establishment. Cremin wrote with neutrality and was simply approaching the subject to ascertain the truth of it. Conservatives didn't notice. They were focused on the economic free market rather than cultural transformation. So Cremin's work would remain in academic circles. Until now.

The commanding heights of culture were secured. In the 1920s and '30s, government-based accreditation was formed to validate school diplomas and control high school to college transitions. Teachers were certified by states through education colleges that were designed by progressive disciples of Dewey. Graduation requirements and diplomas were authorized by states, under progressive education departments. Textbook authors, descended from this professional class of teachers, were trained in the progressive education colleges. All forms of K–12 education—Christian, public, and independent—were now effectively under the influence of the progressive model through the institutions Progressives built using state control.

Many of the affections Progressives co-opted through their American paideia substitute are now considered conservative talking points: American exceptionalism, the pledge of allegiance, a strong affinity for the flag, and patriotism were the carriers they used early on to supplant the Western Christian Paideia. That does not make these things "evil" today—I revere them all—but an honest reckoning with their origins helps us understand the progressive plot.

THE NEW PAIDEIA TRIUMPHANT

"I have no sympathy with the fatuity of the old classical education, and am heartily in favor of an education which will enable the great majority to have a better understanding and control of their actual environment."[14] So said Morris R. Cohen, as quoted by John Dewey.

Progressives had quietly and completely reengineered the very idea of K–12 education. Ideas have consequences. Big ideas have big consequences. Often, the big consequences are delayed for generations. Future voters would think progressively, so Progressives just had to wait for their hard-earned school system to do its work.

And work it did. Our paideia today is progressive. Earlier, we ran through the ideas embedded in the progressive paideia—scientism, Marxism, "equity," and servitude—to name a few. These ideas have yielded their predictable fruit.

Our modern progressive schools are deeply invested in teaching "science" as the sole source of truth in every class—even history as a social science! It's no wonder that "science" is America's new divine center, with high priests like Anthony Fauci, who can decree the necessity of forced vaccinations and the closing of schools, churches, and businesses—and his disciples will act on his words without question. The WCP would have (and did, in past epidemics) balanced public health "science" against other goods, like church, family, and work.

With science on the progressive dais, the state has become its temple.

The progressive paideia asks one Marxist question repeatedly: how can the state fix this problem? Under the WCP, people's problems were viewed in the context of the Bible—what sin caused this problem? And what are we, the local community, *called* to do about it? Under the WCP, if the "town drunk" had impoverished his family, the local parish would confront the sin (drunkenness and irresponsibility) and take his wife and kids to a relative's house. If he didn't shape up and repent, he would have been ostracized by the community. If he did ask for help with his habit, the call was for the community to lovingly give it. Can you imagine this intervention happening in today's isolated suburbs or impersonal inner cities?

The first response of the progressive paideia is to look for "systemic" problems, not sins, that can be addressed by the Marxist state. The drug addict is down-and-out because society has "repressed" him. "Equity" tells us that everyone has the right to be supported in their chosen lifestyle. If we believe that the "system," rather than sin, causes the problem, the state can be the only solution. The state can step in, give him needles, a tent to live in, and a bridge to live under. Or, in a prior failed time, it could build "projects" for people to languish in. For the Progressive, it's a battle between equity and privilege. For the WCP, it's a battle between justice and tyranny.

If "science" is the progressive god, and "the state" is the progressive temple, then "citizens" are a cog in the machine.

Cogs go to work. The progressive paideia indentures a workforce. Perhaps the most obvious observation one can make about the progressive school is that its main purpose is to train for future employment. The WCP asserts that citizens can be free only if they are "liberated" through Christ and education. Freedom requires sacrifices, the first of which is training children how to be free. Education should ensconce tradition, and a healthy dose of skepticism to critique ideas, both new and old. This critique, in light of scripture, develops young minds that will not easily be lorded over by tyrants, but that will also respect the order of God's world. This delicate balance of history, tradition, and order, once upset, yields a massive blow to civilization—and we are just starting to see this explosion unfold around us today.

This book will likely become an object lesson for its own thesis! What happened one hundred, two hundred, or two thousand years ago will be dismissed today as too old to be useful or acceptable as evidence of anything true. Under the American Progressive Paideia, history has dissipated into the irrelevant past.

Our progressive school system promotes more than just a new religion. It has ensconced a new worldview based on that religion, and a new world order. This is paideia. It's a paideia where history is rejected, science is God, and the state is the temple in which the citizen-workers worship, unable and unwilling to be free.

With the control of all the educational levers during the twentieth century, Progressives ended the practices that had sustained the WCP engine and our free Republic. They had control of the plasticity of the child, and they were determined not to squander it on freedom.

With the war declared, the whole framework of our nation was rewritten by Progressives slowly, over time, through the schools. Now everything lines up with the new ethic—in this case, a culturally Marxist ethic.

Starting in the late 1960s, conservatives began to counter the Marxist change. But neither the Christians nor the conservatives addressed education. The flanking maneuver by the Progressives had worked. They occupied the commanding heights and the supply lines—the schools. This allowed them to redirect the population to flow more fluidly into the progressive mold. This is where true indoctrination starts.

6

THE STRAIGHT LINE FROM CRITICAL THEORY TO ANTIFA

Education is not a subject and does not deal in subjects. It is instead a transfer of a way of life.

—G. K. Chesterton

After 1945, the WCP engine was all but removed from America's public schools. The nature of America's schools, now deeply tied to vocational purposes, morphed even further. Vocational needs, after all, change. In 1957, the "space race" was launched when Sputnik was sent into space by the Soviet Union. American schools retooled for math, science, and engineering. Nineteen sixty-two brought the formal eviction of God from the classroom. In 1963, devotional Bible reading in public schools was banned. In 1974, desegregation and busing ironically segregated US cities further, as whites retreated to the suburbs and private schools. These milestones marked the final cleanup in a protracted battle—not over prayer, or the Bible in school, but over the deeper concept of paideia.

But the progressive paideia we've described thus far isn't the sort of Marxist nuttiness we see in schools today. It had a final step of evolution to undergo. With the WCP gone, the new American Progressive Paideia (APP) could be morphed to form almost any culture. But what culture? The Progressives spent the rest of the twentieth century, post-1965, formulating a new paideia based in "critical theory" that villainized Christianity and the West. We'll call this the Cultural Marxist Paideia (CMP), which rose to maturity just after the year 2000.

Paideia, remember, is the fountainhead of culture. By the 1960s cultural revolution, the old WCP was already forgotten in America's schools. The cultural transformation did not start with the 1960s; instead, the sixties were a *result* of this erosion—the cultural manifestation of a project already long under way. This began with the birth of critical theory in the Frankfurt School, a group of scholars who smuggled over Marxist ideas, once again from Germany. Critical theory radiated out from Columbia University and eventually joined with postmodernism, which resulted in most of the crazy reality-denying theories we see gripping the country today. American Christian responses have been woefully inadequate, employing the same postmodern, leftist assumptions in their attempts to fight back. As we've established, all of these theories and movements go way back, but their influence became starkly obvious in American jurisprudence in the 1960s.

FROM THE WARREN COURT TO CRAZY SCHOOLS

Supreme Court chief justice Earl Warren had been an early disciple of the Progressives, having admired and followed Robert La

Follette—politician and the publisher of *The Progressive* (a rival to *The New Republic*, previously quoted). Warren considered himself a Progressive, and he, like Teddy Roosevelt, was a Republican.

Our textbooks would like us to remember the Warren Court as leading the fight against racial discrimination, which was a necessary and noble pursuit—as these white men in black robes gave a generation of previously segregated black Americans an opportunity for a better future. But this is also, nearly universally, understood as the most liberal Court in American history. This Court pioneered the extraconstitutional approach—an approach born of critical theory's "structural criticism." To the progressive Warren Court, founding documents were an *impediment* to progress. The Warren Court saw the Constitution as a guideline; it was living, not law. In many ways, the courts of the 1960s were simply finishing the work Progressives had begun at the beginning of the century.

The decisions were stark, and came quick. The Warren Court issued a slew of rulings that indelibly changed the inside of American classrooms, solidifying a growing (but not new!) political reality in our culture: God was no longer allowed inside. In the 1962 case *Engel v. Vitale*, the Court ruled that having students start their school day with a nondenominational prayer was *unconstitutional*. In the 1963 case *Abington School District v. Schempp*, the Court ruled that Bible reading in public school was *unconstitutional*. And in the 1965 case *Reed v. Van Hoven*, the Court ruled that students praying aloud over lunch was *unconstitutional*. In less than four short years, nine justices fundamentally changed our educational system forever. With three rulings—and more to come—the Supreme Court removed any remaining vestiges of the WCP in American classrooms.

It's ironic, but telling, that the final anti-faith ruling of the Warren Court came in 1965. That same year, Herbert Marcuse, a stalwart of the Frankfurt School—a German Marxist academic movement we will soon learn a lot more about—published his seminal work, "Repressive Tolerance." It came at the same time that a new phase of leftist philosophy, called "postmodernism," was taking hold in academia. Postmodernism, like critical theory, proposed a Marxist alternative theory of morality: oppressor and oppressed. To get there, postmodernists required an anti-Western grand narrative.

As the authors of the book *Cynical Theories* explain, postmodernists believed that "if social injustice is caused by legitimizing bad discourses . . . social justice can be achieved by delegitimizing them and replacing them with better ones."

It wasn't enough to criticize existing Western power structures; an alternative value system had to be proposed. This is the moment—not definitive on a timeline but evident in our discourse—that critical theory metastasized into its authoritarian instinct. This is where Marcuse's "Repressive Tolerance" comes in—the inevitable follow-through of the Marxist Frankfurt School. The basic thesis is that, considering the existing power structures of America and the West, in order to be tolerant, one cannot tolerate intolerance. To Marcuse, also known as the "father of the New Left," the existing power structure—capitalist and Christian—benefited from tolerance. He wrote, "In the firmly established liberal societies of England and the United States, freedom of speech and assembly was granted even to the radical enemies of society, provided they did not make the transformation from word to deed, from speech to action." The norm of "tolerance" only ever benefited the capitalist, Christian status quo, he argued.

You don't have to read too deeply to see how this argument is the precursor to two things, among many: the justification of violence by groups like Antifa (preceded by groups like the Weather Underground) and the need to counteract traditional American tolerance with left-wing intolerance. Concepts like political correctness and cancel culture, the control of language and silencing of speech, are born from "anti-fascist" Marxists like Herbert Marcuse and the Frankfurt School.

Critical theory was all about reflecting on and critiquing society to identify "oppressive" power structures. Postmodernism, an idea popping up around the same time, was all about chucking grand theories or narratives. That sounds good on paper, right? We all want to be freethinkers. The actual applied result of the two ideas is Gen Z kids dismissing objective reality and seeing nothing as authoritative but individual experience. This is why kids ask questions like: *Why should "biology" dictate my sex or gender? Biology has no authority over how I feel. And traditional math? That's racist. The rules of math or hard science must give way if they're deemed oppressive.*

Critical theory and postmodernism form the nucleus around which more modern prescriptive theories revolve—from the sexual revolution, to LGBT glorification, to the most recent example of critical race theory. That is actually the progression: first it was sexual liberation, then it was gender obfuscation, and today it is never-ending racial oppression. In academia, this led to full-blown social justice scholarship like feminist studies, gender studies, queer studies, African American studies, and—today—intersectionality studies, which combines all of them (see Utah State University's "Center for Intersectional Gender Studies & Research"). Ideas that first manifest in our ivory towers showed up later in our elementary classrooms in the forms of books and themes disguised as something else, like a gender unicorn, "diversity, equity, and inclusion," or even an Antifa flag. Identity politics was fully unleashed, replacing Western notions of meritocracy. Self-esteem replaced self-control and self-reliance.

A powerful recent example of this was exposed by Project Veritas, who in August 2021 released a hidden video of a California public school teacher bragging that "I have 180 days to turn them [students] into revolutionaries." Gabriel Gipe was an AP Government teacher at Inderkum High School who had both an Antifa flag and a Pride flag on his classroom wall. He was fired after public pressure, but not before revealing what motivates him and what his true aim was. Gipe said, "I have an Antifa flag on my [classroom] wall and a student complained about that—he said it made him feel uncomfortable. Well, this [Antifa flag] is meant to make fascists feel uncomfortable, so if you feel uncomfortable, I don't really know what to tell you. Maybe you shouldn't be aligning with the values that this [Antifa flag] is antithetical to."

The message to students: comply and conform. This message is receptive to any paideia that supports political tyranny. And it worked. Gipe bragged, "So, they [students] take an ideology quiz and I put [the results] on the [classroom] wall. Every year, they get further and further left. . . . I'm like, 'These ideologies are considered extreme, right? Extreme times breed extreme ideologies.' Right? There is a reason why Generation Z, these kids, are becoming further and further left."

His understanding of the power of education is probably the most telling revelation, as he said, "I think that for [left-wing] movements in the United States, we need to be able to attack both [cultural and economic] fronts. Right? We need to create parallel structures of power because we cannot rely on the state. . . . Consistently focusing on education and a change of cultural propaganda. We have to hit both fronts. We have to convince people that this is what we actually need." Gipe was laser focused on education, like a good Frankfurt School disciple.

This may be an extreme example, but it is emblematic of educators in America today. Their job is no longer to educate in the old sense of the word; it is to indoctrinate. Can you imagine if a public school teacher in America today attempted to hang a cross in the classroom? Or the Ten Commandments? Or, gasp, pictures of Christopher

Columbus or Andrew Jackson? Or Billy Graham? Those would be taken off the wall in one day—yet an Antifa flag, in our public schools, can hang there for months before being exposed. The teacher was only fired because he was exposed, not because of what he was doing. The school district later admitted—in a statement seemingly designed to quell questions from left-wing activists, since the statement also reaffirmed its devotion to equity—that it fired Gipe not just for the video but "because he had violated many policies, Ed Code and more" and that there were "nearly 400 pages of charges and evidence." However, over the course of the previous three years the school had done twenty-five classroom walk-throughs and found "the teacher teaching standards and addressing the curriculum." It seems like Gipe had been a privately reported problem on their radar for a long time (unless the four hundred pages of charges were all compiled in the six weeks between the Project Veritas video dropping and the statement's release), but no one had done anything until he was exposed.

How did today's American classroom become so crazy? It so happens, our story here takes us once again to Columbia University, the leading institution of educational philosophy in the United States. From the mid-1930s to the 1970s, another force was at work with a profound cultural transformation in mind—buried deep in the philosophical echelons of higher education.

THE FRANKFURT SCHOOL BRINGS
MARXISM TO AMERICAN EDUCATION

Before Ibram X. Kendi and Barack Obama, Saul Alinsky and Howard Zinn . . . there was Max Horkheimer, Theodor Adorno, Herbert Marcuse, and the Frankfurt School. I'm ashamed to admit that, before starting this project—and the corresponding FOX Nation series

MisEducation of America—I knew nothing about these names and that school. These forgotten names and others like them laid the groundwork for the postmodernism of the 1960s—and the radical education takeover of today.

These names, encapsulated as the Frankfurt School, represent the origins of a radical left-wing philosophy that was exported from Europe more than eighty years ago and found fertile soil in America's free market of ideas. The Frankfurt School arrived on American soil at precisely the time we had stripped our centralized schooling system of our only defense—the Western Christian Paideia. Its adherents arrived on our shores with a new theory, a theory of scholarship designed to destroy.

You see, before there was "critical race theory," there was simply "critical theory." Never heard of it? You're not alone. The origins of critical theory went largely unexamined, especially in conservative intellectual circles, for many years. Seemingly it popped up out of nowhere as critical race theory; but when the idea of critical theory was established, it was not focused on race. Critical race theory came later. Critical theory wasn't even exclusively focused on the Marxist idea of perpetual class warfare, either. Class warfare had not proven effective enough to these leftists. Neither was sex and gender . . . yet. The original mission of critical theory was much broader. The minds behind the Frankfurt School had a larger goal: rendering obsolete the traditional underpinnings and conceptions of Western civilization. Put more succinctly by the authors of *Cynical Theories*, "The Frankfurt School developed the Critical Theoretic approach specifically to expand beyond critiques of capitalism, as the Marxists had been doing, and to target the assumptions of Western civilization as a whole, particularly liberalism as a sociopolitical philosophy and Enlightenment thought in general."

Anyone reading this just ten years ago, outside of academia, would have ended up with eyes glazed over trying to comprehend another incomprehensible theory arising from obscure egghead departments of higher education. But no one would be bored today, because we can see these ideas have consequences. Today these theories are burning down our cities, driving censorship by big tech, indoctrinating our kids into social justice activists, and dividing our kids into racial groups of "oppressor" and "oppressed"—just to name a few.

Critical theory answers one simple question: if there's no God, how shall we live as a society? Before critical theory, attempts to reorder society around atheism were plagued by inescapable assumptions of God's existence. So, the Frankfurt gang asked a better question: *since we know that there is no God, what is the ultimate good in a society?* With no common goal, or idea of justice, you have war (and we saw a bit of that). So critical theory was born to tear down the remnants of Western Christian culture still carried by the WCP embedded in America's citizens. Critical theory is what you get when you try to actually live out avowed atheism.

The Frankfurt gang looked at Western Christian ideals and noticed that they are all built on hierarchy. There is an order to "goods" that reaches from the lowest act of kindness to an animal to the highest worship of the infinite creator God. Everything is ordered vertically so there are better and worse (higher and lower) ways to live in society, higher and lower cultures, higher and lower stations of authority, and so on. If there is no God, there is no hierarchy—no order. That means that flatness, or equity, is the ultimate good. The Frankfurt School decided the answer was to be "critical" of every social construct so they could "deconstruct" our culture and flatten it. If you wonder why George Soros seems hell-bent on deconstructing our legal system, this is why. Domain after domain of social construct was attacked under critical theory: critical pedagogy (education), critical gender theory (deconstructing biological sex), critical social theory (deconstructing politics), critical language (deconstructing language), and, of course, critical race theory. Each domain needed to be torn down so that it could be rebuilt on the new quality of "equity." We are finding out, right now, where the new god of equity will take us.

Entire books have been written about critical theory—like the one cited above, *Cynical Theories*—and this book is not intended to unpack the entirety of its impact. But what we must understand is the very deliberate, intellectual, and effective way in which European Marxists, socialists, and atheists—centered at the Frankfurt School—exported their unpopular ideas across the Atlantic. So what is this Frankfurt School?

The informal "Frankfurt School" was founded in 1923 and was formally housed at the Institution for Social Research (today known as the "Frankfurt School of Critical Theory") in Frankfurt, Germany. It was founded by a Marxist law professor and represented the first Marxist research center at a German university. Its first director was Max Horkheimer, a Marxist. Just like Karl Marx, the Frankfurt School was focused on radical social change—criticism of all things Western—using social, economic, cultural, political, and educational institutions. You might say, they were some of the original social justice warriors.

The difference between orthodox Marxists and the intellectuals at the Frankfurt School is that philosophers like Horkheimer, Marcuse, Theodor Adorno, and the Italian Marxist Antonio Gramsci—a huge influencer of the Frankfurt School—believed that Marxism had failed to deliver on its egalitarian utopianism. In short, the working class (proletariat) had not risen up to overtake the elite capitalist classes (bourgeoisie). It hadn't worked. Something else must be done.

But their timing was bad—especially for America. As the rise of Nazi Germany took hold in the 1930s, the founders of the Frankfurt School decided it was time to leave. Nazi fascism tolerated no dissent, especially from Marxists and revolutionaries who sought the overturning of existing power structures. Soon after Adolf Hitler became chancellor in 1933, the scholars of the Frankfurt School fled to New York City, in 1935. Soon thereafter, significant members of the Frankfurt School joined the faculty of . . . Columbia University.

At Columbia, instead of being met with skepticism, they were met with open arms. Incidentally, John Dewey had just retired from Columbia in 1930. To the surprise of Horkheimer, the president of Columbia agreed to host the "Institute" and offered up a building for their scholarship. Horkheimer was offered a formal position at Columbia. Soon after, the Frankfurt School was up and running at Columbia University. Exiled Marxists were out in the open and holding court at America's most prestigious teachers college.

They also established a scholarly journal—the first of many journals and books—for their research, titled *Studies in Philosophy and Social Science*. One foreword to this journal, written in 1939 by Horkheimer, is particularly telling. With their printing presses in France under imminent seizure by Hitler's army, Horkheimer explains the purpose of their new publication in America instead of Europe: "Both our Institute and the publishers hoped . . . to help science by enabling authors to write in their own tongue. . . . But this consideration must now be secondary to our desire to devote our work—even in its external form—*to American social life*"(emphasis mine).

He continues: "America, especially the United States, is the only continent in which the continuation of scientific life is possible. Within the framework of this country's democratic institutions, culture still enjoys the freedom without which, we believe, it is unable to exist."

Horkheimer did not admire America's "democratic institutions" or our "culture"—far from it, he sought their destruction—but he understood that America's freedom afforded his anti-Western ideas the fertile soil necessary to flourish.

It was during this time period—during the height of World War II—that the now-American Frankfurt School did their core work on Marxist-based critical theory. Safe on American shores— with American GIs fighting to defend their intellectual freedom—the Frankfurt School went to work. More than a physical location, the Frankfurt School was a radical new form of German intellectualism— laser focused on what they called the "social sciences."

Horkheimer and his Frankfurt School disguised their critical theory under the guise of "social science" (sound familiar?). Science is traditionally understood as objectively observing nature, fielding experiments, and deriving scientific laws about the real world from those observations and experiments. Applying this "science" to human behavior is inherently flawed because scientific generalizations cannot be directly derived from lived experience. This reality did not deter critical theorists, who believed that imposing their scientific (critical) methods on governance, economics, and the human experience allowed them to explain away certain human realities as based on biases and power structures inherent in the historical and ideological context known as Western civilization.

Moreover, critical theorists insist that social "scientists" not be technical observers and problem solvers, but instead self-reflective explorers. This is where ideas like "check your privilege" and "implicit bias" come from. It is not enough to study history or civics; the student must emphasize their own current and historical contribution to the power structure that leftists deem evil at that moment (a standard that is ever "progressing"). As such, in keeping with the Marxist tradition, critical theorists insist that "social science" cannot be content to describe or explain the world, but instead should emancipate students to understand their role in contributing to oppression, injustice, and discrimination. Students must become, in effect, self-loathing activists, "scientists" with raised fists.

Get that? By turning traditional liberal arts subjects into "science," critical theorists focus their efforts on dissecting and then tearing down the societal, cultural, political, religious, and economic layers that utopians believe prevent their egalitarian efforts from succeeding. According to them, it's not that their systems don't work—it's the way we study them and understand them that is flawed. Thus the entire manner in which we study society has to change. Enter the "social sciences." Yes, our modern social sciences—like "political science," previously known as "politics," and "social studies," previously known as individual disciplines like "history, economics, geography, and philosophy"—are by-products of Marxist philosophy.

Let that sink in: the manner in which we study politics, history, and economics in American schools—public and private—today is the product of Marxists. That was always the plan, and it worked. Progressives very effectively used Western appreciation of real "science" to advance their own pseudo-science, all in the service of removing God, tradition, and Western history.

Over time, bolstered by the already eroded standards of higher education, the scholarship and the investigational method known as "critical theory" started to gain acceptance across the United States. To be clear, prior to the Frankfurt School, these activist ideas were anathema to traditional and classical forms of American education. Our founders would have rejected them outright, along with all of our educational institutions until this time. But "critical theory" was sold as something different, and permitted to flourish in the paideia vacuum left by Progressives. Underneath all of it—dressed up as examination of power structures, biases, and comparative politics—the Frankfurt School gained a powerful foothold inside American academia.

One of the defining attributes of critical theory is that, unlike Marxism, it makes no claim of absolute truth. Recall that the WCP is based in the pursuit of unchanging divine order. To critical theorists, there is no such thing as human nature or a vision of "the good life." Critical theory rejects any notions of God, sin, or natural law—rejecting the notion that rights are "endowed by a Creator," as enshrined in our Declaration of Independence. Rather than attempt to meet people "where they are" and improve their condition in life through religion, politics, economics, or culture, critical theorists consider humans and their condition to be socially constructed (by "the dominant ideology")—the result of very complex social processes they alone can interpret. Critical theorists therefore believe their main task is to reveal the societal reasons for our present human reality, then criticize them, deconstruct them, and change them. What those conditions were changed to, at least at the beginning, was secondary. Before "progress" could occur, religious faith, capitalism, and the "authoritarian family"—as it was called by Theodor Adorno—had to be deconstructed.

To critical theorists, the dominant ideology in need of destruction was, effectively, the Western Christian Paideia, because, according to them, that system legitimizes the domination of oppressed peoples. In many ways, critical theory was designed to surpass economic Marxism, opening additional avenues of attack against the West. These attacks go beyond the economic Marxist construct of elite capitalist classes (bourgeoisie) versus the working class (proletariat). Enter *cultural Marxism*.

They hid their intentions well. For example, in a seminal work of the Frankfurt School titled *The Authoritarian Personality*, they chose their words carefully—replacing words like *revolutionary* with *democratic*, to make their arguments more acceptable to American ears. We've seen this takeover of *democratic* from the earliest days of the Progressives. They also replaced traditional Marxist economic explanations with psychological rationales, leaning heavily on the thinking of Sigmund Freud. Under the guise of defeating fascism (remember, like today, the Marxists labeled themselves anti-fascists), these Marxists set about—get this!—describing conservative thinking as a form of mass psychosis. As Jonah Goldberg put it in *Liberal Fascism*, the Frankfurt School's "analysis also held that since Marxism was objectively superior to its alternatives, the masses, the bourgeoisie, and anyone else who disagreed with them had to be, quite literally, mad."

The formula was simple: the entire Western world needed to be deconstructed in the name of anti-fascism, and when their ideas were opposed, their traditional opponents were to be deemed mentally unstable fascists. Sound familiar? Is that really far off from higher education today? Now you know where it all started. It was Marxists, fleeing Nazis, given safe haven in free lands, landing at America's top universities, calling themselves anti-fascists (the forerunner to anti-racists), all in the name of destroying the very place that gave them the freedom to spew their anti-Western authoritarianism. Had the Progressives not suppressed the WCP thirty years before the Frankfurt gang arrived, the soil of American culture would not have been so accepting.

COLUMBIA AND UNIONS EXPORT MARXISM INTO AMERICAN PEDAGOGY

Back to Columbia University. Members of the Frankfurt School did go on to teach elsewhere, places like Harvard University and the University of California, but Columbia remains the most important location pertaining to this work because, by the time the Frankfurt School arrived, Columbia was the home of America's oldest and largest graduate *school of education*. Still today, legions of elite educators—those who shape the curriculum and pipeline of future teachers—graduate from "Teachers College, Columbia University."

In fact, as I mentioned, none other than John Dewey himself— dubbed the "the father of progressive education"—was a professor at Columbia's Teachers College from 1904 to 1930, and remained affiliated long after. The Frankfurt School and America's preeminent teachers college propelled Marxist critical theory straight into America's educational pipeline. From Columbia to your classroom. A quick glance at the Columbia Teachers College website today, on any given day, reads like—you guessed it—a progressive playbook. Who's teaching our teachers today? The Marxists, of course!

As Marxist critical theory snaked its way through America's elite universities, two other institutions—in the late 1950s and early 1960s—forever changed the course of America's classrooms: teachers unions and the Supreme Court. These were two of the commanding heights quickly and quietly seized by the Progressives. Without these developments, one institutional and the other constitutional, the Left would not have been able to consolidate its grip on the classroom, turn- ing abstract concepts like critical theory into mandatory anti-American curriculum. We already talked about the Court, but the unions played an even larger role.

In Chapter 2, I outlined what America's teachers unions have become—the core instrument of leftist indoctrination. The two most powerful unions—the National Education Association (NEA) and American Federation of Teachers (AFT)—have been in existence for more than one hundred years. Today they are arguably the two most powerful unions in America and have become an appendage of the leftist wing of the Democrat Party. Their power has never been so vast, and their politics never so extreme.

But that was not always the case. The forerunner to the NEA—the National Teachers Association—was founded in 1857, not as a union, but as an association of teachers with the desire to better educate children. By 1900, the newly renamed NEA, while active in matters of education policy, was still mostly inconsequential—with only 2,500 members in a country with roughly 500,000 public school teachers at the time. In 1906, the NEA was chartered by an act of Congress. And, far from a left-wing organization, it reflected America: traditional, conservative, and God fearing.

But don't take my word for it. Here's a former educator of twenty-eight years, Rebecca Friedrichs, in her book *Standing Up to Goliath*: "During the 1960s, before the NEA was taken over by unions, teachers spoke out a lot, because the NEA was a positive association formed by teachers to support their profession and the children in their care. A sweet retired teacher reached out to my friend Larry Sand one day and said, 'In the 60s the NEA was not like it is today! I still have booklets given to us in Teacher's Ed for memorization in the classroom. All of them are Bible verses.'"

She continues: "The booklets, *Selections for Memorizing: Growth Booklets*, are full of Scriptures from the Holy Bible, prayers, writings, and poems about kindness, moral character, and even the importance of the Education Triangle [students, parents, and teachers]. They were printed *en masse* by the NEA so that every child in schools across the country could have one every year." Even in the 1960s, the NEA was *publishing* and *promoting* material that contained Bible verses and prayers—because, even if waning, Christian virtue still had a strong pull on America's cultural compass.

But even then, it was fermenting fruit from an already poisoned tree. In the first quarter of the twentieth century, the Progressives, namely John Dewey, had successfully changed the orientation of the NEA—turning it into a lobbying arm for more federal control over education policy. By 1932 the consolidation was nearly complete, with Dewey—the progressive trailblazer and founding father of American public schools—becoming the NEA's "honorary life president." As it happens, Dewey was also the 1916 cofounder of the NEA's chief rival, the American Federation of Teachers (AFT). Yes, the socialist, atheist, progressive founder of American public schools is the "honorary life president" and founder of America's two largest teachers unions.

The trajectory was set for the NEA and AFT when, in the early 1960s, both teachers associations were taken over by the public union-ization movement. For years government employees (here, public school teachers) were not allowed to unionize because, as government employees, they had a monopoly on their positions—therefore public unions could hold the government (and parents!) hostage by going on strike. The government would be on both sides of the bargaining table. But eventually politicians caved and public unions were formed. Worse, the Democrat Party saw the potential and pounced—and in 1962, President John F. Kennedy signed an executive order allowing collective bargaining in the public sector.

Soon after, sensing a massive opportunity to expand union rolls, public teachers associations became the biggest prize. In 1960 the AFT moved to unionize and soon achieved that goal. Their membership more than doubled in just a few years. The same went for the NEA. Despite efforts from teachers to remain a professional association, the NEA soon became unionized as well—and their membership ex-ploded. From there, teachers unions were off to the races—guided by a growing left-wing labor movement that was grounded in left-wing organizing. (The NEA was advised by Saul Alinsky, as you'll recall.) Schools and teachers who had previously been guided by parental involvement and local control were now at the whim of powerful new political entities that were the chief lobbyists for union prerogatives and overarching federal involvement. Soon after, the teachers unions were putting politicians in office and then bargaining with them on the other side—all with progressive aims in mind. Today every major university in America offers "labor studies" courses or concentration, staffed by—you guessed it—labor leaders, keeping the activism pipeline going.

EVANGELICALS FIGHT BACK—BUT ON THE ENEMY'S TERMS

During the second half of the twentieth century, evangelicals responded to the hostility toward Christianity in public schools. In 1950 about 77 percent of the approximately 14,000 private schools in America were Roman Catholic. By 1990 that had dropped to 33 percent as thousands of evangelical Christian schools had been started, bringing the number of private schools to 27,000.

However, there was a serious disconnect. These evangelical Protestant schools were unaware that the classical education model had even existed, since Progressives had driven it into extinction a generation before. The WCP was buried too deep. So, evangelical schools unwittingly borrowed the methods and most of the content from the only form of education that anyone knew at the time—progressive education. This is why today, most evangelical Christian schools are progressive in their educational practice. The classical Christian link between all knowledge, understanding, theology, and philosophy had been severed nearly a century earlier, so evangelicals did not know any better. And they relied upon progressive institutions to train their teachers, inform their curriculum, and earn accreditation. While God was at least in the schools, the pedagogy was still progressive.

Though evangelical schools may not directly teach progressive values, they usually still reduce education to vocational training. Many of these Christian schools do an excellent job competing against public schools and teaching Christianity, but they lack the greater capacity of classical schools to shape a Western Christian Paideia. This is why Christian culture in the church, in our homes, and in our communities is no longer distinct from the emerging progressive culture. We are all educated with the same paideia—the American Progressive Paideia. This is partly why Millennials and Gen Zers are so disconnected from previous generations.

Francis Schaeffer called out this tendency among Christian schools to divide knowledge, as Progressives want Christians to do. He also pointed to another tendency of fundamentalist Christian schools—to isolate and shelter students from difficult topics.

He wrote: "True Christian education is not a negative thing; it is not a matter of isolating the student from the full scope of knowledge. Rather it is giving him or her the framework for total truth, rooted in the Creator's existence and in the Bible's framework, so that in each step of the formal learning process the student will understand what is true and what is false and why it is true or false."[15]

THE PROGRESSIVE PAIDEIA BECOMES A MARXIST PAIDEIA

The original progressive vision was powered by human autonomy. Its objective was societal flourishing. Its means were technology and government. And its gospel promised equality of outcomes, an end to poverty, an end to wars, and an end to human struggle, through social science. The progressive eschatology anticipated a sleek, technology-driven, leisure-filled future. People accepted their view because, after all, science, technology, government, and society had solved some very big problems. We have more time for leisure. These solutions seemed enticing, so Christians joined the culture without realizing what we were sacrificing. These benefits came at a very big cost.

After the mid-1960s, the progressive hangover began. Art and music took to the base, the abstract, and the ugly. The predictable outcome of the anti-authority, free-sex, anti-family, and drug-friendly culture from the mid-1960s did untold damage. The progressive story continues today, but now with more power. For Progressives, unbridled human indulgences are sacred. We can decide what truth is, what gender we are, and even who God is. Miley Cyrus sums up this Gen-Z zeitgeist: "I'm allowed to redesign my relationship with God as an adult and make it how it feels most accepting to me." She said this in the context of sexual freedom. All of this comes at the cost of true happiness. We should be less miserable, but every indicator seems to say that we're not.

C. S. Lewis said that education is about irrigating deserts, not cutting down jungles. When we irrigate a desert, we cultivate what was there—the soil—to grow generations of fruit. It's a natural process. When we build a city, we cut down a jungle and replace it with functional steel and concrete that falls into decay with time.

Progressive educators want to cut down and constrain children to replace their humanity with a mechanical idea of training for a job. Like a man-made city, these mechanical people cannot grow greater by generations. Instead their knowledge decays and their life wears down with their daily labors. They become spent. Their souls become captive. They become slaves. They become miserable. Lewis correctly recognized that by suppressing human nature and turning education into a sort of informational machine, we make students weaker. "The right defense against false sentiments is to inculcate just sentiments," he writes. "By starving the sensibility of our pupils we only make them easier prey to the propagandist when he comes. For famished nature will be avenged and a hard heart is no infallible protection against a soft head."

Why do progressive educators think that they must erect this mechanical, man-made edifice in children's minds? It's because they think there's nothing in the earth to grow. They don't believe the law of God is written on the hearts of man. They don't believe objective Truth exists and is discernible by reason. The Left, especially in our classrooms, has dismissed seeking objective Truth, and replaced it with *their* truth. Modern leftists didn't make this happen overnight. They had progressive forerunners, most of whom they never met, intellectuals and practitioners who, without knowing what the future would hold, went to war with the foundation of Western civilization when those foundations were still strong in America. Separated from their Christian source, older American ideals were "cut flowers"— nice to look at, but destined to die. Without Christianity's WCP root, Progressives dismantled the ethic of our entire American experiment. "Democracy" became shorthand for Marxist social equity. Equal protection under the law became equal outcomes based on shifting measures of "progress" and "fairness." All of this created the conditions for modern leftists to tear down the pillars of our Republic and "reimagine" (their words then, and their words now) a Marxist future.

Paideia, taught in schools and at home, transfers to the culture in the next generation. The effects can be seen by looking back through a generational lens (generations last about forty years). In America's schools, we've seen that the WCP was universally replaced by the American Progressive Paideia in about 1925, with its creed (the pledge), flag, and civics courses. Once the APP had been universally taught in schools, say between 1925 and 1965, its resulting culture dominated for another generation—until about 2005. Because the APP is rooted only in nationalism and American ideals, it had a weakness. The WCP claimed authority from God. The APP claimed authority from the founding fathers and the Constitution—a weaker authority, though still with merit.

Beginning somewhere between 2000 and 2005, the American paideia was replaced with the Cultural Marxist Paideia in America's youth, which obtained its authority from "equity" vested in individual identity. This is a wildly fickle authority upon which to base a paideia. What we now see as "crazy"—people shoplifting without consequences, our cities full of tent towns (by choice), rape in public bathrooms disregarded because of gender identity, riots on the Left dismissed as "mostly peaceful" while protests on the Right are called "insurrections"—makes perfect sense if you assume the Cultural Marxism Paideia. And, if our paideia thesis is correct, the craziness is just starting to gain steam. Think of the power of the American Progressive Paideia to mobilize our military and engender a national response to the 9/11 attacks. Imagine how powerful the Cultural Marxist Paideia will be once it has been taught for a generation—in 2045! Imagine the world your kids and mine are entering. Remember, paideia works one generation down the line. The impact follows behind the schools.

It's happening right now. We are living it. And, I hope, after reading this you will realize the problem is much worse than even you imagined. That is the feeling I've had during this entire project. The theory is more deeply ingrained, the progressive plot more vast, than I even conceived was possible. But, like any recovery, the first step is acknowledging the depth of the problem. Once we know what we're up against, we can design a battle plan—a solution—that is as large as the problem. Nerf guns just won't do.

7

FINDING THE FOUNDING CLASSROOMS

*You see at once that education is essentially
for freemen and vocational training for slaves....
If education is beaten by training, civilization dies.*

—C. S. Lewis, "Our English Syllabus," *Rehabilitations* (1939)

In the *Federalist Papers*, Alexander Hamilton reflected on a revolutionary figure in ancient Greece who tore down statues, leading to the end of the Athenian commonwealth. The founders knew that our system was fragile and factions were dangerous. James Madison also explained that our founders modeled America after Greece and Rome, in *Federalist* number 6: "[they] bore a very instructive analogy to the present confederation of the American states."[16] Why do we have a senate? Why a republic? Why twelve jurors on a jury? Why do our government buildings look like they do? Why an outstretched eagle as a finial on our flagpoles? The Greco-Roman influence on our founding fathers is evident, and so is their Christian view.

Yet, with the rise of our "woke" social justice culture—and triumph of the American Progressive Paideia, now turned Cultural Marxist Paideia—Western civilization itself has become the villain behind nearly every wrong. Whether it's Zinn's *People's History of the United States*, the 1619 Project, or just your average high school history textbook, these "progressive histories" begin their story of America with a blank page—as though our nation sprang into existence ex nihilo. Since the mid-twentieth century, the full history of our Western Christian foundation has been all but canceled—even before "cancel culture" was a thing. To understand our present situation and how we might restore America's Republic, we first need to find our hidden past.

Make no mistake about it: the historical singularity that was America's founding was a result of the culmination of the Western Christian Paideia (WCP). Full stop. Our founders did not stumble their way to the brilliance of 1776; they were forged in the foundry of the classical Christian education of their time. Simply put, without classical Christian education there would be no America. Without the carefully cultivated WCP, which developed over millennia, America's revolution would have landed in the ash heap in history, just like most failed revolutions. Ours, America's, was different—distinctly Western, and rooted deeply in Christianity.

Christianity was an irreducible influence on our founding generation, along with classical philosophy, because it was central to the WCP. These men lived at a confluence in history during which the European Enlightenment challenged the 1,800-year-old relationship between human reason and Christian Truth. In the pre-Enlightenment view, Christian Truth was discoverable through God's revealed word (the Bible) and His revelation through history, nature, and well-trained human reason. This vision formed the core training ground for the WCP.

The political Enlightenment of the eighteenth century caused many to reject the authority of scripture or the church, favoring new institutions of popular government. It caused others to double down on the Truth of Christianity. Two moments in American history reflect this tension.

The first is the Great Awakening, a religious movement in the mid-1700s that emphasized a personal rather than an institutional commitment to Christ. Church institutions and authority were de-emphasized. Benjamin Franklin observed this change. He said of George Whitefield's preaching, "[Residents of our town changed] from being thoughtless or indifferent about Religion, it seem'd as if all the World were growing Religious; so that one could not walk thro' the Town in an Evening without Hearing Psalms sung in different Families of every Street."

On the other hand, as discussed in Chapter 3, we saw the rise of "Deism." This took several forms—but all rejected the supremacy of the Kingdom of Jesus Christ. Freemasonry rose in public prominence to reflect this view. Thomas Paine and Thomas Jefferson were ardent advocates of Deism. And many others, like John Adams, left their traditional Christian churches to join the Unitarian Church, which reflected tenets of Deism.

If one were to place the founding fathers on a spectrum between traditional Christian authority and Deistic rationalism, it *might* be re-flected this way—Christians: John Jay, Patrick Henry, Roger Sherman, John Witherspoon, Benjamin Rush; mixed theology: Benjamin Franklin, Alexander Hamilton, John Adams, George Washington; and Deists: James Madison, Thomas Jefferson, Thomas Paine.

I say "might" because any study would turn up conflicting evidence. This has stirred confusion among those who argue that the framers were Christian and those who claim they were not. In matters of the heart, this is impossible to fully discern. But as far as the paideia that formed in the founders is concerned, a survey of their writing shows that the WCP was clearly the dominant influence in their philosophy, thought, and virtue. They grew up in it, studied it, and practiced it. The respective libraries of the founding fathers, their attendance at schools and colleges practicing classical Christian education, and their own writing make this abundantly clear. Jefferson, a Deist, even rewrote the Bible to better fit his theology. He sensed that the WCP depended on divine scripture, so he attempted to rework it without what he thought were irrational miracles. He found the Bible imperfect, but he also found it necessary, even if he ultimately rejected divine "Logos."

Despite the considerable expanse between Christians and Deists, the American experiment would not have been possible without the long road paved by the WCP. It was the water in which they swam, as they fought the most powerful empire in the world and debated a new republic on a new continent. This historic road left an impressive legacy, as pointed out by mid-twentieth-century scholar John Gardner: "At the time this nation was formed, our population stood at around 3 million. And we produced out of that 3 million people perhaps six leaders of world class—Washington, Adams, Jefferson, Franklin, Madison, and Hamilton. Today, our population stands at 245 million, so we might expect at least 80 times as many world-class leaders—480 Jeffersons, Madisons, Adams, Washingtons, Hamiltons, and Franklins. Where are they?"

The disproportionate number of world-class leaders arising from our founding generation is indeed remarkable to note. Inspired leaders are not created in a vacuum; they are cultivated in a culture. Our founders were reaping what the WCP had sowed, and the results speak for themselves. Such soil is rare, especially today.

That said, the founding of America may have also unintentionally set us on a course away from the WCP that would take more than one hundred years to manifest itself, and another hundred to metastasize. Today our Republic is threatened by a rejection of both reason and Christianity—the two pillars of the WCP on which our civilization stands. While it may be tempting to dismiss a two-hundred-year ideological trend as only of theoretical interest, doing so jeopardizes any chance of reversing our current situation.

The last time the world was completely without the influence of the reason/Christian duo, brutal totalitarian empires cycled every few hundred years—the Assyrians, the Babylonians, the Persians, the Carthaginians, and the Romans, to name a few. Civilizations outside the West remained totalitarian and brutal until colonialism rose in the 1700s—many still are. What about Western democratic socialists, such as those in Europe? It will take time to fully uproot the WCP from what had been a stronghold, but we should not be surprised to see these nations decline into barbarity in the coming decades. The authoritarian response to COVID in Europe (and Australia) foreshadows the coming autocratic, bureaucratic globalism there and around the Western world. God is gone, and the all-powerful bureaucratic socialists are in charge. That said, the roots of the WCP are also very old and very deep in parts of Europe. Tradition slows cultural decline.

To appreciate our current predicament, we can also look back to what the founding fathers believed when they created a government for "We the People." To appreciate the founding fathers' commitment to the WCP, we need to further understand the path taken to 1776.

REASON AND VIRTUE WERE INTERTWINED FOR THE FOUNDERS

*What Athens was in miniature America will
be in magnitude.*

—Thomas Paine

The Greeks first used the word *paideia* to describe the effect of education on their people, especially in the cultivation of young people—the future citizens. Their educational ideal sought to form virtuous, clear-thinking people who would be citizens in their democratic form of government.

The Greek paideia was remarkable in three ways. First, it created citizens who were skilled in reason and logic. They called this "intellectual virtue." Second, they looked to align the soul with the transcendentals of truth, goodness, and beauty so the people would have a vision to "pursue happiness" justly, as our Declaration of Independence puts it. The Greeks called this "moral virtue." Finally, they studied the nature of our world in order to understand, use, and conform to it. They called this "natural philosophy"; what we now call "science" was in this sphere of natural philosophy. With the unified, divine view of reality, the Greeks believed that knowledge and virtue were one and led to understanding. This understanding freed one from being a "slave" to their station in life, and freed them to become virtuous, regardless of their economic status. Raw power was replaced with virtue—something everyone could aspire to.

This understanding is embedded in our founding. Our nation's philosophical bedrock, upon which the founding fathers based nearly all of their great documents—among them the Declaration of Independence, the *Federalist Papers*, and the Constitution—assumed that "the liberal arts, with rhetoric at their head, were originally the civic arts of liberty, the preparation for citizenship in a free city."[17] On one hand, our founding fathers immersed themselves in the classical thinkers like Plato, Cato, and Cicero, while on the other, they were influenced by Enlightenment or Christian thinkers like John Locke, Edmund Burke, John Calvin, and John Milton. All of these figures agreed: liberty was dependent on citizens with "reason and virtue." Moreover, this was cultivated through "liberal education" and Christianity—in the form of classical Christian education.

The thinkers and founders of America were, perhaps more than anything else, concerned that our Republic depended on these two features in citizens—reason and faith. Their own writings and words underscore these pillars of WCP. Consider just a handful of examples:

> "Freedom then of man and liberty of acting according to his own will is grounded on his having reason. . . . To turn him loose to an unrestrained liberty, before he has reason to guide him is not the allowing him the privilege of his nature, to be free; but to thrust him out amongst brutes, and abandon him to a state as wretched and as much beneath that of a man, as theirs."
>
> —*John Locke*

> "In my view, the Christian religion is the most important and one of the first things in which all children, under a free government ought to be instructed. . . . No truth is more evident to my mind than that the Christian religion must be the basis of any government intended to secure the rights and privileges of a free people."
>
> —*Noah Webster, preface to* An American Dictionary of the English Language, *1828*

"If Virtue & Knowledge are diffused among the People, they will never be enslav'd. This will be their great Security."

—*Samuel Adams*

"There are two types of education. . . . One should teach us how to make a living, and the other how to live." Also: "Children should be educated and instructed in the principles of freedom."

—*John Adams*

"If a nation expects to be ignorant and free, in a state of civilization, it expects what never was and never will be."

—*Thomas Jefferson*

"The advancement and diffusion of knowledge is the only guardian of true liberty."

—*James Madison*

"I consider knowledge to be the soul of a republic, and as the weak and the wicked are generally in alliance, as much care should be taken to diminish the number of the former as of the latter. Education is the way to do this. . . ." Also: "For avoiding the extremes of despotism or anarchy . . . the only ground of hope must be on the morals of the people. I believe that religion is the only solid base of morals and that morals are the only possible support of free governments. Therefore education should teach the precepts of religion and the duties of man towards God."

—*Gouverneur Morris, founding father, author of the Preamble to the US Constitution*

"What Athens was in miniature America will be in magnitude. The one was the wonder of the ancient world; the other is becoming the admiration of the present."

—*Thomas Paine*

"And let us with caution indulge the supposition that morality can be maintained without religion. Whatever may be conceded to the influence of refined education on minds of peculiar structure, reason and experience both forbid us to expect that national morality can prevail in exclusion of religious principle."

—*George Washington, Farewell Address*

Note in the above quotes that "knowledge" had a different meaning at the time. Today knowledge is a synonym for information. The historical understanding of knowledge was more like what we would now combine from information, ideas, virtue, and a universal system of understanding, revealed by God through his direct revelation in scripture and informed by the human condition.

Here's Webster's dictionary from 1828: "Knowledge: A clear and certain perception of that which exists, or of truth and fact; the perception of the connection and agreement, or disagreement and repugnancy of our ideas. We can have no knowledge of that which does not exist. God has a perfect knowledge of all his works. Human knowledge is very limited and mostly gained by observation and experience." Also: "Understanding: that faculty whereby we are enabled to apprehend the objects of knowledge, generals or particulars, absent or present, and to judge of their truth or falsehood, good or evil."

The zeitgeist of the Revolutionary era was replete with the idea, borrowed from the Greeks, that educated citizens were the backbone of the Republic. The Greeks postulated that the self-governed must have the ability to think for themselves and be cultivated in virtue, or else fragile self-government would descend into tyranny. Our founders knew that bribes, corruption, clever rhetoric, or the offer of wealth or ease would, if allowed to flourish due to a lack of cultural knowledge, undermine the Republic.

THE PROGRESSIVE VIRUS

When we hear that America's founding fathers read the great philosophers, learned Latin, or studied theology in school, we think, "Of course, that's how they did things back then. But why would we do that now?" We think as if Latin were a living language in the 1700s (it wasn't). Or as if classical philosophy was more of a practical tool for farmers, brewers, millers, or blacksmiths than it is for today's technology jobs (it wasn't). Classical education in the 1700s could have seemed just as "irrelevant" then as it seems now—at least if you judge it by progressive standards. Given the economics of the time, "impractical" education would have been less likely to be widespread. Yet nearly every citizen was educated classically. The real question: why did our founding fathers, and the generations before them, revere such an "impractical" education?

Let's put it into 2022 terms. Think of WCP as a vaccine. Think of progressivism, or authoritarianism—which is what our founders feared most—as the China virus. Without a vaccine, such a virus is free to rip through a society in record speed. Without any defenses, bad ideas can quietly spread without being seen—until it's too late. Centuries ago, the WCP was a ubiquitous and time-tested vaccine, given to Americans at childhood. Given our nation's "herd immunity" through its paideia, the virus almost never had a chance. But as the vaccine was used less and less in America's homes and schoolrooms, the progressive virus was allowed to spread. Today, nearly every school in America is a 16,000-hour superspreader event. Without the WCP vaccine (and waning cultural/natural immunity), our kids are vulnerable. The virus becomes our new normal, with our culture on one giant ventilator.

In Christopher Nolan's 2010 film thriller, *Inception*, the central theme is the power of an idea, once planted, to change everything. There are good ideas, and bad ideas—what matters is how widely they are allowed to spread. Twenty-four hundred years ago something un-precedented happened—an idea changed everything. Recorded hu-man civilization had existed for many thousands of years with few substantive changes. Human civilization was rooted in raw power and superstition. Life, as Thomas Hobbes wrote, was brutish and short. To our eyes, their customs were weird and pagan. People were told what to believe, and they did. Each tribe or nation had a god. And broader people-groups shared multiple gods. Most men were indentured to au-thoritarian leaders. The Greco-Roman-Christian civilization changed all that. Today we take this for granted. And, because we take it for granted, we are about to lose civilization as we know it.

You were probably told that man has slowly evolved socially, away from superstition and toward reason; away from a belief in gods (or even God) and toward personal autonomy; away from totalitarian empires and toward democracy; away from brutality and toward the rule of law. Along the way, enlightened people invented things and science became our trusted companion in any crisis. We have now progressed to become "the great society." And this "great society" will continue if we make it do so. This story arc, as we've seen, is a progressive one.

However, there is another way to tell the story—the Western Christian version.

THREE GIFTS FROM ANCIENT GREECE: ARETE, LOGOS, AND TELOS

A single discovery 2,400 years ago changed the six-thousand-plus-year course of human civilization. The Greeks created Western civilization (and the initial classical paideia) with one simple idea. They called it Arete. This idea, along with the two related ideas of Logos and Telos, made the American experiment possible. We must understand them to understand ourselves. (And don't worry, I didn't learn any of this in school, either—it was long since stripped out.)

Arete and Logos, like our word *paideia*, are not translatable into English. It takes an exploration of Greek thought to understand them. Prior to the idea of Arete, a person's greatness was widely defined by power, wealth, and glory. Egyptian pharaohs; Persian, Babylonian, and Assyrian emperors; and the Shang Dynasty—all were defined by this reckoning. Few have expressed this universal ancient viewpoint better than the English Romantic poet Percy Bysshe Shelley in his 1817 poem "Ozymandias." (Ozymandias was a Greek name for the Egyptian king Ramses II):

> *I met a traveller from an antique land*
> *Who said:—"Two vast and trunkless legs of stone*
> *Stand in the desert. Near them on the sand,*
> *Half sunk, a shatter'd visage lies, whose frown*
> *And wrinkled lip and sneer of cold command*
> *Tell that its sculptor well those passions read*
> *Which yet survive, stamp'd on these lifeless things,*
> *The hand that mock'd them and the heart that fed.*
> *And on the pedestal these words appear:*
> *My name is Ozymandias, king of kings:*

Look on my works, ye mighty, and despair!
Nothing beside remains: round the decay
Of that colossal wreck, boundless and bare,
The lone and level sands stretch far away."

The futility of man's pursuits—like the ruins of an ancient king's statue in a barren desert—intrigued the Greeks. Even during the golden age of Greece (circa 500–400 BC), the colossal statue of Ramses II already lay in ruins in Egypt. The Greeks' own one-hundred-foot-high Colossus of Rhodes lasted a scant fifty years! What if there were a more lasting measure of a man? Something that lasts longer than stone? Something truly infinite? Plato's oft-referenced cave analogy reflected the notion that our world is full of shadows cast by some perfect, ideal reality that is beyond our cosmos. Every thing, every shape, every "form" was simply the shadow of the real thing in the ideal reality. An "ideal" for the Greeks was an "archetype, concept of a thing in the mind of God." They replaced great men with great ideas.

What if this ideal could be, albeit imperfectly, embedded in a person as a set of "virtues"? Not just moral virtues like kindness or fairness, but everything about a person brought into alignment with the ideals of the cosmos. Accuracy in math was a virtue to the Greeks! This all-encompassing idea of "virtue" is the Greek idea of Arete—a man's individual greatness defined not by wealth, power, or glory, but by his virtue. This single, revolutionary idea became the launching point for a civilization, the philosophical descendants of which are still visible in America today. "Virtue" allowed any man—wealthy, poor, slave, or free—to achieve greatness and honor. This was freedom. We see this transformation in Greek culture as they went from early ideas of heroes in battle like Achilles, who was born of the gods, to the Roman general Cincinnatus, a hero because he was a virtuous general and also a simple farmer.

Contrast this Greco-Roman idea with our present ethos—that of scientism. We seek to achieve a utopian perfection by using science to lift ourselves up, not to a divinely inspired vision, but to a vision set by Marxist humanist philosophers who do not believe in the divine. Rather than impressive statues, we build impressive laboratories, some of which create the very pandemics that our science must then solve. Both Marx and Ramses II offer us a shattered visage. Twentieth-century Harvard classicist Werner Jaeger put it this way: "However highly we may value the artistic, religious, and political achievements of earlier nations, the history of what we can truly call civilization— the deliberate pursuit of an ideal—does not begin until Greece. . . . Without Greek cultural ideals, Greco-Roman civilization would not have been a historical unity, and the culture of the western world would never have existed."[18]

LOGOS: WHY THE WORD BECAME FLESH

The second word or idea was, incidentally, itself about words and ideas—the "Logos." The Logos represented a grand architectural blueprint existing only in the mind of God—but expressed for humans in words or ideas. Ideals came from outside of our cosmos, so the Logos was the connection to this reality from the realm of the divine. Language allows us to describe this reality. Logic or reason allows us to understand truths about this reality. But we can never directly experience this metaphysical reality, because we're physical. The power of believing that something truly perfect (not us!) exists is the first step in understanding the Logos.

For example, Greek geometers described a real-world sphere using language: "A sphere is made up of all points equal distant from a single point." The idea of a sphere can be described using words, but it can never be perfectly realized in this world. If you put a billion points, equally distributed, two inches from a center point, it would describe a pretty polished sphere. But two billion would be better, ten billion points better yet, and so on to infinity. No perfect form of a sphere can exist in our universe. Find the most highly machined ball bearing ever made, put it under an electron microscope, and it will look imperfect. Describe the sphere using language and you've described something from the mind of God. When you don't take this idea about language for granted, you can realize its power.

The Hubble Space Telescope's mirror was specified to target an object the diameter of a human hair at a distance of one mile. To do this, it needed a –1.00230 conic constant, or the measure of the arc of the mirror. That was its design on paper. The massive eight-foot-diameter mirror was built with a –1.01390 conic arc. During the manufacture and testing of the mirror, the imperfection was so tiny it went undetected on earth. It seemed perfect. But when put into service in the vacuum of space, the more "pure" environment revealed the flaw. It didn't work. The mathematical specification of Hubble's arc was perfect, but the real thing could never be. Even had the mirror been much closer to working, it would have been imperfect relative to the mathematical description. NASA famously sent astronauts to space to fix the Hubble's mirror, at great expense.

This is a real-life example of the nature of divine perfection as the Greeks saw it. This belief in the divine ideal was not simply a cerebral exercise. It led to impressive feats by the Greeks that were unparalleled in history. For example, the ancient Greeks built mechanical devices so intricate that their complexity was not possible again until the fourteenth century AD, like the Antikythera mechanism—the oldest example of an analog computer, used to predict astronomical positions and eclipses decades in advance. Make no mistake about it, their belief in the "divine ideal" is why you sit in a climate-controlled room with electric lights as you read this.

The Greeks thought the Logos was the key to understanding everything. We may expect this of math and science, but virtue? How can there be perfect justice or fortitude or prudence? Above the entrance to Plato's school in Athens, where most discussions involved ethics or virtue, was engraved "NONE BUT GEOMETERS MAY ENTER." The Greeks believed math and language could access divine reality in all realms of knowledge.

The significance of this Greek view may easily be missed. As with the movie *Inception*, if the Greeks had not planted the idea of a divine ideal for man, the world would be unrecognizable today.

"Arete" is what the Greeks called this type of perfection. The ancient Greeks first invented classical education to cultivate wisdom and virtue (Arete) in people so that they could intentionally perpetuate their culture. To get as close to Arete as possible, the Logos, translated as "word" or even "logic" in English, would describe the ideal man. But to what purpose?

TELOS: HOW THE WEST BECAME CHRISTIAN

The Glory of God is a Man Fully Alive.

—Irenaeus, circa 160 AD

The third word in this triad of the West is "Telos." Greeks observed from nature that everything had a purpose. They believed not just in a functional purpose, like the purpose of claws on a cat, but also what we might call the ultimate end, or reason for existence. From this they postulated that man was built for a greater purpose, or Telos. They argued about this purpose for centuries, but "citizenship" was seen as the leading candidate. Their focus on citizenship eventually gave rise to the republics in Greece and in Rome, and ultimately to the American Republic. All were based on one simple idea: Arete, if cultivated through children's paideia, would create citizens who could self-govern and live in freedom. Without a citizenry cultivated in this liberal paideia, tyranny and slavery would result. The Greeks referred to this type of education as "liberal" in that it liberated minds from the bounds of cultural dogma so the individual could think independently. Thus they called it "liberal education."

As a product of liberal education, the well-known triad of Greek philosophy broke the ancient world order to form the Western order. Socrates taught Plato, who in turn taught Aristotle, who tutored Alexander the Great, who formed the Greek Empire. The Romans saw the power of Greek ideas, adopted them, and their resulting republic overtook the Greek world. But the culture of Rome descended from the Greeks, and remained largely Greek. This is why the Bible refers to gentiles, even in the Roman province of Palestine, most frequently as "Greeks."

The Greek philosopher Socrates broke something else—the world's understanding of the divine. Polytheism had been a feature of nearly every civilization until his time—there were plural "gods," until Socrates identified a singular. Socrates excelled at refining the idea of the divine. He did this through inquiry. He would converse with passersby, asking questions for the purpose of showing them their error through their own answers.

Plato records the dialogues that Socrates had with a number of bystanders, like Euthyphro, Gorgias, and Meno. In these dialogues,

Socrates employs Logos to prove that there is only one God, one ultimate standard of goodness (virtue), and that man cannot know about God unless He reveals Himself to us. These, and many other logical proofs by Socrates, resulted in two things: First, he was put to death by the Greeks for "corrupting the youth" and "atheism" because he argued against the prevailing view of this time (sound familiar?). And second, five hundred years later, he would be recognized as the first proto-Christian. His views became the center of Hellenistic philosophy, in which Christianity was formed.

Consider the fact that the New Testament, written mostly by Hebrews who lived in the Roman Empire, was not penned in Hebrew or Latin, but instead in Greek. The Greek paideia ushered in the Christian era with its philosophy and language. Socratic philosophy about God threw a wrench into the polytheism of the time. And it left the Greeks in limbo. They were "ever learning, but never coming to a knowledge of the truth" (2 Timothy 3:7). There were few answers to be had, but there were many schools of thought—Stoic, Epicurean, Gnostic, Sophist, and more. Polytheism lingered in Greek culture and then in Roman culture through innumerable well-known gods: Zeus, Apollo, Diana, Poseidon, Mercury, Venus, Mars . . . the list goes on.

As we read in Acts 17, Paul entered Athens in about 51 AD. The city was full of idols, representing the Greco-Roman gods and other gods from around the region. The Greeks hungered for knowledge of the divine (Logos). "Now all the Athenians and the foreigners who lived there would spend their time in nothing except telling or hearing something new" (Acts 17:21). Their forum for the discovery of gods and for academic debate about them was the Areopagus—a location, but also the historic seat of the Athenian governing council. Paul was taken to the Areopagus by Socratic philosophers he encountered to discuss the divine. They thought his teaching on Jesus would make for good debate. They presumed Jesus to be yet another "foreign divinity." During his opening monologue of sorts, Paul quoted Epimenides, a Greek poet (circa sixth century BC) who said of Zeus, "In him we move and have our being." Paul replaced Zeus with Christ, the Logos.

When the Roman governor Pontius Pilate famously asked Jesus Christ, "What is Truth?" Pilate referenced this long, illusive quest that framed the struggle in the classical world. Christ answered the question: "I am the Truth." The Hellenists did not understand. At least not immediately. Christ completed the search for the ideal, divine man that the Greeks could never have imagined. Christ was Arete. "The first man was of the earth, made of dust; the second Man is the Lord from heaven" (1 Corinthians 15:47).

This is probably why John included Pilate's question in his gospel—a fitting end to a gospel that begins, "In the beginning was the Logos, and the Logos was with God, and the Logos was God. . . . All things were made by Him; and without Him was not anything made that was made. In Him was life, and the life was the light of men. And the light shineth in darkness; and the darkness did not comprehend it. . . . And the Logos was made flesh, and dwelt among us, and we beheld his glory, the glory as of the only begotten of the Father, full of grace and truth" (John 1, KJV, "Logos" from the original Greek replacing "Word").

John was an apostle to the Greek cities of Asia Minor. It's no wonder that the early church thrived in Greek and Roman cities, despite the governments' attempt to stamp it out. Christianity finally fulfilled this Greek triad of Arete, Logos, and Telos. The Christian Arete became the measure for Christians (Philippians 4:8, 1 Peter 2:9, 2 Peter 1:3, 5).

Never in history has any peaceful movement become so influential so quickly and broadly as Christianity. Divine Providence tilled the soil of the Hellenistic world. Christianity began with twelve humble disciples and soon consumed the greatest empire on earth. Within three hundred years, it had spread throughout the known world.

One reason is that Christ answered the three big Greek questions—Logos: Jesus Christ himself was the Logos, the divine man who called his followers to transform themselves into His image. Arete: through the work of the Holy Spirit, a Christian could approach Christ-likeness. Telos: the chief end of man is to glorify God.

As Christianity spread within the Greek cultural centers, Christians absorbed classical education and directed it toward this new, greater Christian Truth. The concept of the Logos gives us insight into how the Greeks viewed education. Rather than the vocational, information-based concept we have today, the Greeks sought divine Truth, and the related values of goodness and beauty. They proved that the pursuit of the ideal produced a civilization that lasted longer and was more influential than any other culture in history.

In the first and second centuries AD, the early church fathers did not miss this connection. Between 150 and 200 AD, Clement of Alexandria, an early Christian leader and educator, argued that classical and Christian education go hand in glove: "God is responsible for all good things: of some, like the blessings of the Old and New covenants, directly; of others, like the riches of philosophy, indirectly. Perhaps philosophy too was a direct gift of God to the Greeks before the Lord extended his appeal to the Greeks. For philosophy was to the Greek world what the Law was to the Hebrews, a tutor escorting them to Christ."[19]

Justin Martyr, another second-century Christian, points to the connection between the Greeks' pursuit of the Logos (reason) and

Christ's fulfillment of their pursuit: "[Socrates] exhorted them to become acquainted with the God who was to them unknown, by means
of the investigation of reason, saying, 'That it is neither easy to find the
Father and Maker of all, nor, having found Him, is it safe to declare
Him to all.' But these things our Christ did through His own power.
For no one trusted in Socrates so as to die for this doctrine, but in
Christ, who was partially known even by Socrates (for He was and is
the Word . . .) not only philosophers and scholars believed, but also
artisans and people entirely uneducated."[20]

In the second century, Clement addressed an early form of the
separation of faith and reason that we saw in the late 1800s: "There
are some people who . . . do not consider it right to have anything to do
with philosophy or dialectic (reason)—more, they refuse to engage in
the consideration of the natural world at all. All they ask for is simply
and solely faith. . . . So here I affirm that the expert is the one who
brings everything to bear on the truth. He culls whatever is useful from
mathematics, the fine arts, literary studies, and, of course, philosophy,
and protects the faith from all attacks."[21]

By the time of the First Council of Nicaea, held in 325 AD, the
church fathers had a long tradition of classical Christian education.
Ambrose of Milan, Augustine of Hippo, John Chrysostom, and
St. Jerome, among countless others, were church fathers with classical educations who originally expressed the doctrines that nearly
all Christians believe today.

By the Middle Ages, classical Christian education was in common practice. This education spread with missionaries to convert all
the peoples of Europe. Unfortunately, from the fall of Rome in about
400 to the rise of Britain in the 700s, Europe descended into political
disarray. Classical Christian education would play a central role in its
recivilization.

WHY GREECE AND ROME FAILED, AND WHY AMERICA SUCCEEDED ... FOR A TIME

As you may know, the first recorded democracy was in Athens in around 500 BC. It ended around two hundred years later. Rome's republic was founded at almost the same time as the democracy in Athens—around 500 BC. It fared longer, lasting until the rise of Caesar Augustus in 27 BC. These two republics were based on a Western paideia. Besides "liberated" minds (paideia), self-governance was believed to require a collective national Telos (purpose). Citizens needed to share a common purpose above their own self-interest, around which to center their lives. Otherwise they would vote in their self-interest, which would eventually result in tyranny and collapse.

The ancient Greeks made Arete, or the ideal man, their higher purpose. This abstraction proved too mercurial and individualistic upon which to base a nation (sound familiar?). Thus Greek democracy was relatively short-lived. The Romans placed their Telos in *Senātus Populusque Rōmānus*, or the "Senate and People of Rome." This gave the ideal of a republic itself a nationalistic purpose. Nationalism, as a good purpose, has limits. Nations decay into factions—and the Roman Empire fractured into provinces. Once factionalized, people vote in the interest of their faction. When this happens, the system decays and erodes. (Again, sound familiar?) James Madison realized this, and that is why factions are a centerpoint of concern in the *Federalist Papers* (*Federalist* 10, for example).

America's founding fathers, when they looked to the Greeks and the Romans, realized the problem of Telos and the nation-state. But they had something the Greco-Roman republics did not. They had the Western Christian Paideia. Its Telos was an eternal Kingdom that had no end and was "catholic" (universal, whole). The problem, as they saw

it, was that Christianity had factionalized. They lived closer to a time
when the English Civil War and the Catholic/Protestant tug-of-war
had cost many lives and had torn apart Europe. We've already seen
how the founding fathers addressed this by forbidding a specific state
church (First Amendment) and, for some of them, proclaiming Deism.
Yet, at the time of America's founding in the 1770s, the Kingdom of
Christ had been the central Telos in Europe and much of western Asia
for a thousand years. And the Western Christian Paideia was deeply
set in the education of nearly everyone.

Just about one thousand years earlier, between 700 and 800 AD,
a fractured and disorganized Europe became united around a single
Telos—the Kingdom of Christ. In Britain, Alfred the Great, the king
from whom all British monarchs today descend, united Britain under
the cross of Christ. He used classical Christian education as his instrument to unite the English people. Alfred mandated Latin, translated Aristotle, and created schools for Christians. A generation or two
earlier, a monk named Alcuin from the northern English city of York
founded "cathedral schools" for children across Britain. Alcuin's work
began to establish the WCP, with a generation or two of influence
before Alfred used this WCP to unite the Anglos.

On the continent, a similar Telos emerged. Charlemagne the Great
recruited Alcuin from Britain to plant classical Christian schools across
Germany. Charlemagne established the seat of his empire in Cologne,
Germany, but his vision was for a Christian kingdom, not an empire.
Alcuin's schools, by 1100, had become prevalent across Europe and
they began to organize. They helped give rise to the Scholastic Age,
beginning around 1200 AD, which in turn gave rise to the colleges
at Oxford, Bologna, Cologne, and in Paris. These "colleges" gathered
classical Christian scholars together and eventually created "universities." These universities, in turn, educated the merchant and artistic

classes and gave rise to the Renaissance, which was the inspiration for the rise of the Enlightenment and the American experiment. The remnants of this structure are seen, albeit in decay, in our university system today.

America's founding was based on a thousand-year project to cultivate the WCP in citizens.

Charlemagne ruled his empire, later dubbed "the Holy Roman Empire," between 800 and 880 AD. The Holy Roman Empire lasted officially until 1806—almost exactly one thousand years. We saw earlier that most or all of Europe's nation-states flew flags with Christian symbols. These states were primarily products of the Holy Roman Empire. For the first half of its existence, the Holy Roman Empire was referred to as a *universum regnum* ("whole kingdom") or *imperium christianum* ("Christian empire"). Over time, the Holy Roman Empire and greater Britain influenced all of what we now call Western Europe, from the tip of Italy's boot to the Scandinavian countries. Its eastern border skirted through Poland and down through the Balkan states, which is why this line defines the East-West division of Europe today.

Few of us know or at least recall much about the Holy Roman Empire. That is because modern historians tend to speak in terms of political power rather than religious influence. Also, Progressives all but removed the study of medieval history from schools. Historians today tend to minimize the scale of religion or culture as the base of power. They fail to recognize that the Holy Roman Empire and the United Kingdom were based in Christendom before politics. The most important thing about the world was not who ruled on the throne of a German city-state, or the British monarchy, but rather the training of everyday people as citizens of Christendom. The Holy Roman Empire lived on through the Western Christian Paideia, which was cultivated into the citizens of Europe through this heritage.

As Western civilizations grew, the orchard of classical Christian education near the city nourished it. It may seem unrealistic that classical Christian education played such a central role in creating the world we enjoy today, but, if you think about it, supply lines don't appear to matter much in a battle, until they collapse. The church became the school for well over a thousand years, and through the Puritans, classical Christian education was the basis for early American schools. America's first public school was Boston Latin School, originally a classical school. These schools formed the paideia of our founding fathers, who depended upon this schooling to sustain the Republic. And they had little reason to believe that this long-practiced form of education would disappear. If they made one key mistake, for which they can be forgiven, it was their assumption of an ever-present Western Christian Paideia.

If we fail to recognize the importance of paideia, as it is developed in schools and families, we'll cede victory to those who did—the Progressives. With the loss of the WCP, America, and Western civilization itself, must find the path back.

To start our course back—as we move into the final section of the book—we will contrast the progressive and classical views of education in concrete terms, unpacking four of the most noticeable "lost arts." Through modern (progressive) eyes, these lost arts are barely recognizable—but that was not the case for America's founding fathers. Classical Christian education was a gift to America at our founding, and can be a gift to us again.

PART III

A SOLUTION AS BIG AS THE PROBLEM

8

REASON AND VIRTUE

Two Towers of Freedom

*Since both knowledge and virtue require the
concept of transcendence, they are really
obnoxious to those committed to [materialism].*

—Richard M. Weaver, *Ideas Have Consequences*

During the twentieth century's Battle for the American Mind, Christianity became an early casualty in the public classroom. The Western tradition of education withered under the progressive siege. Classical Christian education, the source of the Western Christian Paideia (WCP), was all but stamped out. America was vulnerable.

Progressives breached four of the WCP's core battlements, or towers—strong points in our defense that protected America's republic: Reason, Virtue, Wonder, and Beauty. Four words that, because of this leftist breach, sound almost alien to modern ears. When I started this project, words like *virtue, wonder,* and *beauty*—as it pertains to education—sounded simplistic and outdated. I could not have been more wrong, and Progressives wanted it that way. They had molded my brain, too. But before we get to those, the largest battlement to fall was reason itself.

THE FIRST BATTLEMENT: REASON

If you had applied to the University of Michigan with a perfect score on the SAT in 2001, you would have received 12 additional points on your application. If you were a minority applying, you would have automatically earned 20 points toward admittance because of your race. In 2003 the US Supreme Court found Michigan's admission standard troubling and declared this type of racial preference discriminatory and unconstitutional. The Court's decision, as much as I agree with it, set into motion a course of events that would put a nail in the coffin of "reason" as a valued part of the American paideia.

From its widespread adoption in the 1940s until after the 2003 Michigan decision, the SAT measured one thing: reasoning. It had two 800 point scores—one in Verbal Reasoning, the other in Quantitative Reasoning—which added up to a perfect score of 1,600. No reasoning test can fully measure wisdom, or clear thinking. Even so, as a proxy, the SAT was widely successful for its purpose. While other content-oriented tests can be studied for, aptitude tests like the SAT measure more deeply embedded reasoning ability in a student. Reasoning tests like the SAT have been repeatedly validated as a predictor of college performance. A 2007 review of more than one thousand academic studies confirmed the predictive value of verbal and quantitative reasoning in academic success. "The [1999] SAT is a statistically and practically significant predictor of college performance, a stronger predictor than high school GPA, and the SAT remains a significant predictor after adjusting for income and racial/ethnic group."[22] Even so, the SAT ran into scrutiny during the 1980s and '90s because the results of the test seemed to differ by race.

We've already seen that the progressive gospel promises equality of outcomes—today known as "equity." Equality of outcome—or equity—means that reasoning itself must yield to the progressive vision. In 2020, the University of California's task force on admissions recommended the elimination of the SAT as an admission standard. The progressive gospel was echoed in comments by the UC's own task force that the test was racist. John Perez, chairman of the UC board of regents, said, "I believe this test is a racist test, there's no two ways about it." This was despite their own review of the data: "Our review of the existing literature suggests that racial bias in the SAT, at least the version of the SAT in place in 1999, is, at most, a minimal problem."

Andrew Conway, a psychology professor at Claremont Graduate University, clarifies the dissension: "Now, it is possible that university officials think 'the test is racist' because certain racial/ethnic groups, on average, score lower than other groups on the SAT. This is true. . . . However, similar group differences tend to be found in UC's grade point average (GPA). Does this mean that UC schools and/or the UC faculty are racist? This logic would imply that any measure that shows a group difference is racist. Taken by itself, this is a very narrow definition of racism—the context for what causes those differences is ignored."[23]

Herein lies the problem. Underlying causes—like broken families, poor schools, and socioeconomic factors—are ignored and thus the very essence of "reason" itself is dismissed as racist. It's as though the Left now actually believes the amount of melanin in one's skin is related to one's reasoning capacity! It's the "soft bigotry of low expectations," as presidential candidate George W. Bush phrased it in 2000. The institutional and structural makeup of college in America was founded on the WCP, which placed well-honed reason just below the revealed word of God as a source of Truth. Despite the leftists' control of colleges over the past hundred years, they cannot unmake their heritage. It is still embedded in how they operate. Thus the catch-22: the college system is built on reason, but they must reject reason because it's an artifact of Western culture.

Charles Murray's book *The Bell Curve*, released in 1994, set off a firestorm of riotous protests that eventually led to Murray being "canceled." His thesis referenced the SAT among other reasoning and intelligence tests to show that reasoning ability was a function of some combination of heredity, environment, and culture. One can understand why "heredity" got him into trouble. "Culture" was also off-limits in a multicultural world. For years, educators had known of the environmental factor as children develop. Educational Progressives tried to address environmental differences during the 1970s and 1980s through government programs and early childhood education, with programs like Head Start and Perry Preschools. But to no avail. Murray had poked a sore spot. Progressives had to respond.

Murray's critics countered that the SAT, as an artifact of "European culture," was racist, and thus biased against non-European cultures. At first Progressives claimed that vocabulary used on the test was too "white." Murray refuted this. Then they claimed that the type of thinking the test measured was verbal instead of spatial, which he and others again addressed. By July 2020, critical theory had found its sweet spot with critical race theory, and Progressives pinned everything on systemic racism. *Newsweek* exposed an exhibit at the Smithsonian's National Museum of African American History and

Culture in Washington, DC, that claimed that the idea of "rational cause and effect" was an outflow of "whiteness." The exhibit went on to label just about every part of Western civilization—like individualism, traditional families, and hard work—as a "white" construct. This idea is widespread in critical theory, now considered orthodoxy among Progressives. The real target, in bold type, is Western Christian civilization. A civilization spawned from the WCP.

In his book, Murray vetted nearly every possible angle to explain the difference in reasoning among different ethnicities. In his final analysis, Murray attributed the reasoning differences to what we might ultimately see as paideia: "Given a chance, each clan will add up its accomplishments using its own weighting system, will encounter the world with confidence in its own worth and, most importantly, will be unconcerned about comparing its accomplishments line-by-line with those of any other clan." Murray was knocking on the door of the Battle for the American Mind, though he showed little sign of realizing it. He seemed to realize that there was something deep about culture—not just the surface values or the attitudes that cultures exhibit, but something deeper.

Murray identifies "East Asian" cultures as the highest group on the SAT, so the narrative that Eurocentrism is the motivation behind the cultural argument is unsupported. The bottom line is that culture seems to be a sizable influence on reason. If Murray had been a classical historian, he might have called this influence "paideia."

HOW COMMON CORE CORRUPTS SAT RESULTS

Just months after the 2003 US Supreme Court decision striking down racial discrimination in the University of Michigan admissions process, Progressives proceeded to flip the script on the SAT. For decades, colleges had been making wild attempts to overcome the "reasoning" effect measured by the SAT. Undaunted by reason or court decisions, the Progressives decided to change what the SAT measures.

David Coleman launched an initiative called the Common Core in 2004. In 2009 the Obama administration promoted the Common Core curriculum objectives for K–12 schools. As we covered earlier, it was adopted in more than thirty states. Many criticized this standardization of K–12 education as a power grab by the federal government, and the events that followed Common Core's adoption made the Progressives' true intent more clear.

In 2012, the same David Coleman took over the leadership of the College Board, the organization that administers the SAT. In 2016, Coleman redesigned the SAT around Common Core knowledge and skills. The significance of this move brought Coleman's intention with the Common Core into sharp focus. To understand what he was doing, we need to revisit the backstory of the progressive programs throughout the 1970s, '80s, and '90s.

As Murray pointed out, programs like Head Start—a government program to "promote the school readiness of infants, toddlers, and preschool-aged children from low-income families"—were not succeeding in the goal of helping underserved students get into college by increasing their reasoning skill. And they cost over $1 billion annually in the 1980s. (Remember, reasoning tests were designed so they could not be studied for.) These tests depended on innate reasoning ability, but it was discovered that "innate" wasn't really innate. Reasoning ability was embedded in children through factors like their exposure to books, parents with higher levels of vocabulary, and good schools. These advantages spanned their whole childhood. Head Start was a decent idea, but it didn't influence reasoning enough and thus college admissions still were disproportionately white. At first, this meant we needed to give underserved students a "hand up" through programs like Head Start. When this didn't work, the Progressives made their pivot: reasoning tests themselves were racist; therefore the SAT was racist. The solution: design a test that could be studied for. Then anyone could be taught the content. You could memorize the answers like any other rote test. Kids could be programmed to answer like machines, without demonstrating preparedness for complex reasoning problems they would encounter after graduation.

Now, with Common Core content, the SAT measures what information and skills students are taught—not how well a graduate can reason. With the new SAT, anyone with access to Khan Academy preparation courses can study information and improve their score. But knowing "information" is not reasoning. The old SAT looked for the long-term, complex development of reasoning. Reasoning cannot be studied for—it's built up in a more complex way, as we shall soon see. This "way" descends from the distant classical Christian origins of the American educational system. Good schools, at least until the 1990s, still used vestiges of the seven liberal arts. These vestiges were minuscule, but they were enough to create an advantage on the SAT for white kids from good neighborhoods.[24]

So, rather than fixing the disparity in the schools, "verbal reasoning" was removed from the test to make way for fact-based questions that could be taught in high school. "Quantitative reasoning" was replaced with math skills.

Coleman reveals this transition, saying, "Assessment without opportunity is dead. We at the College Board have decided it's not enough to say these problems are not our fault. We just make the test. We're not responsible for inequities in test prep, course access, or stagnant performance. It may not be our fault, but it is our problem. We have to redesign everything we do to foster opportunity. . . ."

Imagine the SAT as a race where you want the competitors to each hit a certain speed without help. The pre-2000 SAT was like a speedometer linked to the drivetrain of a car—it simply reflected the vehicle's speed; it did not make the car go faster. The new SAT no longer measures reason; it measures a student's memorization of the Common Core. Now the speedometer is trying to be the engine. To switch metaphors, the SAT tail is now wagging the collegiate dog. Instead of measuring the attributes that predict success in college (reasoning), the new test tells colleges how well the student has memorized the Common Core—information without a well-established correlation to college success. Some colleges are all too happy to embrace outside influence, as long as they meet their diversity, equity, and inclusion objectives. Other colleges are going "test optional" to more quickly reach their diversity agendas without court fights.

The Michigan case, the University of California, and the SAT takeover are just a few among countless assaults on the battlement of reason. One hundred years earlier, we saw Progressives redesign the school system to deliver training useful for industrial jobs but void of the traditional training in logic and clear thinking. It took Progressives nearly a century to finally excise reasoning from the educational infrastructure. Did they set out to do this? Yes and no. Early Progressives valued reasoning, but didn't see its purpose for the common laborer. They asked: what does a factory worker performing repetitive tasks need with formal logic? Progressives did not want factory workers to be scholars. Voters who could easily be persuaded to support progressive regulation and government entitlement programs could greatly help the progressive cause.

Today, attacking reason as a vestige of Western culture is their new approach. Reasoning has the effect of advancing some cultures—paideias—over others, so in the name of equity, we must replace reason with other cultural values that do not come from the West. This sentence might have been challenged by Progressives not that long ago. Critical theory is changing that.

Progressives made three fundamental changes to diminish reason in America's schools. First, they removed logic and rhetoric from the curriculum. Second, they stopped using the Socratic method, or the requisite study of world history, philosophy, and theology. And third, they divided subjects into silos without a unifying frame. In short, they completely hollowed out the classical Christian education framework that had birthed the American experiment. To learn more about how these work in an actual school—a school you can choose—keep reading.

THE POWER OF DEPTH

What you sow, that you will also reap.

—Galatians 6:7

Two high school students at a classical Christian school were working on a video package for an elective course. The video was about school uniforms, and they solicited interviews from kids in public school. One public school student said on camera that uniforms "would cause his soul to shrivel inside him." The student reporter editing the video made a passing comment: "He must have a fragile soul." The other, without looking up, let out a brief "Ha, yes, I think they all did," in reference to the three other students they interviewed. Their banter was not meant to demean, and their attitude wasn't prideful. It was more of a curiosity. They were genuinely flummoxed by the lack of depth they encountered in the day's foray to the local public mega-school. After all, these classical students talked about the human soul nearly every day, and in a way that informed the bigger questions of human flourishing.

16,000 hours is a lot of time. If you spend a good portion of it on deeper, more weighty topics, you develop depth. Classical Christian schools do this by reading original sources, not synthesized textbooks. They do it by studying languages and cultures that are among the deepest in history. They engage their classmates about ancient philosophers who ask deep, and timeless, questions. The discussions often pour into the hallway. When this happens for thousands and thousands of hours, depth happens.

Civilization is under siege. If you study a siege, like when the Roman general Titus besieged Jerusalem in 70 AD, you'll note that the process takes a long time. Starvation, a siege wall (to keep people from escaping), siege engines, and constant volleys of arrows do their work for months or even years before the battlements begin to fall. When the four corner towers (battlements) fall, all that is left is the burning and pillaging by the invasion force. The first battlement, "reason," is a rubble pile among our youth today. The second battlement—virtue—has taken a while to fall, but we have seen the results in our streets and communities—starkly so in the past few years. Certainly, broken families and empty churches have played a role. But the Christian school has, through the history of the West, been the guardian of civility—passing on virtue to the next generation.

THE SECOND BATTLEMENT: VIRTUE

Virtue is not the absence of vices or the avoidance of moral dangers; virtue is a vivid and separate thing, like pain or a particular smell.

—G. K. Chesterton

The vision of an innocent man on his knees begging for mercy, only to be roundhouse-kicked in the head by an Antifa protestor—while onlookers cheer—is reminiscent of a line of Christians on their knees being beheaded by Muslim terrorists. The former was in Portland, Oregon, in August 2020. The latter took place in Libya in 2015. The lack of civility during the so-called protests in 2020 surprised many Americans. Such barbarity is usually far away from our shores. But today it's not. Speeches, signs, and graffiti were riddled with the F-word, not to mention the burning buildings and rampant property destruction. "Protesters" even showed up at a hospital wishing death to a pair of police officers being treated for injuries following an ambush. The captured and complicit media dubbed these "mostly peaceful protests."

In the mayhem of the summer of 2020, we saw the abuse of the police, destruction of property, and the assault of innocent bystanders. Countless people were murdered, either during the unrest or in the lawlessness that grew out of "defund the police." This was not the fringe. The Black Lives Matter chairman of New York said on national television, "Give us what we want, [or] we will burn down this system." Our elected governments joined in—and not just one or two of them. Mayors in New York and Washington, DC, endorsed "Black Lives Matter" and painted their slogan on their streets. The NBA and

NFL painted it on their courts and fields. Presidential candidate, and now vice president, Kamala Harris encouraged people to donate to the bailout fund for rioters. Seattle and Portland allowed rioters to declare lawless "autonomous zones" in their cities. Statues were torn down. This widespread institutionalized support for a lack of civility is unique in American history.

Contrast these protests with the 1963 March on Washington for Jobs and Freedom. A quarter-million people converged on the National Mall in a civilized protest. Dr. Martin Luther King's "I Have a Dream" speech did not dwell in anger or threats, but rather appealed to God's hand in freedom. MLK pointed to the Bible, and the promise of America's founding documents. Despite Malcolm X's call for violence at the time, the march was peaceful. Not every protest in the 1950s or '60s was peaceful, of course. And the police committed acts of real racism back then. However, one major difference is evident: local governments—while far from blameless—were not complicit in the riots back then. When elected governments encourage incivility, civilization's days are numbered.

Civility, of course, is rooted in the virtue of citizens. The Western Christian Paideia was marked by the aspirational pursuit of this quality. The progressive takeover of school changed that. The schools of the 1930s, '40s, '50s, and '60s cultivated American patriotism, with some associated nationalistic virtue. The older virtues from classical Christian education were fading, lingering primarily in the homes.

C. S. Lewis points to this loss in his book *The Abolition of Man*. He laments the loss of the cultivation of the WCP in education: "In a sort of ghastly simplicity we remove the organ and demand the function. We make men without chests and expect of them virtue and enterprise. We laugh at honour and are shocked to find traitors in our midst. We castrate and bid the geldings be fruitful."

THE REVOLUTIONARY IDEA OF THE AFFECTIONS AND VIRTUE

*The only way to dispossess [the heart] of an old
affection, is by the expulsive power of a new one.*

—Thomas Chalmers

Ethical shifts are among the most difficult to engineer within a culture. To achieve our present shift, we've seen Progressives resort to changing words—a proven tool of propaganda.

The Western Christian basis for virtue transcends humanity. It does not change. It is framed in the Bible and developed through the great texts, and is universally applied to all people. Disputes between branches of Christianity sometimes brought conflict around the perimeter, but every Christian sect saw virtue in the same way. For Progressives, this vision had to change. So they slowly but surely replaced the word *virtue* with the word *values*—and grounded those values in the individual and society rather than God. The road to this new term *values* was long but important. Let's jump back to when Thomas Hobbes, Jean-Jacques Rousseau, and John Locke developed concepts of "natural law" and the "social contract."

"Natural law," or the law of good and evil imprinted on every person innately, was put into humans by God, at least according to Locke. Scripture backs up this idea, loosely, in Romans 1. Lewis references this concept in *The Abolition of Man* as "the Tao." Reason was seen as a product of natural law, and thus could contribute to an ethical frame.

This innate knowledge of goodness was challenged by moral skeptics like David Hume, who believed ethics were sourced from one's emotions. Unhitched from the divine, modernism and postmodernism sourced ethics completely from the individual. *Your truth,* not the Truth. Well, almost completely. "Everyone doing what's right in his own eyes" has its limits, especially when building a utopia. So Progressives borrowed from "social contract" theory to construct their own ethical frame. Thomas Hobbes recognized that without an agreed-upon legal system based upon natural law, the human condition would be "solitary, poor, nasty, brutish, and short." He opened the door to a social contract detached from the divine. After all, if our shared values need simple agreement, they can be sourced from anywhere. Progressives realized that this contract need not be divine in origin, but rather could be an agreement between those in a society. As laid out in previous chapters, the ethics of the Progressives are both pragmatic and ultimately Marxist. All they had to do was get society to play along with a new contract and a new order based on Marxism.

Christian virtue is different in two ways. First, there is no contract. There is law, passed down from God. Man's institutions are good or bad insofar as they conform to this law. Our cultures are good or bad insofar as they conform to the principles of the law. Second, virtue is not a conformity to the law, but rather an alignment of the will with the divine. The will is driven by affections of the soul. These affections, when aligned with God's, cause man to desire the law.

Virtue is not a synonym for morality or values. We are so absorbed in progressive culture that the previous sentence seems foreign. I've used the word *values* for years, while assuming I understood what it meant. In fact, in my previous book, *American Crusade*, I used the term *values* more than fifty times; the word *virtue* occurs only four times. We're all infected.

Values are just "things we believe." They're like answers on a memorization test, and they're self-defined. Virtue, properly understood, is rooted in the affections of a person as they align to God's affections.

A virtuous person loves the right and the good. Virtue is not behavior, though it nearly always results in behavior. Actions are the outworking of a person's virtue, which is cultivated into his or her character. Under this Christian ethical system, any given choice is a function of virtue. For example, knowledge and sound reason may prompt you to invest in a particular company. The virtue of sound reason, to the degree it is possessed, will make this a good or a bad decision from a financial point of view—and from every other point of view. Virtue applies to everything, not just what we think of as moral decisions. However, even moral decisions are complicated by the hierarchy of virtues.

In the Law of Moses, lying is declared a sin. Yet not much later in the Bible, a prostitute named Rahab is honored by God for lying to her city's officials to save a few Israelite spies. Her lie ultimately results in the destruction of her city. Yet she is seen as virtuous in Hebrews 11. Her faith and trust in God was a higher good than the sin of lying. Another example: in scripture, we see that it is good to feed the poor. But the greater good is that Jesus is worshipped (Matthew 26, Mark 14, John 12). Even lies or not feeding the poor can be virtuous, when they are ordered against other affections. When Jesus was asked "what is the greatest commandment," he said the first was to love God, and the second to love your neighbor. Notice, they are ordered. If loving one's neighbor supersedes loving God in some way, then loving thy neighbor is not properly ordered. Once the ethics of Christianity are understood in this way, a whole new virtue forms in how we relate within our communities. This may seem to some like an odd form of "moral relativism." But, in fact, because the right or wrong is always tied to a divine ideal, it is far from a floating, personal standard. God's ways are *always* rooted in hierarchy—in this case higher and lower goods. The world was viewed through this lens, in the classroom, from before Augustine until the twentieth century.

Writer and theologist Kaitlyn Schiess captures this well, saying,

There is a long history in Christian education that focuses on the formation of the affections, alongside the training of the intellect. This reflects one of the religion's foremost insights about human nature. Augustine famously wrote, "You have made us for yourself, and our heart is restless until it rests in you." That is, humans navigate our way through the world via the things we love—the stories about the world that captivate us, the desires that motivate us, the material or spiritual goods that attract us— and we need guidance to make sure that the things we love are ordered beneath our ultimate love of God. Christians have often described sin as misdirected love—loving the wrong things or loving the right things in the wrong way. Christian education, then, has historically focused not merely on delivering the right information, but also on giving students the tools—music, prayer, storytelling—to shape our loves.

Amen.

Schiess is addressing an error descending from fundamentalist Christianity. We saw this fundamentalism rise out of the separation of Christianity into liberal and fundamentalist strains late in the nineteenth century. The quote above is part of a *New York Times* editorial she wrote on ethical problems with the leadership at Liberty University.[25] Fundamentalists frequently make Christian morality into a list of dos and don'ts.

Everything from manners, to our precision in math, to the quality of our reasoning ability, to our appreciation of beautiful music and art begins with the proper ordering of our affections. There is nothing more true about the created universe than this hierarchy. Do you remember from math class that there is an order of operations—like multiply before you add? This is a fleck of our entire universe, which is designed with an order. Ordered affections, driven by virtues, define our paideia.

The real breakthrough idea is that we love these "goods" in an order, and that order dictates what we do. Augustine asserts this order in *On Christian Doctrine*: "But living a just and holy life requires one to be capable of an objective and impartial evaluation of things: to love things, that is to say, in the right order, so that you do not love what is not to be loved, or fail to love what is to be loved, or have a greater love for what should be loved less, or an equal love for things that should be loved less or more, or a lesser or greater love for things that should be loved equally."

This Augustinian view from 400 AD defined the social and religious economy of the Western Christian world through the nineteenth century. We see it repeated often. Here's an example from Jonathan Edwards in the eighteenth century. He writes in his treatise on *The Religious Affections*: "True Christian fortitude consists in strength of mind, through grace, exerted in two things; in ruling and suppressing the evil and unruly passions and affections of the mind; and in steadfastly and freely exerting and following good affections and dispositions, without being hindered by sinful fear or the opposition of enemies."

These ordered affections span all of life and were the bedrock of Christian virtue—until they were systematically removed. Education cultivates a paideia. The WCP is the product of an educational system dedicated primarily to the cultivation of virtue—but probably not the idea of "virtue" as most people conceive of it.

COUNTERINTUITIVE THOUGHTS ON VIRTUE

For some clarity, the following four examples will show four laws of virtue that are counterintuitive to the modern ear, but nonetheless true.

One, a virtue is a "golden mean," not a "do or don't": when we say someone is a "free spirit," we generally mean that he goes through life letting his whims direct him. The ancients would have called him intemperate (a vice). We all know someone who tends to be driven to excess in the pursuit of financial success. He would also be intemperate. The actions are opposite—whimsical versus goal driven—but the vice is intemperance. Every virtue has a "vicious" (vice) antithesis. Virtues and vices operate on a scale that has a "golden mean," or a point at which our virtues are rightly ordered. Note that there is nothing wrong with working hard in your career or following a whim. Both can be virtuous. But there is always an ethical reality in how our affections are prioritized against one another—how we order our affections.

Second, obedience out of *duty* is the lowest form of virtue. I'll use an everyday example of a simple virtue: completing tasks. Everyone wants to finish an important task (like writing this book). Some people force themselves to complete tasks out of a sense of duty (an affection for doing what one ought to do). But those who actually accomplish tasks regularly have an affection for completion set deep in their soul. If you have a highly ordered affection for finishing a task when you start it, then the culture of your home or office will exhibit productivity. It overpowers other lesser affections, like surfing Netflix. It comes from something deeper than a lecture or a lesson, or even willpower. It comes from joy. This is a virtuous paideia at work.

As always, C. S. Lewis puts it better: "A perfect man would never act from a sense of duty; he'd always want the right thing more than the wrong one. Duty is only a substitute for love (of God and of other people) like a crutch which is a substitute for a leg. Most of us need the crutch at times; but of course it is idiotic to use the crutch when our own legs (our own loves, tastes, habits, etc.) can do the journey on their own."

Third, a good affection, if not rightly ordered, is a vice. Take for example the virtue of completing a task, and how it can become a wrongly ordered love. When our neighbor shows up to ask for help while we're completing a task, we may become frustrated. But we may act out of duty. We do the right thing and help. If our loves had been rightly ordered (if we were virtuous), we would not be frustrated but rather we would love to help our neighbor in that moment, forgoing the completion of our own task. This is the difference between duty (morality) and virtue (a rightly ordered love of the good, true, and beautiful). We may love completion, but we love our neighbor more. Boy, is this a lesson I need to learn in my own life!

Fourth, and finally, affections drive your actions, even if you think it's reason. Once you understand this concept of virtue, you realize that all human choices—moral and otherwise—are tied to affections. Two engineers once met to try to solve a manufacturing problem. Lab tests showed that a particular part was routinely measured in the low end of the prescribed tolerances, but stayed within them. The two engineers strongly disagreed with each other. For one of them, the fact that the parts were measured within tolerance made the course clear—move forward. For the other, a redesign was necessary because the part was too close to one edge of the tolerance. For one engineer, tolerances were there for a reason. He loved justice more than security: *the rules say it's okay, so we must move on.* For the other engineer, the grouping near the low end was just too risky. She loved security more than justice. This "scientific" decision was made, in the end, because of ordered human affections for two different people, not science or engineering. Both engineers loved security and justice, but their orders were reversed.

When you think about it, this is how all decisions in life are ultimately made—according to ordered affections.

This is a small and deliberately technical example. Who you marry, how you drive, what church you attend, what career you pursue, even how you get ready in the morning is a function of affections, cultivated in paideia. Decisions big and small originate here. We too often think these are just preferences that we're born with. They're not. Or we think we are autonomous beings who make decisions based purely on our reason. We don't. At least not entirely, or even primarily. Education, informally and formally, influences how our affections are formed and ordered.

We're told today that every individual is unique, and personal preference is indelible. But this isn't entirely true. While we are indeed unique, we are also products of the families and cultures that birthed us. Each of us has cultivated virtue that modifies our natural, sinful, and divinely imaged selves. The WCP recognized this tension between the individual and the culture. It uniquely fuses the two through the affections. These affections are trained in classical Christian schools. You can see how this works in the classroom in Chapter 10.

Since "rightly ordered affections" or "virtues" are one key outcome of the WCP, we can now look at how Progressives corrupted this function of education.

HOW PROGRESSIVE EDUCATION UNDERMINES CIVILIZATION

The Left is in a war against nature.

—Tucker Carlson

You may remember that Progressives reappropriate words to make their vision more palatable. Progressives replaced the word *virtue* with *values* late in the nineteenth century and early in the twentieth. Virtues come from God; values come from within you.

While progressive liberal clergy were teaching the social gospel, based in "values" instead of "virtue," fundamentalists in the late nineteenth and early twentieth centuries forgot "virtue" and made lists of "morals." The two sides of Christianity were both influenced by the progressive agenda. "Morals" were the zeitgeist of the age for a brief time; however, they were neither virtues nor values, so they waned throughout the twentieth century. They were pharisaical codes from well-meaning Christians who had lost their memory of virtue. Why did people want pharisaical rules rather than affections? We can speculate. First, possibly because affections are cultivated through deep and arduous means—true education that, over time, cultivates a person's affections. And second, pharisees feel like they can "do good." Pursuing virtue is about imitating the divine Logos, which requires repentance and transformation. The Enlightenment had distilled everything to earthly "facts"—or a list of dos and don'ts. This made "measurement" of those morals simple, and within the ability of anyone to "do." It's harder to "be." Ordering your affections in the context of your character is more challenging than behaving a certain way.

In the following chart, Google measures historical documents to see the frequency in the use of particular words in publications. It provides a proxy view of the timing and magnitude of the change from the Western Christian Paideia (virtue) to the fundamentalist Christian paideia (morals) to the American Progressive Paideia (values). The crossover points reinforce our story—in about 1825, the moralism of the Second Great Awakening rose (the beginning of the evangelical movement), peaking in about 1850. "Virtue" declined slowly but steadily through the nineteenth century as the WCP was slowly converted to the moralism of the evangelicals. Between 1905 and 1915, overlapping the Progressive Era, atheistic humanism "values" replaced both. As the generational effect of paideia in the schools took hold, values soared and never looked back. By 2000, the Progressives (and conservatives!) have their values, evangelicals have their morals, and virtue has fallen out of use. Language, in this case, tells us much about the progressive history.

PROGRESSIVES' PSEUDO-VIRTUES

Progressives replaced the old idea of divinely originated virtue with a new ethical system: anything goes between "consenting adults" and "your rights end where my nose begins." In other words, unless you directly hurt someone else, your values are just as valid as anyone else's. This ethical construct often goes by the pseudonym "tolerance" or post-modernism. In reality, it was a transitional form. Once Progressives waited out the lingering effects of the WCP over the course of the twentieth century, tolerance no longer served their purposes.

"Tolerance" had given progressives the space they needed in polite culture to develop and advance their progressive paideia. At the dawn

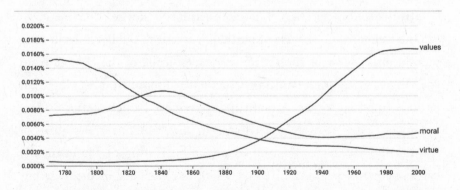

Use of Words in Publication Over Time as a Proxy for American Attitudes
(https://books.google.com/ngrams)

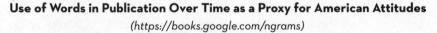

of the twenty-first century, tolerance has become nothing more than progressive doublespeak for intolerance. Over the past twenty or thirty years, Progressives have established a new set of pseudo-virtues around race, gender, and oppressor/oppressed identities. These "virtues" share with the original term a sense of absolute orthodoxy. Hence the term "virtue signaling" when these are on exhibition. But these "virtues" are based in cultural Marxism, not Christianity. This new paideia based in pseudo-virtues is far more "intolerant" than anything from the WCP. For this reason, we call the rising paideia of our time the Cultural Marxist Paideia (CMP).

Louis Markos, professor of English at Houston Baptist University and a classical scholar, notes that "the secular-progressive architects of our modern schools were not foolish enough to [eliminate virtue]. That is why, after purging their schools of traditional Judeo-Christian— and traditional Greco-Roman—virtues, they replaced them with a set of five pseudo-virtues to fill up the virtue-shaped vacuum in our hearts: tolerance, inclusivism, egalitarianism, multiculturalism, and environmentalism."

Progressive pseudo-virtues are based on expected contributions to society (to each according to his need, from each according to his ability), a materialistic worldview (no God and no purpose), individualistic affections (do what's right in your own eyes), a separated concept of God who makes us feel fulfilled (therapeutic religion), and an enforced social contract to guide us (no right and wrong, just agreed-upon progressive standards). All of us—as products of the same progressive pipeline—have been pulled into portions of this vision at some level, myself included.

The WCP's ethical system included a true form of tolerance that recognized authentic virtue could not be imposed from without. So, shaming people in Western culture was mostly limited to public activities (actions, not speech!). Because these actions were seen by all in public, they set a standard. Things like, *No swearing in front of women. Wear appropriate clothing. Discipline your children. Take off your hat when you pray. Stand for the national anthem. Don't be drunk in public.* This type of cultural expectation supported virtue on a societal level, but was tolerant of your personal convictions.

The American Progressive Paideia turned Cultural Marxist Paideia is now based in pseudo-virtues that do not include Christian tolerance. They now want to control what you believe and think. Jeering, roving bands of "protesters" today demand that diners at a restaurant or on the street "say the words" or "hold up their fist." "Canceled" is the new shaming—on steroids—based on thought crimes or speech crimes, not just public action. The new priests of the progressive gospel control corporations, sports teams, and government bureaucracies, to name a few. You'd better take a knee during the national anthem, or else! Violence against certain kinds of people with certain beliefs is just fine. They are privileged and had it coming. Not every left-leaning American is willing to rationalize violence yet, but this is where we are headed. "Burn it down" is not entirely figurative. The medieval church, even with its highly publicized intolerant exceptions, was not this committed to the wholesale indoctrination of civic society. Nor did it have this wide a power base.

9

WONDER AND BEAUTY

Learning to Love the Right Things

To enjoy the things we ought and
to hate the things we ought has
the greatest bearing on virtue.

—Aristotle, *Nicomachean Ethics*, Book X, 1172.a17

As we begin this chapter, and before we get to the next battlement, I hope you'll indulge an important foray into popular culture—and the examples they provide on the topic of virtue.

At one point in the 2000 movie *Gladiator*, Commodus—the antagonist—rails at his father, Marcus Aurelius, just before killing him: "You told me once that I must develop virtues like Fortitude, Temperance, Prudence, and Justice. I don't possess those virtues, but there are others. . . ." We know that progressive Hollywood would never come up with material that good! It turns out these cardinal virtues appear around nearly every corner in Western history. In the fourth century, Augustine combined them with faith, hope, and love to create the historic seven Christian virtues. They adorn ancient and medieval architecture, stained glass, paintings, and literature. These virtues were a centerpiece of the WCP.

Today we might say "Mike's a banker, and a middle-aged father of three." But historically, "virtues" were used to describe. Ancient kings or nobles were called things like "Richard the Lionhearted," or "James the Just," or "Frederick the Wise." Titles described the essence of who someone was, in terms of virtue, or sometimes who they wanted to be.

If you take the time to understand how these seven virtues influenced our world, you can see why Christians have historically made them an educational centerpiece. These aren't the only virtues, of course. But considering the condition of our Republic—currently obsessed with Commodus's "other virtues"—they would be a good start. Contrast the Christian virtues with the progressive pseudo-virtues: celebrate anyone's choices, as long as they conform to socially acceptable orthodoxy on the environment, gender fluidity, sexual liberation, Marxist economics, critical race theory, or climate change zealotry, to name a few. Rather than your soul, you are defined by your race, gender, sexual identity, and "correct" political beliefs. The list goes on.

CULTIVATING THE MORAL IMAGINATION

The most important area of imagination is moral imagination. Good stories are the fertile flowerbed of the moral imagination.

—Vigen Guroian[26]

To most of us the words *moral* and *imagination* seem unrelated to each other. This is because the progressive paideia casts the "imagination" as unbounded and free. "If the imagination were obedient, the appetites would give us very little trouble." wrote C. S. Lewis. In the WCP's economy of affections, imagination becomes a vision of God's ideal, not your personal ideal. By training children to discipline their imagination and aim it toward divine ideals, we bless them with a lifelong gift of a moral imagination.

Pastor Patrick Twagirayesu runs a group of schools in Rwanda called Bright Future Schools. Patrick was alive during the genocide of 1994 as his family fled to a nearby country. He treasures education in a way few Americans can.

"Consider an illiterate Christian Rwandan peasant, one who might easily have been a killer in the genocide. This peasant believes the gospel and loves Jesus, but embodying the gospel requires the ability to understand how the gospel shapes all parts of life, the eyes to see how genocidal ideology contradicts Christianity—even when the leaders he has been educated to blindly follow tell him God wants him to kill Tutsis. The unschooled person has been prevented from growing the spiritual, intellectual, human capacity for asking moral questions, applying ideals to situations, or contemplating different narratives of action. An uneducated person . . . is like a man who cuts down the pillar that is holding up his own house and burns it for warmth, thinking he has done a good deed."[27]

We see here the need for the capacity to imagine, to contemplate that which you have not encountered. To imagine the moral reality of such a claim as "kill Tutsis" is dependent on growing the capacity to ask moral questions or contemplate different narratives. Classical Christian educators call this the "moral imagination."

Literate children who imagine and wonder with divine truth, goodness, and beauty as a goal are the most dangerous people to progressive vision. If we want to cultivate these types of children, we need to return to stories for children from an earlier time. The twentieth century did much damage to the stories that sparked wonder and the moral imagination for children. Walt Disney did much of that damage.

Ask anyone on the street, "What is the moral of the Pinocchio story?" The answer will almost certainly be "Don't tell a lie or your nose will grow." This comes from the Disney retelling of the story. But it is a minor subplot in the original 1883 novel by Carlo Collodi. Children's classics in our era have been altered and simplified morally, drastically changing their potency, their depth, and consequently their impact on the moral imagination.

In the classic children's book, we see Pinocchio following his foolish heart time and again, creating pain for his father, Geppetto, and his mother, the Blue-Haired Fairy (a Christ figure in the work). Pinocchio's sinful and foolish heart repeatedly overcomes his good intentions. People who love him get hurt because of his selfishness. Finally, when he finds his lost father in the belly of a great shark, he is overcome by love for his father. He begins to self-sacrificially nurse him back to health, and for the first time, he thinks more of someone else than himself. He works hard without complaining. He earns milk for his father by pumping water for a gardener. He earns enough money to buy himself a new suit, but when he learns that the Blue-Haired Fairy is sick, he sends the money to her instead. His love starts to grow. It is only then, when he learns to love others more than himself, that Pinocchio finally becomes a real boy. We can hear the resonance with Ezekiel 36:26: "I will give you a new heart and put a new spirit within you; I will remove your heart of stone and give you a heart of flesh." Pinocchio's story brings this home for children in a heartfelt way.

In 1964, Walt Disney continued his neutering of great stories. He was disappointed with Bill Peet after he created an initial, faithful interpretation of Rudyard Kipling's classic *The Jungle Book*. Disney wanted something less lush and moody, and less serious. He hired a new director, Larry Clemmons, to direct *The Jungle Book*, with one condition: "The first thing I want you to do," instructed Disney, "is not to read it. I want you to have fun with it." The product, released in 1967, bears out the result of Disney's request. In Disney's released version, the monkeys steal an innocent Mowgli, prompting his "friends" Bagheera and Baloo to save him. At the end of the battle with the monkeys, Bagheera and Baloo discuss what happened (Disney's version):

> **BAGHEERA:** Mowgli seems to have man's ability to get into trouble.
> **BALOO:** Keep it down, you're going to wake up "little buddy." He's had a big day. It was a real sockeroo. It ain't easy to learn to be like me . . . you know.
> **BAGHEERA:** Associating with those undesirable, scatter-brained apes? I hope Mowgli learns something from that experience.

The scene ends as Baloo tucks him in. Through the rest of the show, Mowgli's crisis is in finding a friend he can trust. It turns out to be a girl.

In Kipling's 1894 original, the story infuses transcendent virtue. After Mowgli has been found befriending the monkeys, he's scolded by his guardians, Baloo and Bagheera. Mowgli's pride and rebellion bring him to disrespect his teacher, Baloo.

> MOWGLI: [The monkeys] gave me nuts and pleasant things to eat, and they carried me up in their arms to the top of the tree, and said that I was their blood brother and should be their leader someday.
>
> BAGHEERA: They have no leader. They lie. They have always lied.
>
> MOWGLI: They were kind. . . . They stand on their feet as I do. They do not hit me with their hard paws. They play all day. . . . I will play with them again!
>
> BALOO: Listen, Man-cub, I have taught thee all the Law of the Jungle for all the people of the jungle, except the Monkey-folk who live in the trees. They have no law. They are outcast. They have no speech of their own . . . they are without leaders. They have no remembrance. They boast and chatter and pretend that they are a great people about to do great affairs in the jungle, but the falling of a nut turns their minds to laughter and all is forgotten. . . .

After Baloo, Bagheera, and Kaa (the snake) rescue Mowgli from the monkeys, the beaten and battered guardians chasten Mowgli after he mocks their injuries.

> BAGHEERA: His nose is sore on thy account. As are my ears and sides and paws, and Baloo's neck and shoulders . . . all this from your playing with the [monkey people].

MOWGLI: True, it is true. I am an evil man cub and my
stomach is sad in me.

But Baloo knows he must follow the law of the jungle. Mowgli must still be punished: "Sorrow never stays punishment." Bagheera proceeds to spank Mowgli with his paw.

Kipling's story cultivates a view of laws and civility that is sorely needed today. These examples are but the tip of the iceberg in the recurring moral simplification and dumbing down of great stories, which yield shallow, neutered moralism in our kids. In Collodi's and Kipling's stories, we see the important virtues of self-sacrifice, loving others, avoiding bad company, seeing through deception, the value of law, and the necessity of punishment as justice. Disney left us only with the desire to belong, and telling the truth. Morally simplistic stories fail to inspire virtuous kids. Standing athwart this shallow and hollow "morality," classical Christian schools restore the reading of original children's classics instead of modern interpretations or modern books. Truth, after all, is timeless.

Progressive schools lack a "bible," which cripples the training of affections in every subject, not just religious ones. In one classical Christian classroom where Jack London's *The Call of the Wild* was discussed with sixth graders, the different mode of teaching is instructive. The teacher wrote on the board, "It's idle to separate a fool from his folly." During the ensuing conversation, she guided students through a discussion on how to deal with the vice of foolishness. The passage dealt with two fools who rushed into a snowstorm. The teacher made a connection with Proverbs 27:22, where the fool and his folly cannot be separated. A fool does foolish things, so trying to persuade a fool to do something wise is futile. This kind of pursuit is impossible in public schools today.

THE THIRD BATTLEMENT: WONDER

*All mortals tend to turn into the thing
they are pretending to be.*

—C. S. Lewis

Those who enter a classical Christian classroom are frequently taken aback. They expect to see structure and order—which they do. But they also expect the children to be regimented and disinterested. When they see the opposite—when they see joy—they are surprised. Classical Christian schools believe something about children that the Progressives fundamentally reject—that every child is made in God's image for His purposes. This makes life and children wondrous.

James K. A. Smith observes, "Behind every constellation of educational practices is a set of assumptions about the nature of human persons—about the kinds of creatures we are. Thus a pedagogy that thinks about education as primarily a matter of disseminating information tends to assume that human beings are primarily 'thinking things' and cognitive machines. . . . In contrast, [teaching] that understands education as formation usually assumes that human beings are a different kind of animal."[28] Consider how in *Star Trek*, the ultralogical Spock always seems befuddled when a situation requires emotion to understand. He has to learn that life isn't just a set of textbook questions that a computer could answer just as well as a human. It has to be *ordered* emotion, but a totally dispassionate, logical approach to life leads to an anemic imagination. Emotion that is not bridled by transcendent virtue leads to aimless wonder. As we see Spock's character develop over the course of the franchise, his most defining virtue becomes loyal friendship—a virtue that resonates with a rightly ordered moral imagination.

I know this sounds foreign, but imagine that the point of school is to inspire wonder. Not aimless wonder, but the type that pushes children to engage their minds on matters much bigger and more important than jobs, or skills, or even themselves. Imagine students with a honed sense of reason and a capable way with words. Imagine faithful, hopeful, and loving students who serve their given purpose instead of their personal desire. Imagine students who value and seek lifelong friendships. These students would have a life-giving vision for learning and they would know the joy of wonder.

These promises are bold and require a form of education that breaks nearly every paradigm that, today, we assign to "school." When we hear "wonder," we're tempted to think of fantasy books or clever inventions. In truth, wonderment was the engine behind Western ingenuity, art, and culture, as well as the WCP (the Greeks wondered what it would take for people to self-govern). This kind of wonder is only fantastic in that God's world is full of fantastic discoveries. This kind of wonder is born of curiosity about how God built things. This kind of wonder is not an unbounded wonder, but a wonder conformed to the pursuit of an infinite God.

Great accomplishments begin with great vision. This is where true education begins. Subsistence cultures train children only in practical skills like fishing, or logging, or farming—hands-on, easy to see. The central feature of progressive education is the same—vocational training—although today this training is in fields like science, engineering, or business. In both cases, these skills are valuable for survival, but they limit the soul. Subsistence cultures rarely grow, improve, or change for the better (think back to the Afghanistan example). For education to be wonderful, it must be saturated in two things: First, children must have a framework that submits to God's standard of truth, goodness, and beauty—not a subjective view of things. Second, children need the tools for learning. Without them, learning is frustrating, boring, and deflating. English poet Dorothy Sayers called these the "Lost Tools of Learning." We'll come back to her description soon.

"CHILD-CENTERED" EDUCATION IS WONDER-*LESS*

The mainstream of early progressive education stifled wonder by focusing on the practical—training for jobs. Later, other progressive innovators built on that approach. They wanted to free the child to imagine in an unbounded, open field driven only by the child's curiosity. John Dewey and educational progressives like William Heard Kilpatrick believed we should make education "child centered." This means that education stops looking out toward the bigness of God's world. Now education comes from within each child. As you might imagine, both purpose and truth shrink.

A Christian worldview provides an essential structure for wonder. Wonder is like organizing a child's soccer game: without teams, coaches, rules, boundaries, and referees, the fun is pretty short-lived. But when you apply structure, the fun is just beginning. Classical Christian education cultivates wonder, but within the bounds of divine standards of Truth, Goodness, and Beauty.

Wonder is the pining that emerges in order to understand, and motivates the most earnest learning. It levitates life. As adults, wonder gives us a more accurate way of understanding how things fit together around us. When we encounter something, do we just accept it? Or do we wonder who did it? How did they do it? Why did they do it? What does it mean? And how does it fit in with the greater Truth system? These questions are not asked in a cynical or critical frame. When we go about life seeking to know answers like these, we create a tapestry of understanding that lasts throughout life.

MYTH OR MY STORY

"My story," as in a personal story, is a popular item with Millennials and younger generations. Myth is a different thing. Myth is the story that makes you, rather than the other way around. The progressive idea of story strips myth away. Myths require that we submit to something old or outside of us. Myths can help calibrate our culture to divine ideals.

These ancient foundations of myth are important if you want to catch the classical Christian vision of education. Two of the twentieth century's greatest storytellers were C. S. Lewis and J. R. R. Tolkien. Both men were keen students of ancient myth. Dorothy Sayers and G. K. Chesterton shared this appreciation of myth. Both were renowned authors of mystery novels. Nearly all nineteenth-century authors were saturated in myth. The classical idea of myth is powerful because it connects with the transcendent.

Every child's heart is tuned to pursue the ideal, and the infinite. "He has made everything beautiful in its time. Also He has put eternity in their hearts, except that no one can find out the work that God does from beginning to end" (Ecclesiastes 3:11). About a thousand years after Ecclesiastes was written, the Logos of Christ brought eternity into education. Almost two thousand years later, the Progressives took it back out. They brought us pragmatism (if it works, it's good) and progressivism (make your own way that works, don't pursue outdated ideals), as well as "child-centered" learning (unbounded wonder that leaves students hollow). It's no wonder children are languishing in our government schools. Children were made for the infinite and they are being treated like finite machines.

Perhaps the greatest historical example of myth appreciation is the famed Roman emperor Caesar Augustus. Augustus looked at his empire and was concerned that Roman culture seemed to be overshadowed by Greek culture, even though the Romans were the conquerors. He believed he knew why: the Greeks had more inspiring myths. Augustus commissioned Virgil, the greatest poet of his time, to write a myth that would provide Romans with the same wonder and imagined greatness as the *Iliad* and *Odyssey* had provided for the Greeks. It took Virgil the rest of his life to compose what has been called the greatest work of poetry in history: the *Aeneid*. The *Aeneid* helped secure Roman culture in history. If you doubt it, consider something as fundamental as the origin of the alphabetical characters used on this page—they are not Greek.

This third battlement, wonder, was an early casualty of the Progressives. It has been rubble on the ground for more than sixty years. This is why the concept of wonder in education is so foreign to us. But there is one battlement that fell even earlier. Its loss has done untold damage to our culture, and our flourishing.

THE FOURTH BATTLEMENT: BEAUTY

That all art must be moral is the rule until the 19th Century, when it cuts loose from moral significance, from regard for virtue in the maker's character, and from the expectations of the public.

—Jacques Barzun[29]

There's nothing like watching your football team's best wide receiver catch a pass just beyond the defensive safeties, with nothing but open field and a footrace to the end zone. Art is the "open field" left by our culture's vacuous sense of beauty, defined by paint swirls and boring functional architecture. If we can reacquaint the church with beauty, Christians can once again capture the imagination of the culture.

Postmodernism has little to offer in the way of beauty, so the field of art affords an opportunity for Christians to win the footrace just beyond the "safeties" who curate today's abstract art museums. In an effort to make art "avant-garde," our world has made art irrelevant to most people. Frankly, much of it has lost its beauty. Modern art now resides in museums and galleries before it's ever hung on someone's wall. Music, the performing arts, and movies are, perhaps, the exception. And the quality of these have suffered as film artists and musicians fail to develop good stories (the Fast & Furious series is on its eleventh film, after all). They have chased sensationalism as the shiny object of entertainment, not realizing that by doing so, they cultivate into the audience a craving for more of it. Taste for art in the medium has diminished.

If you take any part of this book on faith, this may have to be it: as twenty-first-century Americans, we have a more corrupt view of beauty than probably any generation in history. This is a bold statement, and it would take volumes to develop a convincing argument. The topic is simply too deep and too wide. Many books have been written on this, including Francis Schaeffer's *Trilogy*, Gene Edward Veith Jr.'s *State of the Arts*, Dorothy Sayers's *The Mind of the Maker*, Leland Ryken's *The Liberated Imagination*, Stratford Caldecott's *Beauty for Truth's Sake*, and Ned Bustard's *It Was Good: Making Art to the Glory of God*. The soul of classical education is in viewing human creativity as part of the divine image placed upon us. Classical schools emphasize training students to do art well.

BEAUTY IS *NOT* IN THE EYE OF THE BEHOLDER

On a crystal-clear day in Seattle, you can see something regal and surreal—Mount Rainier towering more than fourteen thousand feet above the city. If you live there, it's not something you pay attention to. But for visitors, it's spectacular. The catch? A crystal-clear day in Seattle is very rare. The same can be said of our final ascent to the furthest and perhaps most misunderstood mountain that feeds our Christian cultural river: aesthetics. We've seen that the ancient Greeks and early Christians weighed truth and goodness alongside a third measure—beauty. For them, beauty was integrated into their world. Today we struggle with this because we believe beauty is subject to our tastes. We cheapen it. So beauty becomes an early casualty of progressive culture.

"Beauty is in the eye of the beholder" is a popular saying. Would Christians say, "Truth is what you make it" or "Goodness depends on the person"? Christianity is so obviously incompatible with these statements about truth or goodness that the point has already been made. But if you say, "Beauty is in the eye of the beholder," most Christians will pause. Many will agree. Why? Because different people have different tastes? Many Christians have embraced the radical individualist view that aesthetics are relative. In truth, the beholder's eye can only recognize beauty rightly if it has been cultivated to do so. Our natural preferences may be flatly wrong when it comes to beauty, as with truth and goodness. While all humans tend to be naturally attracted to beauty, our sinful nature bends this attraction to ugliness. So, for Christians, beauty needs to transcend our personal preferences and yield to God's.

Are you still wrestling with this idea of absolute beauty? The question to ask: if God thinks something beautiful that I think is ugly, which one of us is right? Either God can have no opinion of beauty (a theological impossibility, since he created creatures who do) or God's opinion can be transcended by an individual person (also a theological impossibility). Beauty is in the eye of God. We can become great artists when we realize this, and pursue real divine beauty just as a philosopher pursues truth or a theologian pursues goodness.

Sadly, because the art world assaulted Christian ideas of transcendent beauty so long ago, and most Christians in the last century saw art as something neutral, Christians have forfeited a field that they once dominated. The result has been the near-total collapse of a Christian domain of art, and a bad reputation for contemporary Christian art and music in the creative marketplace.

Whether in music, sculpture, painting, theater, poetry, movies, literature, dance, architecture, or countless other art forms, we've reduced these today to personal preference. That, in turn, has reduced them to curiosities and monstrosities. Christians created Handel's *Messiah*, da Vinci's *Last Supper*, Michelangelo's Sistine Chapel, Rembrandt's *Storm on the Sea of Galilee*, Bach's "Toccata and Fugue in D Minor," and countless glorious cathedrals in cities like York, Paris, London, Cologne, Rome, and Istanbul. The list is nearly inexhaustible—the beauty unparalleled in all the world. So why do we see so much beauty, but question whether beauty exists outside of the individual's experience? Because we have had a paideia cultivated in us that's based in a lie.

Ancient Pythagoreans discovered the ionic scale (the notes that make up the white keys on a piano), in the fourth century St. Ambrose wrote early hymns, medieval monks invented notation to move music geographically, later monks discovered harmony, Bach perfected harmonies and timing and so much more, and the neoclassical composers advanced music to Handel's *Messiah*, Beethoven's *Ninth Symphony*, and Tchaikovsky's piano concertos. Yet students today rarely encounter this height of music. They wallow in lower forms in church, on Spotify, on YouTube, and in the vast expanse of the internet. Of course, low forms of music are enticing at times. But our kids need cultivation in the great, not just the popular.

At many classical schools, students from the fifth to eighth grades perform slightly abbreviated but otherwise authentic Shakespeare plays. Students draw and paint, paying close attention to line, color, value/light, form/shape, perspective/space. They also focus on reproducing Western masterpieces. In the classroom, this means students spend much more time on the standards of beauty than they do on self-expression or original works. We want them to appreciate masters. If you visit Hope Academy, a classical Christian school ministering to inner-city kids in Minneapolis, you'll see beauty. It resides in an old hospital building with plenty of concrete-block canvases—or walls. The students have reproduced masterworks on those walls. It is sheer beauty.

The methods and content of classical Christian education are clearly different from what you encounter at other conventional schools—Christian, private, or public. But the difference extends deeper. It extends to the model of teaching itself. To successfully cultivate a good, true, and beautiful imagination, we need to start by rejecting the progressive ideas. Progressives want to free the child to imagine. They believe that children's natural creativity is stifled by constraints—that children are naturally good. Classical Christian schools cultivate imaginations, but they do so, as with everything, by subjecting the child's imagination to God's absolute standards of Truth, Goodness, and Beauty. Sometimes we need the help of outsiders to see this.

The deepest and most remote gorge in North America is Hells Canyon, at the border of Idaho and Oregon. In it you can find the ruins of abandoned homesteads built more than one hundred years ago. The cabins and shacks are rotten and forgotten. But the orchards of fruit trees that were planted by early settlers are still bearing fruit. In fact, the fruit has often seeded other trees. Cultivation is powerful because it has staying power. This is why the Progressives still hold our culture in their educational grip. And this is why Christians need to be as committed to cultivation of the moral imagination as the Progressives were when they started their takeover.

With all four of these battlements—reason, virtue, wonder, and beauty—either crumbled to the ground or nearly so, our defense is lost. We cannot defend the fortress of Western civilization any longer. But we can rebuild it. When Nehemiah returned to rebuild the walls of Jerusalem after the Babylonian exile, he set some men to work with shovels, and he set others with swords to defend their work. Conservative politicians, courageous media members, faithful judges, and future election victories may buy us some time. They are the "swords." But they cannot rebuild the battlements of our city. And they are too few to defend it without the battlements. Parents and classical Christian educators must be about the work of rebuilding the battlements and adjoining walls. This will take a radical transformation of family, church, and school. What does a radical rethinking of school look like? We tackle that now.

10

HOW CLASSICAL CHRISTIAN EDUCATION WORKS

A classical education provides a model
for the way the mind works, as well as for
the way a student will think as an adult.

—David Hicks[30]

When the *Costa Concordia* capsized off the coast of Italy in 2012, something happened inside. The behemoth cruise ship with more than one thousand cabins listed 90 degrees and half-submerged. To those inside, the world changed. Walls became floors. Escaping passengers leapt chasms created by what once were hallways. Multifloor restaurants became swimming pools, with what had been a stage suspended overhead. The scene can hardly be envisioned or imagined. But if you had lived inside the bowels of this capsized ship for one hundred years, it would seem normal and the *upright* ship would be nearly impossible to imagine. American schools have been capsized for more than one hundred years. To imagine classical Christian education, we must first realize that everything about it will seem foreign. Yet as we slowly right the ship, things will, oddly, seem to make a lot more sense.

Parents who first visit a classical Christian school immediately notice a difference when they cross the threshold of the front door. The mannered students and ordered classrooms stand in stark contrast with the frenetic nature of many public schools. What parents may not realize is that the differences go much deeper. Here we'll explore some of those differences as we walk through a representative classical Christian school.

When you walk into a classical Christian school, you'll inevitably see uniforms, hear children greet you politely, and possibly see them stand when you enter the room. The rooms are orderly, and the décor reflects classical art with, invariably, a few columns somewhere. The décor is also more refined—appointed like a well-decorated living room rather than the brightly painted rooms with wall-to-wall posters typical of a conventional school. The children will be joyful and engaged, but with an uncommon sense of decorum. Beyond the superficial, if you spend more time you'll notice that Latin seems to be sprinkled throughout. From down the hallway, recitations in unison may be about anything, from Bible verses to great men of the Middle Ages. If you stop around second- or third-grade classrooms, students with singsong voices will be reciting jingles as they diagram sentences to gain a precise understanding of grammar.

At this point, you may think, *Okay, I get it. But this just sounds old-school, like something out of a period movie. Why is old necessarily better?* If you share that question, this chapter is for you.

A German exchange student once visited a classical Christian school for six months. When asked of his experience, he commented, "It was good. But everything was about religion. I know this is a Christian school, but why was God in every subject, too?" He experienced classical Christian education as it forms paideia—the truth about everything, underlying how you think about everything, so it influences everything. The deepest purpose of classical Christian education (CCE) is to cultivate Christian wisdom and virtue in students. For the past one hundred years, the West has oriented school around subjects that lead to vocation, and today indoctrination. To outsiders, like this exchange student, the classical method seems odd. For parents who do choose CCE, they go to great lengths not to return to the capsized ship. This often means they accept compromises in lifestyle or career just to be near a good classical Christian school.

HISTORY IS EVERYWHERE

As you walk into a CCE school, you will see history everywhere—on the walls, in the entryway, in the books, and in costumes at school events. Ancient, Greek, Roman, Egyptian, Byzantine, early Anglo-Saxon, medieval, French, German, Asian, and on it goes, right down to American history. And always alongside is biblical and church history. Classical Christian schools orient their years, months, and coursework around a historical context.

You've probably heard the axiom "He who fails to study history is bound to repeat it." This is really more of a progressive idea than a Christian one. History, in the progressive mind, is *merely* a dead artifact of backward times. It is like a road over which we've already traveled on a way to a more enlightened place, relevant only as something to avoid. This is why progressive schools teach so precious little history, and why what they do teach is laced with spin that creates heroes and villains according to a progressive reckoning. Classical Christian schools take a different view, all with the understanding that human nature—imprinted on our hearts by our Creator—does not change.

CCE studies the world as a single, connected system; a single story unfolding from beginning to end. Heroes and villains are both flawed and to be admired because all people are. In this environment, the timeline of history connects the parts of human knowledge into a wider system of knowledge that can be understood, as students, in an imperfect yet rewarding way, trace God's hand through time.

The empire of Persia, with its king Xerxes, who fought the famed three hundred Spartans at Thermopylae, is taught alongside the books of Esther (a servant of Xerxes), Daniel, Isaiah, Ezra, and Nehemiah, all of which intersect with Babylonian and Persian rulers of the time. Julius Caesar's assassination is avenged by his adopted son, Caesar Augustus, who appoints Herod the Great to build the second Hebrew temple, into which Jesus walked before the empire crucified him under the reign of Augustus's stepson, Tiberius, whose lineage would end in 68 AD with the suicide of the Christian persecutor Nero, followed by Vespasian, the emperor under whom Herod's great temple was destroyed, just as Jesus had prophesied about thirty-seven years earlier. An innocent Socrates is tried and executed in the Athenian courts by a jury of peers, from which the US jurisprudence system drew its inspiration, and some 450 years after Socrates' death, on the traditional location of the Athenian court, the apostle Paul would argue before the Socratic philosophers of Athens that Jesus Christ was raised from the dead.

No other faith can claim integration with recorded history like Christianity. No other form of education integrates everything so naturally—history, literature, language, philosophy, theology, science, art, mathematics, and music—into a single system of understanding. And from this integrated study, classical Christian students gain perspective and wisdom as they evaluate story after story through the lens of a Christian viewpoint—not as indoctrination, but rather as they investigate the historical narrative. Could it be that Progressive schools study so little history because they cannot avoid the historicity of Christianity?

In 390 AD, the Roman emperor Theodosius attacked a village called Salonica for rebelling against the local garrison. Historical facts like this seem to be of little consequence today. Why study them? Even if you learn the facts in grade school, you'll probably never use them, right? CCE's integration of every subject into a historical context provides a unique window into the consequences of ideas. When a student immerses himself in the mind and ideas of historical people, a sense of perspective emerges. Ambrose, Bishop of Milan, threatened Theodosius with excommunication for his role at Salonica, which reshaped the role that Christianity would play in government to the present day. What should the relationship between the state and church be? Rather than adhering to a trite phrase "separation of church and state," CCE students know the source, and why the idea of separation is not what it's presented to be by the Left. As a Christian, should you take a political position? Should you speak boldly about the course of our leaders, as Ambrose did? Rather than being told what to think, CCE students have the tools to think well.

This gift of historical perspective anchors students, especially in times such as these, to something deeper. Today, youth seem too often distressed and fearful, and often aimless. (No wonder "self-esteem" training is all the rage in our progressive schools.) Today's youth can be easily given to protest, but they can rarely articulate why they are protesting. They are well trained for jobs in many cases, but they are unable to make wise decisions on their own. Perhaps this is why an increasing number of colleges and businesses seek CCE graduates.

Wisdom is as important in business as it is in life. In 1939, C. S. Lewis said in "Learning in War-time" that "[a] man who has lived in many places is not likely to be deceived by the local errors of his native village: the scholar has lived in many times and is therefore in some degree immune from the great cataract of nonsense that pours from the press and microphone of his own age." In today's highly politicized universities, this problem is more pronounced than ever. Viewing our lives today as part of a longer narrative helps to make sense of it all, and make sense of everyday decisions.

FEWER SUBJECTS; INTEGRATED SUBJECTS

[Classical Christian education is] more like a web than a chest of drawers; there are no subjects that are unrelated to others . . . the boundaries [between subjects] are light and fluid and emphasize the inter-relationship of all knowledge.

—Dr. Christopher Perrin, Classical Academic Press

Classical Christian education treats subjects differently. In Chapter 5, we learned that the fathers of modern American "social sciences" hijacked education and redefined nearly every area of study, shattering education into dozens of specialties. Course names like "social studies," "sociology," "anthropology," "psychology," "geography," "political science," and even "economics" are all artifacts of the social science transformation. These reduce knowledge to information, learned for a test, compartmentalized, and easily forgotten. The narrow silos of knowledge are not interrelated, so they offer little wisdom. If you think about it, integration in a social science worldview based in atheistic materialism has no point. An integrated world makes no more sense to an atheist than a pile of random rocks at the bottom of a hillside— things just happen to be the way they are. There is no deeper or higher meaning to be discovered in anything. Any attempt to integrate, say, "psychology" with "political science" in order to trace common examples of God's hand across the disciplines is pointless if there is no master architect.

For example, our founding fathers integrated "politics" and "theology" when they realized that sinful nature (a Christian idea) leads to tyranny whenever power is concentrated (a political reality). As a result, we got divided powers in government, a republic not a democracy, and a Bill of Rights. Social sciences do not integrate, so they give democracy an open, unlimited pass. This leads to the pure foolishness of mob rule—something our classically educated founders understood, and warned against. But students educated only in social studies will not be wise enough to anticipate this reality. They, too, will be trained specialists who know little outside their focused discipline. Wisdom is hard to achieve when you have tunnel vision.

Sadly, even the vast majority of *conventional* Christian schools have latched on to subjects like "social studies." If these classes were "in name only," they might still escape the progressive zeitgeist in education. Unfortunately, the methods and content in these schools nearly always reflect progressive education. Their Christian teachers are trained in progressive colleges. Their accreditors, from Christian associations, are linked with progressive accreditors. The state standards to which these schools conform reflect the subjects required by progressive educators. These standards often drive textbook choices that are, of course, progressive. Classical Christian schools reject the social studies schema and the progressive educational institutions that govern education—public and private.

In secondary classrooms at CCE schools, teachers are widely read in the classics and great ideas. The economics of Adam Smith, Marx, or Keynes relate to the politics of Jefferson, Lenin, or Roosevelt. And these ideas descend from the ideas of Hesiod, Xenophon, and Aristotle, among others. Of course, Matthew 20, 2 Thessalonians 3, and Mark 10:23 shed the light of Truth on the economic discussion. The conversation in the classroom is about all of these people and ideas and scriptures at once, without false partitions. It's not about information. The real objective is to train minds to think through the ideas carefully.

This Socratic approach may appear inefficient. It takes hours of inquiry and discourse around a table to arrive at knowledge that would take only minutes to simply lecture at students, as they sit in rows of desks. So why do CCE schools do it this way? It exercises the mind. A liberated mind is one that can entertain thoughts without accepting them (real tolerance). This art is harder than you might imagine. The skill can only be built through practice.

Francis Schaeffer wrote, "Today we have a weakness in our education process in failing to understand the natural associations between the disciplines. We tend to study all our disciplines in unrelated parallel lines. This tends to be true in both Christian and secular education. This is one of the reasons why evangelical Christians have been taken by surprise at the tremendous shift that has come in our generation."

FEWER TEXTBOOKS, MORE GREAT BOOKS

History can be dangerous. In the hands of a skilled writer like Howard Zinn, our past can become a weapon to be used in the present to move students toward conventional dogma. George Orwell famously said, "He who controls the past controls the future. He who controls the present controls the past." This is a sobering thought, given the media and big-tech grip on our nation at present.

How does CCE address this? CCE lets the past tell its own story. We'll go back to the previously mentioned battle at Thermopylae. A standard college text on Western civilization describes it this way:

> A Greek force numbering close to nine thousand, under the leadership of the Spartan king Leonidas and his contingent of three hundred Spartans, holds off the Persian army at Thermopylae for two days. The Spartan troops were especially brave. When told that Persian arrows would darken the sky in battle, one Spartan warrior supposedly responded, "that is good news. We will fight in the shade!" Unfortunately for the Greeks, a traitor told the Persians of a mountain path they could use to outflank the Greek force. King Leonidas and the three hundred Spartans fought to the last man.[31]

This account from one of the best textbooks on the subject is accurate but it can be no substitute for an account closer to the time of the event: the ancient Greek historian Herodotus:

> By this time the spears of the greater number were all shivered, and with their swords they hewed down the ranks of the Persians; and here, as they strove, Leonidas fell fighting bravely, together with many other famous Spartans, whose names I have taken care to learn on account of their great worthiness, as indeed I have those of all the three hundred. . . . The Greeks four times drove back the enemy, and at last by their great bravery succeeded in bearing off the body [of Leonidas] . . . One man is said to have distinguished himself above all the rest, to wit, Dieneces the

Spartan. A speech which he made before the Greeks engaged the Medes, remains on record. One of the Trachinians told him, "Such was the number of the barbarians, that when they shot forth their arrows the sun would be darkened by their multitude." Dieneces, not at all frightened at these words, but making light of the Median numbers, answered, "Our Trachinian friend brings us excellent tidings. If the Medes darken the sun, we shall have our fight in the shade." . . . The slain were buried where they fell; and in their honour . . . an inscription was set up which said, "Here did four thousand men from Pelops' land Against three hundred myriads bravely stand."[32]

On the surface, these are similar tellings of the story. But, very subtly, Herodotus reveals something of his culture's paideia in this short example. This revelation is the best material for a Socratic discussion. Why would someone memorize the names of "worthy men"? What makes a man worthy? What makes men worthy to Herodotus? The fact that Herodotus reveres the valiant Dieneces reflects the Greek heroic ethic of his culture. What was this ethic? How did it motivate? What ethic do we revere in America today? We see that the Greeks thought any outsiders, even the sophisticated Persians, were "barbarians"— another reflection point on their culture. How should we see outsiders? Immigrants? The textbook extracted the facts. The source from which the facts are drawn—the writings of Herodotus—reveals much about the Greek paideia. From this, students learn to critique their own paideia. Across an expanse of reading, this regular engagement with historical cultures helps students gain wisdom in the nature of men. This type of wisdom is more important today than it ever has been.

There are other reasons to focus on original sources. The Latin term *ad fontes* (to the source of the spring) is used to describe the virtue of reading the original source or a close translation, rather than depending on a textbook. When interpreted by modern scholars, the story tends to change to fit the current narrative. Of course, Herodotus was not objective, either. But students can more easily spot the bias of ancient writers because they were born of a different age, as revealed in the questions above.

Today, scholarship has all but quit trying to be objective. Textbooks have descended into mere progressive propaganda. Original source material is often banned in an effort to cancel the culture of the West. The solution is to go back to the sources; they are much more interesting anyway.

Great books have another function: they cultivate virtue. You cannot teach virtue simply by telling students "this is good" or "this is evil." Of course, that's part of it. But CCE schools do not strive to train students to "know good from evil" (Genesis 3). Rather, they seek to develop a love of the good and a hatred of evil in students. John Milton said education should seek to "repair the ruins of our first parents." In other words, knowing what is good is insufficient. To repair the damage, we need to create an affection for goodness.

What is a "great book"? It is a book that has stood the test of time, usually by contributing an original idea to the conversation about Truth, Goodness, and Beauty that descends from at least three millennia of the Western Christian tradition. In general, these works have entered a "canon" by wide recognition. Unlike the Bible, with its sixty-six books confirmed by a formal church council in the fourth century, no council has formally designated the great books. Publications like Harvard Classics and the Loeb Classic Library are collections of great books as determined by a college or an individual scholar.

Something close to a council was formed by *Encyclopaedia Britannica* in the 1940s. It was led by Mortimer Adler, the editor of the encyclopedia and professor at the University of Chicago. Also involved was Robert Hutchins, who helped promote the great books. Adler assembled a group of thirty-five scholars who were paid to read and produce a list of great ideas on behalf of *Britannica*'s effort. The group established 500 ideas, which were eventually reduced to 102 "great ideas." From these ideas they gathered the books that most contributed to them. It took more than 400,000 man-hours to establish the fifty-four-volume set, *Great Books of the Western World*, published in 1952 and representing more than seventy-five authors, dating from ancient Greece to the present. The Bible was not included in Adler's set but was heavily referenced because Adler viewed it as superior to the great books, and it was widely influential across all areas of study. In the 1980s, Adler became a Christian. He released the second edition of *Great Books* in 1990, adding more religious thinkers like John Calvin, and more story-based content. To that end he added pieces from F. Scott Fitzgerald, Ernest Hemingway, George Orwell, T. S. Eliot, Samuel Beckett, and others. This sixty-volume set is widely viewed as a close-to-canon of the great books. It has a near-universal overlap with other lists, such as Harvard and Loeb. Classical Christian schools use this canon, or one like it, as the mainstay of their secondary curriculum.

CHILDREN LOVE A CHALLENGE

Have you ever watched children skip over stepping-stones or try to jump the cracks in the sidewalk? They love to see how far they can jump. Sometimes parents challenge them in this. Academics is the same way. Progressive educators want to place the stones a safe distance apart so no one skins a knee. Thus they use materials that are dumbed down so that students won't be discouraged. The result: students become bored.

Of course, to reach great works like Homer, Aeschylus, or Sophocles by middle school, K–6 students need to be primed. In the last chapter, we saw that cultivating a moral imagination, and a love of the good, requires good stories. In progressive schools today, rarely do children read "chapter books" before junior high or high school, if at all. Mostly they read "readers," or short booklets written specifically for the classroom by ensconced educators, not recognized authors. These readers offer hollowed-out stories of little artistic value. Recently, many of these stories have been saturated with LGBT and CRT influence. They simplify reading skills to offer a manicured experience that can best be described as tedious. It's no wonder so few children love to read in our age!

Most great books for children were written between 1800 and 1960. And, in those days, kids read books. Long books. So it makes sense that Robert Louis Stevenson, Hans Christian Andersen, Charles Dickens, Laura Ingalls Wilder, C. S. Lewis, J. R. R. Tolkien, and George MacDonald wrote longer works. They wrote in a more complicated form, with more nuanced and penetrating virtues.

At a classical Christian school in the second or third grade, students read books that were written by these great authors. It often stretches them, and this rigor concerns some parents. When young children are challenged to jump at an achievable but challenging pace, at first they say, "I can't!" But, with encouragement, they'll meet the challenge. If you expect more, children will achieve more.

MORE STORYBOOKS, FEWER FACT BOOKS

In Madeleine L'Engle's 1962 classic, *A Wrinkle in Time*, a dystopian society lives a gray existence attempting to create a perfect world with no poverty, no pain, and no sickness. But they, in fact, are miserable slaves. Charles Wallace, the youngest child of a visiting group of three sent to destroy the "darkness," is of particular brilliance. Charles does single combat with the "darkness" (IT). But IT has a defense. IT uses Wallace's love of encyclopedic knowledge to captivate and immobilize him. Facts about molecules. Facts about literature. Facts about everything. Charles Wallace becomes a slave to particulars. He is neutralized by information.

L'Engle was a professing Christian whose metaphor of American progressive education is thinly veiled. The book begins with a droning teacher who writes formulas on a chalkboard. As in her story, America's brightest, like Charles Wallace, are distracted by gifted-and-talented programs that feed them even more information.

C. S. Lewis warned us about this tendency to dehumanize education. Eustace Clarence Scrubb, the early antagonist in *The Voyage of the Dawn Treader*, is described as a boy who "liked books if they were books of information and had pictures of grain elevators or of fat foreign children doing exercises in model schools," but later says "you would have recognized it [a dragon] at once, but Eustace had read none of the right books." Our kids need to know what heroes are and how to become one. This is more important than knowing things that, in our age, we can look up with Google.

Dorothy Sayers describes the peril that we leave children in if we do not spend time teaching them to read well. "We let our young men and women go out unarmed in a day when armor was never so necessary. By teaching them to read, we have left them at the mercy of the printed word. By the invention of the film and the radio, we have made certain that no aversion to reading shall secure them from the incessant battery of words, words, words. They do not know what the words mean; they do not know how to ward them off or blunt their edge or fling them back; they are a prey to words in their emotions instead of being the masters of them in their intellects . . . young men and women are sent into the world to fight massed propaganda with a smattering of 'subjects.' We have lost the tools of learning. . . ." Sayers puts her finger on the importance of verbal reasoning. In doing so, she describes the classical Christian way of educating.

THE HEART OF CLASSICAL CHRISTIAN EDUCATION: THE TRIVIUM AND QUADRIVIUM

When visiting the youngest CCE classrooms, you will notice few differences between students there and at other schools; but the older they get, the more exceptionally mature they seem—especially compared to their progressive-school peers. In classical schools, the trivium— grammar, logic, and rhetoric, the first three of the seven liberal arts— changes *with* the child. And as it does so, it *changes the child*. It makes them active learners, thinkers, and articulate leaders. Think of the trivium as a skeletal frame for all learning—the bones of the "arms, spine, and legs" to which all other human studies attach.

Dorothy Sayers brought the seven liberal arts into focus with her 1948 essay, which in 1981 inspired the rebirth of classical Christian education. She prescribed a return to the trivium, which trains students in reasoning and persuasion, and the quadrivium, discussed shortly, which trains students in a philosophical form of science.

In the first art of the trivium—the grammar phase—students in grades K–6 hone their use of language and knowledge as a foundational skill, sharpened in preparation for the next art. While the grammar phase described by Sayers ends in about sixth grade, grammar continues to be emphasized through the study of classical languages in secondary school. Students in middle school advance their linguistic skills to the intersection of language and mathematics—the "logic" phase. The study of logic takes apart, analyzes, and applies the human capacity of reason so that students can recognize good arguments. Once this is well practiced, students move on to the final phase—rhetoric—to integrate these specialized logic skills with language. Often oversimplified as meaning public speaking, rhetoric is actually the fusion of grammar and logic into the art of persuasion. Rhetoric as a capstone completes the most basic art of discovering truth. These three arts—the trivium—are practiced throughout K–12 in classical Christian schools.

1st–6th Grade: The Grammar of Everything

Sayers calls this the poll-parrot stage because students are content to take in new information, memorize it, and recite it—either as song, poetry, or even as a simple recitation or chant. If you don't give them something to chant, they'll make up ditties on the playground to jump rope by. As adults, we may be put off by the thought of standing in a row and rattling from memory the states and their capitals, the periodic table of the elements, or the famous men of the Middle Ages. But at this age children do it with pride and a smile on their face.

In classical schools, students memorize great poetry, hymns, songs, the Bible, and other literary pieces to impress a stamp of beauty, timelessness, and culture on their soul. An older generation, educated in the 1930s and '40s, when they still practiced this type of memory work, seemed to always have a quip, or a turn of phrase, or a poem at the ready. They could always fling out "Brevity is the soul of wit" or "Neither a borrower nor a lender be." Sadly, sixty years from now, most grandparents with a 2000s-era education will tell their grandchildren all about renewable energy. By then the grandkids will look quizzically at the older generation and wonder, *What other kind is there?*

7th-9th Grade: Logic: Teach Them to Reason and Understand

Dorothy Sayers made the point that adolescents love to argue, so we should teach them to argue well. CCE calls this the logic or sometimes dialectic stage. During this phase, students are trained in formal and informal logic, which is normally taught from ancient sources. Works by Aristotle are employed as texts to train in the logic of causes, fallacies, and sound reasoning. Conversations between Socrates and those with whom he dialogues demonstrate in real-life situations how to reason well. Students practice logical exercises through events like *disputatio* (public discourse and debate) and a type of declamation where a two-sided, brain-teaser-like case is presented with an ethical catch-22 for the students to argue. "Logic," as a course, is just the tip of the iceberg. For classical schools, logic is not just a course, it is infused in the way all courses are taught in grades 7–9, and logic is expected to be mastered in grades ten and up.

With the advanced reading skills that students gained from earlier grades in a classical school, these students can comprehend the complex ideas present in ancient literature. They can read philosophers and playwrights like Euripides, Socrates, and Aristotle and understand their reasoning. Skeptical? Most people are. But when they see what average kids can do when they get an extraordinary education, they become believers. When students are stretched, they grow.

10th-12th Grade: Rhetoric

From the ninth to twelfth grades, students in classical schools engage big ideas. One parent of four classically educated students said it well: "The most important part of classical education is high school. The best part of what [CCE schools] do is in the School of Rhetoric." In this phase, students finish their core writing skills, particularly in English grammar and usage. They also begin to learn the fundamentals of rhetoric. A classical school's rhetoric program is built on an ancient training form called the Progymnasmata, which has fourteen exercises culminating in the defense of a thesis. This system was passed down to us from the ancient Romans, mainly sources like Cicero and Quintilian, and remains a mainstay in some college rhetoric programs and many law schools. These tools apply to all coursework in the CCE high school, not just rhetoric class.

If you wander into the school of rhetoric, things may seem even more alien. First, you'll notice students are engaged in discourse, discussion, and debate a significant portion of the day. This typically takes place around a large "Socratic" table. Rather than teachers asking all the questions, a teacher asks a big ethical question like "Should Charles Colson have taken the fall for Nixon?" The question in this example may follow a reading from Jefferson, Machiavelli, Aeschylus, or the book of Genesis or Daniel. Students then engage the question with each other, around a table. Students agree or disagree, support their arguments from the reading, and ask more penetrating questions until the table begins to find an answer. Often these questions begin with "should." The teacher engages with corrective questions to ensure that the answer is consistent with biblical wisdom. This process exercises students' powers of reason and develops an order to their loves, which forms "virtue," as we discussed in the last chapter. Rather than being told what right and wrong are, they come to understand how to reach right conclusions in countless real-world situations.

By the time students in CCE schools are seniors, they defend a thesis as a major part of their education. The thesis may be four or five pages in some schools, but it's often fifteen to twenty-five pages, depending on the curricular approach. Students use some data to support their thesis, but they also depend heavily on great texts they have read. During their six to seven years of great books study, students keep journals of quotes and thoughts from the many great books they read. These journals are called "commonplaces" and are indispensable in the thesis defense process. In fact, keeping a "commonplace" is one of the fourteen exercises of the Progymnasmata—and these journals were kept by many of our founding fathers and survive to this day!

In math, students blend their understanding of formal logic with its natural brother, mathematics. This helps them build a solid understanding of mathematical ideas, not just skill in processing math problems. Science becomes more inquiry based as students read the works that form the basis of all science, including Archimedes, Galileo, da Vinci, Newton, and even Darwin. Students become more capable of evaluating and understanding the limits and proper functions of science. These skills have proven to prepare students well for careers in science.

THE QUADRIVIUM

These last four liberal arts—the quadrivium—provide a domain of real-world study upon which the trivium can be applied. Today we might call this science, except that the quadrivium is pursued for a different purpose. Science seeks to understand nature so that it can control, manipulate, or utilize it. The quadrivium seeks to encounter God's wisdom by looking at nature, thereby drawing closer to Wisdom Himself. The four arts of the quadrivium are arithmetic (the study of numbers), geometry (the study of space), music (the study of ratios and proportions), and astronomy (the study of motion). Note that all of these four use mathematics and physics to understand the nature of things, which the Greeks believed were basic reflections of the transcendent Logos, or language of God.

The apostle Paul, writing to a Greek city, asks, "Has not God made foolish the wisdom of the world?" He hints at the intersection of Athens and Jerusalem: "For Jews demand signs and Greeks seek wisdom, but we preach Christ crucified, a stumbling block to Jews and folly to Gentiles . . . you are in Christ Jesus, who became to us wisdom from God, righteousness and sanctification and redemption, so that, as it is written, 'Let the one who boasts, boast in the Lord.'" The wisdom pursued for the WCP cannot be the domain of the seven liberal arts without Christian revelation. We're told in Proverbs 9, "The fear of God is the beginning of Wisdom." Many parents recognize that, unlike Christian schools that append a chapel or Bible class to a progressive course of study, every CCE classroom is saturated with Christian understanding.

DEAD LANGUAGES COME ALIVE

If you time your visit to a classical Christian school right, you will find several courses that are unique to CCE. Of course, there's Latin. Other schools teach Latin, but it's required at CCE schools, and taught at a younger age. You will likely find ancient Greek as well. Why study these ancient languages? The answer begins with an obvious question: Who do you want to communicate with? Do you believe that communicating with the staff at a restaurant on vacation is more important than communicating with some of the greatest minds in history? Progressives tell us that today, we are more enlightened than we were in the past, so why learn a dead language from the past?

Thus, in their view, Mandarin Chinese or Spanish is more relevant, or practical, than Latin.

CCE educators realize that our world extends not just east and west, but also backward in time. Cicero (the world's greatest orator), Julius Caesar (arguably the greatest military mind of all time), Marcus Aurelius (one of the greatest political leaders of all time), Virgil (called by many the greatest poet in history), Ovid (one of history's greatest storytellers), Augustine (the father of Christian doctrine), Jerome (the chief translator of scripture), and a host of historians, philosophers, and theologians all spoke and wrote in Latin. Isaac Newton wrote his postulates in Latin, as did nearly all scientists of his time. Embedded in these languages are the cultures of Greece and Rome. Because translations are susceptible to idea-bias from our time, it's more important than ever for us to preserve our culture by preserving its languages.

Latin has also proven to be a key ingredient to academic success. Today, even a few public schools have reinstated their long-abandoned Latin programs. Students who take Latin score an average of 150 points higher on the SAT. An estimated 65+ percent of English words are Latin in origin. Science, law, medicine, and many other academic disciplines depend heavily on Latin. Dorothy Sayers explains that "[a] rudimentary knowledge of Latin cuts down the labor and pains of learning almost any other subject by at least fifty percent. It is the key to the vocabulary and structure of all the Teutonic languages, as well as to the technical vocabulary of all the sciences. . . ." The precision of a child's words—how they say them, write them, and read them—is affected by Latin because it is an inflected language. Why study Latin? Douglas Wilson states it well: "Their Latin might revert to zero, but their English will never be the same."

CHRISTIANITY IS ESSENTIAL TO THIS CLASSICAL MODEL

[I do not] seek to understand that I may believe, but I
believe that I may understand. For this too I believe,
that unless I first believe, I shall not understand.

—St. Anselm, Archbishop of Canterbury, twelfth century.

Some see the term *classical Christian education* and assume it is classical education with Christianity added in. This mistake leads some to attempt classical education in a secular or public charter school without the Christianity—as though Christianity can be extracted and taught at home or after school. In fact, CCE is a single, unified form of education that anchors itself in Christianity. Charter schools cannot truly do classical education because they can teach nothing of transcendent truth, biblical revelation, or God, not to mention the truth system of Christianity. These types of schools often suspend classical education in midair, engaging Latin, the great books, and the trivium but without any more understanding of God than the Greeks had.

St. Anselm's ancient prayer can seem puzzling. While the wisdom of our age tells us that we must use reason to understand things like Christianity, the truth is that our reason, without the revelation of the scriptures and our belief in Christ, leads to unending despair. It cannot bring us understanding. It must first be anchored to the historic faith of our fathers.

The age-old saying "Theology is the Queen of the Sciences," reveals a deep truth about education. *Belief in God's revelation must precede truly knowing anything.* Otherwise, we can only peek through a pinhole in the door at the creation around us. Without someone on the other side of that door filling in the big picture, we cannot truly understand anything.

THE "AROMA" OF A CCE SCHOOL

What if education wasn't first and foremost about what we know, but about what we love?

—James K. A. Smith, *Desiring the Kingdom*

Education is teaching our children to desire the right things.

—Plato

We may not realize that our house has an aroma until we walk into another person's house and immediately notice theirs. Occasionally we walk into a house and smell fresh-baked bread. Classical Christian schools hope to foster an aroma like fresh-baked bread through the culture of students, and the families that are part of the school community. To achieve this, uncommon wisdom is required.

Uniforms, hairstyle, makeup, and even manners in CCE schools combat the "look at me" mentality that nearly always defines other school environments. This is a beginning, but the culture goes deeper. It depends on some things you might not expect. For example, classical Christian schools intentionally reject lowly and lazy habits, and instead try to build higher habits in children.

Daily class routines that include great art, great music, excellent poetry, and other beautiful elements help develop students' habits, and thus their love of higher and greater things. While words cannot describe this aspect of the aroma, beauty is another centerpiece in CCE schools. Manners, intentional liturgies, and pathways of thinking have fallen out of favor because we live in an individualistic culture. Deep down, we believe each of us is "the captain of our soul," important in his own right, ruggedly independent, and a "firework." Conforming to a corporate habit stifles us. But if we believe that habits can elevate us because they train us to love higher and better things, we can attain what no individual can.

Many CCE schools use "house programs" or other student leadership groupings to elevate wisdom within the school. These "houses" typically include students from seventh to twelfth grades, so that the school is more like a family, with students of different ages sharing life together. The houses are led by the upper-class students, typically not elected by the student body but rather appointed by faculty. This helps to ensure that wisdom prevails within the student community. Between houses, habits, an emphasis on beauty, and the academic programs at CCE schools, the whole "house" enjoys the aroma of fresh-baked bread.

G. K. Chesterton said, "Education is not a subject and does not deal in subjects. It is instead a transfer of a way of life."

We should take notice. Especially if our kids just rode off in a yellow bus to get their "way of life" from the wrong people, telling the wrong story.

Paideia establishes culture, or enculturation. The trivium adapts the method to the age and results in the powerful life tools of persuasion and clear thinking. Great art, music, and literature develop a more refined taste in students for deeper, more beautiful things. Scripture's lens takes all of this captive to the mind of Christ, and calls students to align their world to their Christianity, forming a strong Christian worldview. Through close teacher relationships and Socratic discussions, students become like their teachers, growing in maturity and goodness—and they learn to think well. Very well. Stories and true literacy bring students to a love and affection for God's standard. Writing, vocabulary, reasoning, and being well-read are by-products of it all. The paideia of Christ is cultivated in the next generation.

The descriptions in this chapter only scratch the surface of classical Christian education and its potential to reverse the Cultural Marxist Paideia. Most classical Christian schools are still learning how to recover this lost tool of education.

Some might think it's mad. School is going to fix all of this? But, if you're a student of history, you know it's happened before—repeatedly. How did Rome convert to Christianity? Largely through the leadership of classically educated Christians. When eighth-century England was in crisis, what did Alfred the Great do to unite the island under Christianity and repel the Vikings? He mandated Latin, translated Aristotle, and created classical schools for Christians. At about the same time, Charlemagne could not civilize the northern Saxons on the continent through war, so he called in Alcuin, a monk who started not military outposts or forts, but classical Christian schools in monasteries in the Saxon lands. They were Christianized and the Holy Roman Empire enveloped them. This led to the scholastic movement of the 1200s, leading to the Renaissance and ultimately to the Reformation. If we have the patience and the resolve, classical Christian education can again establish a paideia that will turn the tide in America.

When David Goodwin first uncovered the following quote from Lawrence Cremin, I had to read it a couple of times to realize the importance of what this Columbia professor was saying:

"If education was to be the principal engine of an intentionally progressive society, then the politics of education would have significance far beyond the control of schools. Or child saving institutions. Or communication organizations; in the end, it would hold the key to the achievement of the most fundamental political aspirations—in effect, the key to the American Paideia."

Cremin won a Pulitzer Prize for this thesis in the early 1980s. He did not live to see the radical "political aspirations" that would surge onto the scene in 2020, nor did he predict the complete takeover of the Cultural Marxist Paideia. Cremin's American paideia—what we have called the American Progressive Paideia—has been transformed slowly over the latter half of the twentieth century and the early twenty-first. Since 2005 we have seen the rise of the Cultural Marxist Paideia, signaled by the advent of the Common Core, the restructuring of the SAT, and the rejection of reason, virtue, wonder, and beauty. As Cremin predicted, the politics of education has had great significance beyond the schools. It holds the key to nearly every political change we've seen in the past sixty years—and we've seen many.

As America changed, conservatives and Christian Americans were subject to the whims and the winds of the "cult of culture." In most cases, we lightly resisted—insisting everything would eventually be okay—and instead allowed the progressive winds to sweep us, and what we believe, away. As often happens, we have been trapped without our knowledge, in two senses of the term. Now we're at a crossroad. Critical race theory and LGBT+ indoctrination in schools is just the beginning. If we continue to allow our children to be educated in schools that cultivate the Cultural Marxist Paideia—as we are right now—the situation will become much worse. We will lose our country, and our freedoms.

To turn the fate of this present culture, we need a battle plan. And we have one.

11

A BATTLEFIELD ASSESSMENT FOR RETAKING THE AMERICAN MIND

*Where do correct ideas come from? Do they drop
from the skies? No. Are they innate in the mind?
No. They come from social practice, and from it
alone.... Once the correct ideas characteristic of
the advanced class are grasped by the masses,
these ideas turn into a material force which
changes society and changes the world.*

—Mao Zedong, 1963

*We cannot understand the West apart from
the Christian faith, and we cannot understand
the Christian faith as we live it today without
understanding the history and culture of the
West. If future generations fail to learn to love our
Western culture heritage, we will lose it.*

—Rod Dreher, *The Benedict Option*

The title of this book—*Battle for the American Mind*—was chosen with a great deal of intentionality. The mission to liberate the minds of America's future citizens is not a debate, an academic argument, or even a clash of worldviews. It is a battle. A war—a war over correct ideas. And our goal is to win back every single hour of the 16,000 hours in which our kids are educated, from kindergarten to high school graduation. The classroom is our battlefield, the hearts and minds of our kids the prize. The very survival of the American Republic, and the greatness of Western civilization, are at stake. And, right now, we are losing. The Cultural Marxist Paideia has seized the commanding heights.

But, as the previous chapter laid out, we have rediscovered our most powerful cultural weapon: classical Christian education to re-vitalize the Western Christian Paideia. It had been lost for decades, swallowed up by a progressive educational takeover that controls every single aspect of the current educational pipeline. But the light of WCP is not extinguished, at least not yet. In fact, today it is actually growing (more on this very soon). While the culture around us rots—and it feels like the Left's educational Death Star is stronger than ever—there is a resistance gathering.

We are outnumbered, and outgunned, but we are not yet de-feated. To continue the Death Star analogy, I'm reminded that while the Death Star represented the height of the Empire's power in the fictional Star Wars series, there were dedicated Jedi rebels regrouping on a hidden military base on the fourth moon of Yavin. The Rebel Alliance was down, but not out. There was no way Luke Skywalker and his fellow Rebels could fight the Empire head-on; that was a death sentence. They had to find another way, by identifying a full picture of the threat they faced and finding secret vulnerabilities that could be exploited. They had to *survive* the Empire, *regroup* their rebellion, and *reconstruct* a lasting alternative. In the movie they did . . . and *won*.

We are in the same place. Down, but not out. We have laid out the overwhelming advantage now possessed by cultural Marxists—now it is time to plot our counterattack. But we cannot afford to be hasty or pursue half measures. Charging the "commanding heights"—the leftists' educational Death Star—with Nerf guns will not suffice. We don't want martyrs, we want victors. Armed with a solution as big as the problem—classical Christian education—now we need to build a plan capable of delivering that solution.

RECAP: THE SITUATION

In the US Army, the primary mission-planning format is an operations order (OPORD). Commanders issue OPORDs so all the units in any particular mission are on the same page. The first paragraph of every OPORD is called the "situation." Of particular importance in that section is the "enemy situation" paragraph—which outlines the capabilities of the enemy. Specifically, Army planners are trained to war-game both the enemy's "Most Likely Course of Action" and "Most Dangerous Course of Action." It's a useful exercise because it forces you to both understand the capabilities of your enemy as well as challenge your assumptions about their next moves. Do they think they are winning or losing? Are they planning something larger, or licking their wounds? How much do they know about your capabilities, and how might they change their approach to neutralize your strengths? Or exploit your weaknesses?

The planning process forces you to be ruthlessly self-aware, and as situationally aware about the enemy as possible. If this book has done anything so far, it has increased your situational awareness about the nature, depth, and strategy of our enemy. We know that, over one hundred years—and today pressing their advantage with 16,000 hours of indoctrination—the Left has a stranglehold over American education. The government has a monopoly on the minds of our kids, with the vast majority of American classrooms progressive, and growing more so by the year. We know that.

But, as we look to the future of the progressive agenda, how ruthlessly self-aware are we about our side of the equation? How is our morale? What are our capabilities? How many troops do we have? And what, if any, is our strategy? Almost everything we have done over the past hundred years has failed to blunt the Marxist advance, so what are we going to do differently today? We need a solution—a strategy—big enough to overcome not just the Left's "Most Likely Course of Action," but also their "Most Dangerous." I believe—in this case—they are one and the same. The Left's most dangerous course of action is also their most likely.

That course of action is as follows: They keep doing what they are doing. Maintain control of all the institutions they control, and wait for the ultra-woke students of today to become the teachers, administrators, and politicians of tomorrow. Think government schools are bad now? Wait until the current anti-America, anti-faith generation gets an opportunity to press their advantage. Their Achilles heel, however, is their belief that their power is inevitable. They are wedded to a bureaucratic and bloated system, a system that benefits their grip on power but also prevents them from making necessary changes should they find themselves under threat from an alternative educational system. If we, patriots and Christians, do not mount an effective counter-campaign, they will be deadly. If we do, they will be dangerous—but hamstrung by the weight of their complacency. We must know ourselves, and them, in order to build that alternative.

So, *what do they think of themselves?* They know their schools don't deliver excellence, but they also know they have full control. Ultimately student outcomes are secondary to job security, political power, and more funding. Their funding streams are vulnerable, as is their union membership—should "right to work" ever become widespread. They also know that many parents, given a cost-effective alternative and the freedom to choose, would likely choose something else. Therefore, their most important goal is to prevent educational competition by denying parents the freedom to choose other alternatives. They are aware that many of the things they are teaching are unpopular, hence they use creative names and limit public oversight. They assume the "public school thing" is inevitable, and "traditional values" (especially God) will never be allowed back in.

What do they think of us? We are a nuisance, but not a threat. We are also outdated and constitutionally ("wall of separation") incapable of changing the trajectory of curriculum or school culture. As long as parents are not allowed to use public money (taxpayer dollars!) to choose faith-based schools, our outside schooling system will be marginalized—especially since most private schools are largely progressive and nominally Christian. Our inability to abolish the Department of Education when it was first created shows what little ability we have to politically defeat their federal educational initiatives. Of course, they also believe we are racist and sexist for advancing anything other than their left-wing orthodoxy. To our advantage, they have little consideration for classical Christian schools.

What do we think about them? They are arrogant and complacent, but remain effective. They are ruthlessly focused on control of the classroom and press their advantage at every turn (COVID-19 mandates are a recent example). Any minor victories by us—say, parents exposing CRT at school board meetings—have very little impact on their overall trajectory. In most cases, it solidifies their perception as untouchable. As such, they believe they are invincible and inevitable—which has caused, and will continue to cause, them to overreach. Their progressive plans and theories go well beyond common sense and basic decency, inducing useful backlash from parents and politicians. Their ultimate goal is to ensure that the government, not families or faith, molds the values of the next generation. Maintaining the government school monopoly is their obsession. They believe they are better, smarter, and more "virtuous" than us—based on their social justice view of the world.

What do we think of us? While the "COVID-(16)19 effect" has awakened many American parents—including apolitical parents—to the takeover of our schools, most parents are still largely resigned to our current reality. Our response is still limited to school board meetings, calls for school choice, and watchdogging our kids' curriculum. Most parents still feel resigned to fighting the system from within, even if our efforts feel futile. Worse, many well-intentioned parents have bought into the vocational construct of education—*school is to get a job, that's it. STEM is the future, get with it!* This unfulfilling and ineffective cycle continues to keep us demoralized—so we focus more on our families, our churches, and our kids' activities. And while these are worthy efforts, they are not enough. Moreover, with hot-button policy issues like socialist spending, open borders, rising inflation, defunding the police, and more—education remains a secondary political issue for most conservatives.

In short, we are not yet up to the task. But that is because we mostly feel alone. Our morale is low and getting lower. And so we look for a way out. Private schools are an option, but they are often too expensive and just as "woke" as public counterparts. Homeschooling is an important option, but very time intensive and not everyone is cut out for it. Many people have public charter school options, which, while better than core public schools, are still completely devoid of the WCP and God is certainly not allowed. Some people have heard about "classical Christian" schools, but most have the wrong impression—an impression we aim to change with this book.

The nonclassical Christian "other-than-public school" options are limited, and often feel barely better than the local public schools that, after all, we pay property taxes to support. So, even though most Christian and patriotic parents know the schools are infected with left-ism, many charge ahead within the status quo, holding their noses and saying their prayers. It is personal survival, not a winning strategy. And it is certainly not sustainable, merely passing the same losing hand to the next generation. With this approach, we lose. We lose America— and Western civilization.

INSURGENCY

So, what do we do? A conventional military commander might look at this "situation" paragraph and yell: *Retreat!* I actually agree, in part. We need to retreat from government schools—and other "woke" private options—completely. We need to leave them, as soon as is feasible. There is nothing there for Christians and patriots. We are not winning there and have no prospects to win there for multiple generations. We have to admit a hard truth to ourselves: we are not special. No matter how much you may try, it is nearly impossible to counteract the leftist social justice agenda of public schools, especially with the cultural rot that surrounds school. A few hours a week in church—Sunday school and Wednesday nights—don't stand a chance against more than forty hours a week in progressive schools. I am a living example of this . . . and that was thirty years ago. While my veneer as a youth was Christian, my public schooling core was purely secular. And many of the choices I made later in life reflect this bifurcation during the formation of my character. My paideia was *progressive*. I never had a chance, and I want a better foundation for my kids.

But retreat, alone, is not the answer. Retreats are useful as a means to not be completely defeated. We retreat only to survive the current moment. General George Washington executed multiple daring retreats in the service of winning the Revolutionary War. But retreats are only useful if they are followed up with a plan to regroup. So, what is the most effective military tactic that can be employed when you are outnumbered, outgunned, and have been defeated on the conventional battlefield?

Insurgency.

Our only option is insurgency. Our only chance is to become educational insurgents in our own country. Throughout history, insurgency has been the preferred tool of the "weak against the strong," the "have-nots against the haves." Insurgents don't play by the old rules, because the old rules are used to protect the status quo—in our case, the Marxists who have taken full control of America's education system. We are the new radicals, the new revolutionaries. We must choose insurgency, since all other options are a path to certain defeat.

I know a great deal about insurgency strategy as a former senior *counter*insurgency instructor in Afghanistan. My job was to study our enemy—the insurgency that was the Taliban. That was in 2010. The Taliban controls Afghanistan today, and America is gone from that battlefield. Insurgencies can work, if they are executed properly. The Taliban insurgency, while long in battlefield terms, was brief compared to what we face on the American cultural front. It took progressives a hundred years to consolidate their grip on the American mind—our insurgency may take just as long.

The best definition of insurgency I encountered during my study of the subject was by David Kilcullen, in his book *Counterinsurgency*. He defines insurgency as "an organized, protracted politico-military struggle designed to weaken the control and legitimacy of an established government, occupying power, or other political authority *while increasing insurgent control*" (emphasis mine). The definition need only be modified slightly to fit our use. Obviously our struggle is not military, but instead politico-cultural. We are not looking to topple our government, but instead to defeat the monopoly of government-run schools—and the leftist unions who are their occupying power. In the meantime, we increase our control by building an alternative educational model. First we survive, then we regroup and reorganize while weakening the control and legitimacy of our foe, and finally we replace their power structure with reconstructed schools based on freedom and faith.

I know, it sounds daunting. Easy to study or write about; much more difficult to do. Thankfully, and this is a word of great encouragement, the insurgency has already begun—and you didn't even know it. Neither did I, until I met David Goodwin. I'm not talking about parents at school board meetings or (important) books that warn us of American Marxism. I'm talking about the foundation of an alternative education system that is growing in strength every year because it is grounded in the Western Christian Paideia.

THE INSURGENCY HAS ALREADY BEGUN

After years of educational warnings by great thinkers like C. S. Lewis (*The Abolition of Man*) and Dorothy Sayers ("The Lost Tools of Learning"), among others, in 1981 a Christian academic, David Hicks, first published *Norms and Nobility: A Treatise on Education*, calling for the restoration of classical Christian education. Hicks used the book to dismiss the notion that classical education is elitist and irrelevant, arguing instead that it serves as a feasible model for mass education of liberated people. The book reclaimed the idea of a "Christian paideia" and proposed a curriculum to revive classical Christian education.

At about this same time, an ecumenical group in Indiana founded a classical Christian school, the Trinity School at Greenlawn. Another classical Christian school, Cair Paravel Latin School, sprang up in Topeka, Kansas. Logos School in Moscow, Idaho, rose in prominence and helped launch the Association of Classical Christian Schools (ACCS) in 1994. The classical Christian movement seemed to emerge across the country simultaneously in small, start-up schools apparently unaware of each other.

In 1999, Susan Wise Bauer published *The Well-Trained Mind*, which encouraged classical Christian homeschooling. Also in 1999, *The Devil Knows Latin: Why America Needs the Classical Tradition* was published by the University of Colorado scholar E. Christian Kopff. The year 2001 saw the publication of *Classical Education* by Gene Edward Veith Jr., an academic and leader in the Christian worldview movement, and Andrew Kern, president of the Circe Institute. In 2009, Stratford Caldecott penned *Beauty for Truth's Sake: On the Re-enchantment of Education*.

Publications continued, and more schools were started. The annual ACCS conference grew, both in numbers and in advocates. Christian leaders like R. C. Sproul, Chuck Colson, Os Guinness, Nancy Pearcey, Albert Mohler, John MacArthur, Alistair Begg, Eric Metaxas, and Rod Dreher saw and supported the transformational potential of classical Christian education. The early insurgents were gathering, far from the public eye.

In 2002, a modest 17,420 students were enrolled in roughly 125 classical Christian schools across America. A decade later, in 2012, that number had doubled. In 2020, there were 50,000 students in classical Christian schools. In the 2021–22 school year—the year this book was written—that number jumped to over 60,000 students, filling more than 300 schools across America, including schools in 44 of the 50 states. The school that three of my kids currently attend—Liberty Classical Academy in White Bear Lake, Minnesota—was founded in 2003 by parents seeking an alternative. It has grown ever since, through sheer determination and faith in Christ. Chances are, there is a school near you—and you don't even know it.

In the 1970s, there were zero classical Christian schools in America. That was, simply put, the real rock bottom for American education. The Western Christian Paideia was gone and buried. But as the Progressives pushed their advantage, Christians forged an alternative. Little did they know, they were the original insurgents—they had no money, no support, and no network. We stand on their shoulders today. Our battle plan today only stands a chance because of the foundation they built. We are further along than you thought—but also further behind. While there might be 60,000 American kids in classical Christian schools today, that number is dwarfed by the 48,100,000 American kids currently enrolled—trapped—in government schools.

The Death Star lives . . . but the rebels have gathered.

THE PHASES OF INSURGENCY

The study of insurgencies often starts with the writings of Mao Zedong, the famous Chinese communist revolutionary. Chairman Mao—an avowed Marxist—was the founding father of the Chinese Communist Party, waging an insurgency to seize control of China. He was ruthlessly effective, and his writings on guerrilla warfare, or insurgency, are still studied today. To simplify, Mao believed insurgencies were waged in three phases. Phase 1 is the organization and preparation phase, which includes building cells, recruiting new members, and establishing an underground network. Phase 2 is the guerrilla warfare phase, which includes targeted sabotage, delegitimizing attacks, and establishing a parallel structure. Phase 3 is conventional warfare and includes taking control, achieving political objectives, and defeating the enemy.

My experience in Afghanistan is once again instructive here. After the fall of the Taliban in 2002, their remnants scattered into the countryside and into Pakistan. They were militarily defeated but were determined to survive and reorganize. The United States worked to create a new government and new military, focused on capabilities and legitimacy. At first the Taliban held back. Soon after, they conducted sporadic attacks and, due to the corruption of Afghan authorities, started reestablishing "shadow governments" in the countryside. They didn't need to run the official government; they instead had to delegitimize the Afghan government while increasing their psychological grip— their connection—to the population. Over time, they took over small villages and fought the Afghan military when it served to bolster their narrative.

It was not until America's exit was imminent that the Taliban started waging all-out conventional warfare against the Afghan government and security forces. From the beginning, the Taliban followed their old adage, "The Americans have the watches [meaning technology], but we have the time." They waited us out, built their own "shadow government," and allowed the foreign-backed Afghan government, which did not reflect the Afghan paideia, to delegitimize itself. It took the better part of a decade for the Taliban to go from Phase 1 to Phase 2, but their transition to Phase 3 was swift. The Taliban knew the population, because they understood the Afghan paideia. Eventually the population was coerced into supporting the strongest, and most legitimate, tribe.

The most dangerous moment for any insurgency is when it attempts to move from one phase to another. Move too soon—without population support or robust networks—and you are vulnerable to being crushed by the group in power. Wait too long and you allow the existing power structure to gain even more power and legitimacy. Also, sometimes an effort that is viewed as a battlefield loss is actually a strategic victory. The North Vietnamese Tet Offensive in 1968 is a textbook example of this. Even though the American military was able to decisively defeat the Viet Cong on the battlefield, the perception in the American media was devastating. North Vietnamese insurgents knew that political will was critical for American success, and the sheer size and scope of their offensive rocked the American psyche. America won in military terms, but lost strategically. The Tet Offensive led to the release of the Pentagon Papers . . . and the rest is history.

In addition to understanding phases and timing, according to official US Army doctrine, insurgencies share several common dynamics—leadership, objectives, ideology, geography, and external support. Without any of these, the effort is likely to fail. Successful insurgent leaders know how to make their case to the people and gain popular support—while breaking the ties to the existing power structure (public education). Objectives need to be clear—in the short term (building awareness), medium term (building capacity), and the long term (universal educational tax credits). Ideology is our strength, with CCE building on the two-thousand-year heritage of the WCP (with constant appeals to Heaven). Geography means taking, and holding, key terrain—that means building new schools. Finally, external support. This is a huge one. Without serious outside financial support, such as millionaires and billionaires pulling their money from the Ivy League and pouring it into classical Christian education, our insurgency will eventually fail.

Below is an outline of what our educational insurgency could look like. It is intentionally focused only on the realm of education, but does not dismiss the substantial changes that will need to be made across our culture—from social media to Hollywood to churches to our families. The battle for America outside of the classroom is urgent and critical, but this plan is designed to reorient future American citizens toward the WCP, which made America great from the start.

Phase One: As mentioned above, we are not starting from scratch. Forty years ago, when the classical Christian movement started, we were in early Phase One. Today we are in the middle to late stages of Phase One. Schools have been planted, and a network established. Now they need to grow, and our largest impediments to growth today are *awareness* and *misconception*. Most parents are simply not aware that classical Christian education exists or they falsely believe that traditional Christian and Catholic schools are sufficient to blunt the progressive advance. Moreover, the misconception that *classical* means outdated or elitist must be dispelled. CCE is for all walks of life—think wise welders, not "woke" welders. A great piece of ammunition here is the fact that, across the board, students educated in CCE—regardless of race or class—far surpass their counterparts in SAT scores. The numbers don't lie.

As the CCE movement grows, it will be attacked and mischaracterized. Parents, politicians, and influencers need to be armed with the knowledge and background to advocate for the CCE alternative. *Hence, the reason for this book. We hope you share it!* Individual schools, the Association of Classical Christian Schools, thought leaders, pastors, and media personalities need to spread the word—not just about the problems, but about the solution staring us in the face.

Simultaneously, the campaign to discredit the public school system, and the union infrastructure that controls it, must continue on a slow burn. Parents agitating at school boards is a good start, as is widespread exposure of critical race theory in the schools. Outside groups need to sue to get access to curriculum, parents need to record conversations with teachers, and older students need to keep pulling out their phones to record radical teachers. Concerned parents need to run for the local school board, not because they think they can change it—but to conduct reconnaissance and expose it. Think Project Veritas for public schools.

Parents, over time, need to develop an "ick factor" when it comes to their view of public schools—which we need to rebrand, lock, stock, and barrel, as "government schools." If apolitical parents feel like "school" is being unfairly maligned, it may backfire. But when, over time, parental frustration grows regarding what, and how, their kids are being taught—they will start looking for alternatives. Parents need to come to the conclusion: Why don't I have the *choice* to use my tax dollars to send my kids to any school? Not just the local public school. Many already are. A June 2022 national poll by the Trafalgar Group asked, "How should parents who oppose Critical Race Theory in public schools respond if it becomes part of their children's curriculum?" Twenty-nine percent of parents responded they would teach their kids at home, without interfering at school, and 28 percent said they would remove their children from public schools in favor of private, religious, or home schooling. Millions of parents, ripe for a change. Our movement can draft off of this dissatisfaction, but we need the capacity.

The key here is to be tactically patient. Just as the Frankfurt School did when it first arrived on our shores, we need to use our freedom while we still can. In order to move to Phase Two of our insurgency, we need to have the capacity to absorb tens of thousands, and then hundreds of thousands, of new students. New schools need to be built—in your community and mine. Existing schools need to expand. Online CCE options—of which there are many—need to grow. All of this requires fund-raising . . . with an eye toward Phase Two, when a full-on push for private school tax credits is advanced. That is how, in Phases Two and Three, the CCE movement can reach full potential.

Finally, churches need to get involved. Pastors need to preach paideia—the importance of education—from the pulpit. Too many churches, including most I've attended, leave the application of education up to "other people." We have forgotten that for two thousand years the Western Christian Paideia was chiefly fostered by the church. At the end of the day, Christianity will survive without America, but America cannot survive without Christianity. With Progressives dominating the commanding heights of culture, the church—properly understood—remains one of our last fortifications. It needs to get out of the Sunday and Wednesday business only, and into the Sunday through Friday business.

By the end of Phase One, the educational establishment should be starting to get a sense that CCE is a threat to their stranglehold on the American mind. The Battle of Ia Drang in the Vietnam War—made famous by the movie *We Were Soldiers*—provides a decent analogy here. When the Americans air-assaulted onto the battlefield, their intelligence suggested a manageable enemy presence. Instead they were met with thousands of additional North Vietnamese troops—their sheer size masked by an intricate maze of underground tunnels. Our network of tunnels—our schools—need to be well developed before we can go on the offensive.

Phase Two: Armed with a network of schools, and with thousands of CCE graduates going into higher education and the workforce, our insurgency can start to go on the offensive—challenging the viability, legitimacy, and monopoly of the government school system. This is the phase during which government schools should start feeling the pinch—in terms of numbers, in terms of dollars, and in terms of their very survival. The pinch starts with the continued exposure of their Marxist agenda, and then morphs into serious advocacy and political campaigns to level the playing field.

The Left had their "defund the police" movement—we should have our "defund the unions" movement, galvanizing freedom-loving policy makers to end the public union boondoggle. The idea of "public unions," as discussed earlier in the book, was never constitutional. (With *Roe v. Wade* on the constitutional ropes today—after fifty years of being falsely "settled law"—there is reason to hope that long shots are not lost causes.) Legal challenges should be brought across the board, and—at a minimum—caps should be placed on how much money public unions can contribute to political candidates. At the federal and state levels, "right to work" legislation should be passed that allows teachers to leave their unions, or at least not pay union dues. The unions need to be isolated and attacked, a tactic Saul Alinsky explains in *Rules for Radicals*. The unions are the problem, not the teachers. Stripped of their power base—which is campaign cash to Democrats and bargaining power in Washington, DC—their influence can be shaken.

Speaking of power, mega-school districts have become a massive impediment to local control and school choice. Governors and school board members should fight to break up large school districts that were expanded to ensure left-wing control. Loudoun County, Virginia, is a classic example—and also the forefront of the battle against critical race theory. The schools there have grown by 400 percent in the past thirty years, from 14,000 students in 1990 to 83,000 in 2020. Meanwhile, just nine school board members oversee all curricular decisions. So while parents protest, school board members ignore them. Large school districts claim to be efficient, but they really just become insulated—hiding behind an ever-growing bureaucracy and shielded from public scrutiny. If larger school districts were broken up, parents would have more sway—allowing more conservative areas to educate accordingly.

Another policy avenue to pursue is getting video cameras placed in the classroom. If we have cameras in school buses, on police officers, in courtrooms, and on public streets, then why not in public classrooms? We pay for the instruction time, we should be allowed to see it. The camera would be trained on the teacher, not the students—and would allow all parents to see what is really taught. The more we allow the world to see what is happening inside government schools, the more parents will clamor for an alternative.

Finally, the key element of this phase is to implement universal educational tax credits at the state and federal level (tax credits are preferred over "vouchers," in that the former are paid by parents whereas the latter is money directly from the government). It's school choice—on steroids, and should be priority number one for every freedom-loving politician for decades to come. *It's a no brainer.* The average expenditure per student in public elementary and secondary schools for the 2018–19 school year was $13,187. Public school resources are allocated by the number of kids who attend, except currently, that money does not follow the student if they choose to go elsewhere. A true educational tax credit program would drive a stake through the heart of government schools—solving two problems at once. It would lead to a mass exodus from government schools, and allow millions of American families to afford to send their kids to classical Christian schools. The average annual tuition for classical Christian schools is well below $13,000—ensuring financial viability for new schools to start, and allowing parents to vote with their feet.

The I-pay-property-taxes-so-my-kids-should-use-the-local-school excuse would be gone. At the same time, government schools would be
forced to *compete* for students and money, incentivizing them to revisit
their failed educational model.

This massive sea change would not come without years of constitutional challenges, but at this point, if our insurgency has begun to gain
popular support—which every insurgency must—the public pressure
for such a change could be immense. Then politicians—our lagging
indicators—will catch on. Remember, it is freedom *of* religion, not
freedom *from* religion. Parents would be given the option to take their
tax credits to any school—public, private, Christian, Jewish, secular,
homeschool, or other. Of course, our hope (and plan) is that most parents are clamoring to get their kids into the best *local* classical Christian
school. And, by now, those schools would no longer be small—but
instead just as large as public schools, complete with competitive sports
teams and powerful alumni networks. Not to mention creating millions
of liberated citizens.

Phase Two could end up being a very long phase. These things don't
happen overnight. Who holds the presidency will matter. The compo-
sition of the Supreme Court may matter even more. And for CCE to
ultimately succeed, an entire alternate framework for the educational
pipeline would need to be established. New teachers colleges, based on
CCE, would need to be founded. More classical colleges and universities
would need to be founded, based on the new demand. Tests like the SAT
would either need to be restored to their original purpose (reasoning) or
replaced with an alternative test—like the Classic Learning Test (CLT),
which was established in 2015 to reset the conversation around testing
and entrance exams. We must build an entire parallel structure, while
tearing down the fake prestige of progressive cathedrals like Harvard,
Princeton, and elite high school boarding schools.

Phase Three: It's doubtful that anyone reading this book in 2022 will be alive when this comes to fruition; maybe, just maybe, we will see it as aging grandparents. With the government school system in retreat (and the Department of Education abolished!) and tax credits in full use, classical Christian education would provide the core of America's education—providing America the opportunity for a diverse America to once again live out our motto—*E pluribus unum*—out of many, one. I was never trained to read that Latin phrase, but my descendants will be. In the end, liberated citizens who love God, love freedom, and seek wisdom and virtue will chart the future for our nation.

In order for any of this to happen, Jesus Christ has to be at the center of all of it. Without constant prayer, faithful application, and the full Armor of God—this insurgency will fail. An important note is required here: simply putting your child in a classical Christian school won't ensure their souls are saved. Just as some parents were astonished to find that homeschooling their children didn't produce the perfect results promised by the religious right of the 1990s, there is no silver bullet. For example, CCE is about paideia formation, but it is not itself Christianity. Christianity without a Christian paideia is given to error and weakness. We see this in the church today. A Christian paideia without actual conversion to Christianity has certain benefits. Western civilization thrived with many unbelievers who nonetheless had a Christian paideia cultivated through home, church, and school. It's also been said that classical education without Christ creates clever devils. In this era, a new strength is needed. The church and home must row in conjunction with the school to bring children to the faith, and cultivate them to be salty citizens of the Kingdom.

If we don't keep Christ the King as the center of our earthly efforts, our insurgency will never leave Phase One. But as Romans 8:31 encourages us, "If God is for us, who can be against us," and all things are truly possible through Christ, who gives us strength (Philippians 4:13). America will need a spiritual revival to undergird an effort of such magnitude; so after you read this book, join us in prayer as we run this race together.

INACTION IS NOT AN OPTION

Now, back to reality—at least for now. It is motivating to picture what the future *could* look like, but right now, we are in a firefight. We are pinned down, caught in an enemy near ambush. The enemy has the high ground and is shooting from concealed and fortified positions. We are on the "X," in the kill zone. Our families, our kids, our country, and our faith are in the crosshairs. We can talk strategy all we want, but our reality right now is tactical. Hand-to-hand combat, face-to-face.

As a former infantry platoon leader, the only thing I know you *cannot* do when you are in the kill zone is to hunker down and hope you survive. Inaction ensures death. You must act, even before you know where the enemy is or exactly what to do. Your only hope is to quickly find cover, and throw your grenades—fragmentation grenades to stun or kill the enemy, and smoke grenades to conceal your counterattack. In most cases, in a near ambush, there is no option for retreat—only to charge at the enemy.

Statues are coming down. Books are being canceled. Our history is being erased. Vice has become virtue, and virtue has become vice. Our country is upside down, and the Marxists are looking to finish us off. That family back in North Carolina, the ones who got me started on this project, got out of the kill zone. They got me out of the kill zone. And now it's time for you to do the same. Will you?

12

AN EXHORTATION FOR PARENTS

Radical Reorientation

The most difficult part of this book is exhorting parents and grandparents to choose a different educational path for their children without shaming them for how, and where, their kids have been educated thus far. Everyone reading this wants the best for their kids, and the best for our country. That's a given. And we all come at this subject with our own background, biases, limitations, and hesitations. That includes me.

My parents were both public school kids; heck, my father was a public school teacher. I was a public school kid—and proud of it. I always swore my kids would be, too. The history of public education in America is rich and deep. If it was good enough for me—as we say— then why isn't it good enough for my kids? Many of us worked very hard to move to "good schools" in the right zip code. I did the same.

I pay the property taxes, too; lots of them. Almost all of us defaulted to the inevitability of public school, and that does not make you a bad parent. It makes you the product of a deeply embedded system that has shaped all of our lives for more than a century.

I also have a chip on my shoulder as it relates to "fancy pants" private schools. You know, the ones with the fancy uniforms and family legacies. I don't like the so-called elite status, and I don't like the arrogance. Families pay their way in, in the hopes that their (average) kids will go to "elite" universities. From there, they believe, they will be set for life. That was my view of most private schools, and, frankly, it still is (excepting classical Christian schools, which reject these forms of elitism). Using money to get a progressive high school diploma in order to get privileged kids into a progressive university just reinforces the failing status quo—pumping more "good kids" into a system designed to turn them into obedient social justice warriors. This privileged path only reinforces the progressive pipeline and power structure.

We all come at the subject of education—of "school"—with our own backgrounds. The Left calls this concept "implicit bias." They cynically apply it to race and gender, but it's very true when it comes to schooling. The goal of this book has been to challenge our long-held assumptions—our biases—about what we think is good for kids, and good for this country.

This book is not simply about dismantling government schools or trashing elite schools; it is about *you*. Your kids. Your grandkids. My kids. My future grandkids. Ultimately, their future is in only one set of hands: *ours*. Knowing what you know, seeing what you are seeing, feeling what you are feeling—what will you do about it? Will we make excuses for ourselves and think we can "fix" government schools? Will we pretend that somehow our government or private school is actually not captured by cultural Marxists? Will we retreat to Christian or Catholic schools who "sprinkle" faith on top of otherwise progressive education? Will we spend our money on vacations and cars—and the latest gadgets—but not on the best possible education for our most precious gift?

These are real questions. Questions we all ask ourselves. And the answers are not easy. The answers require risk, sacrifice, and change, which are not easy to muster, and not easy to manage. But if, as parents, we believe our most important charge on planet earth—our legacy—is the children we raise, then what risk would we not take? What sacrifice would we not make? What change would we not endure to forge faith-filled and patriotic children?

Maybe it's just me getting older, but those three questions answer themselves. I would do anything to provide that for my kids. And so would you. So why, instead, do we outsource nearly all of the most important job we have to secular, progressive, and anti-American government schools? Again, for some, it's habit. For others, it's financial. And for many, it's that we continue to lie to ourselves—that everything will be fine.

We love our children. We teach them forgiveness. We take them to church. We pray with them. We teach them patriotism. We reinforce family. We teach them virtue. And those are all things parents should do for their kids. Yet we ship them off to school *knowing* that what they will encounter there—eight hours a day, five days a week, and nine months out of the year—reinforces *none* of those things. We ship them off to Democrat camp . . . every day. We are complicit—to use another word of the Left—in the undoing of our own beliefs. We are willfully blind to the indoctrination of our kids, because it's easier, cheaper, and more comfortable to excuse it away.

THE KIDS ARE NOT ALL RIGHT

Just doing what we are doing, and hoping our kids turn out "just fine," is not a strategy. I know many good families, good parents, who believe that living in a good neighborhood, with other good families, and going to "good schools" will insulate their kids. Instead, the story unfolds otherwise. The school tells students their parents' beliefs are backward; they are young and naive if they hold traditional values, it's much easier to follow the crowd, social media reinforces every "woke" message, Hollywood does the same, and, voila, you have a high school graduate you don't recognize. Or, just as bad, a falsely fortified graduate who heads off to college and is completely consumed by the next level of "woke" educational and social pressure. If I had a dollar for every parent or grandparent who lamented as much to me during my travels, I would be a very rich man.

If you think about it, why should we be protesting at our local school boards? Who has the time to constantly watchdog the superintendent, the school board, the principal, every teacher, and the curriculum? Maybe a handful of parents, but as I shared earlier in the book, my own mother did the same—and nothing changed at the high school. Nothing is changing in the school districts where parents are protesting today. My good friend and cohost of *FOX & Friends Weekend* Rachel Campos-Duffy put it best, saying on our show, "Why do I want my kids in a school where I have to spend my time—which I have little of—protesting against what the school teaches? Why do I want to perpetually fight the very system I am entrusting my kids with?" She is exactly right, and I hope you ask yourself the same question.

The answer: stop doing it. Pull your kids out. Choose a radical reorientation for your life, and the life of your kids. I promise you this: you will not regret it. I'm not saying there's a silver bullet that will solve your every problem—or save every soul—but you will at least give your kids a fighting chance. No school or system is perfect, including classical Christian schools. But, what if, instead of worrying what your kids are learning and undoing the damage done to them, you could joyfully send them off to school knowing that everything you believe, everything our founding fathers were taught, would be taught in that school? It is the most liberating feeling in the world. Now every conversation you have at home reinforces what is taught at school—and vice versa. It is a game changer; a life changer.

This *does not* mean that your kids will be "sheltered." I hear this excuse for inaction all the time, and I don't want sheltered kids, either. This does not mean shying away from the big topics, or not discussing the sins of our past. Every classical Christian school in America takes on the big topics, and examines the reality of human nature. But, instead of throwing our kids into the cultural deep end and hoping they find the right answer, classical Christian education builds a foundation of virtue and knowledge—a lens through which students are prepared to explore and engage with our past, present, and future with *wisdom*. If you missed it, I refer you back to Chapter 10—it's all there.

RADICAL REORIENTATION

When I say radical reorientation, I mean it. Find a school that reflects your values, and visit it. You will be blown away by what you see. Then, once you find that school, move to it (you can find more than three hundred such schools at classicalchristian.org). If you have to switch jobs, switch. If you need to pass up a promotion, pass it up. If you need a longer commute, drive it. If you need to take another job, take it (by the way, every classical Christian school I've ever encountered has a generous scholarship program for families who cannot afford it). If you need to skip vacation to pay for it, skip it. *Oh, but my kids will miss their friends.* If I know anything, kids are resilient (ask a military family). They always make new friends—and they will meet friends, and you will meet families, who share your passion for faith and freedom.

One teacher I interviewed for this project, who switched her own kids from public school to a classical Christian school and initially drove forty-five minutes each way to make it happen, describes the sea change this way: "There was no screaming. There was no yelling. There was no throwing of things. The kids respected the teachers. The kids respected each other. It was weird, because it was a culture of not just information and teaching to the test but character formation. When you have those two things underneath all of that, it's not just teaching to the test. It's not just, 'I need to memorize this.' The cram-pass-forget model. You won't believe this, but they [the kids] will come to love learning so much they will ask to do their homework."

Another parent, whom the teacher recruited to have her child attend the same Christian school, describes her reaction this way: "We're like, 'Okay, lady. That's fine. You don't have to go that far. They'll never *ask* to do homework.' First day of school, first day, there's a forty-five-minute drive. Ten minutes after she [their daughter, the new student] left, she was in the backseat, 'Mom, could I do my homework?' We just about crashed the car, like, 'What?' No kid I've ever heard asking the parents to do their homework. At that point, we knew that she wasn't exaggerating. We didn't think she was at all. The thing is that the teachers all the way down, from admin all the way to the bottom, created such a special environment. We said to ourselves, 'We have to do this.' We can't afford it. I have two kids. We have to figure out a way to afford this and make it work somehow." They made the sacrifices—driving forty-five minutes each day and reaching beyond their financial means—and their kids flourished.

Finally, this brings me back to the family in North Carolina whom I introduced in Chapter 2. Amita Sherwood and her husband, Doug, made the same choice for their two precious little girls. Neither Amita nor Doug attended classical Christian schools themselves, but as parents, after doing their research and growing in their faith, they moved their children to one at their first opportunity, gifting to their daughters an educational foundation that they never had themselves. Sandhills Classical Christian School is located in Whispering Pines, North Carolina, just 7.5 miles from Pete's Restaurant, where I first met them. My conversation with Amita that morning during *FOX & Friends*—during which she extolled the virtues of CCE and encouraged me to investigate further—is what led me to David Goodwin, spawning our partnership. I recently spoke to Amita and expressed my gratitude. She is now chairman of the board of Sandhills, still giving back. Not only has she changed the lives of her two daughters, but she is a frontline leader in our insurgency.

Around the nation, people are waking up and doing just this. People whose names you would know, from walks of life as far afield as professional sports, politics, media, and even blues and rap artists—not to mention the thousands of working parents—are moving their kids and/or putting their support behind classical Christian schools. One powerful example is a former NFL player who, after accepting a coaching position at the University of Alabama and receiving multiple offers to coach in the NFL, decided to give all of that up in order to move with his wife and kids to the classical Christian school that fit them best. For them, that meant leaving the center of the football universe and moving, in their case, to a place without a huge football program. When I spoke with his wife about the decision, she summed it up this way: "Our friends asked us: 'Why would you give that up? It's the NFL, it's Alabama!' I think it's God's grace, we got to go to

Alabama, because I think He showed us what life could be like and what so many people are going after and how empty it is. How these coaches that are celebrities and these players that are celebrities in the NFL and all these things, how empty their lives are and their families are falling apart, their marriages are falling apart, they don't have a relationship with their kids. We just have such a bigger perspective of what we want and that's not it."

If you take the time to see it, you will feel the same way. Once you see a classical Christian school, the first thing you will say to yourself is, *I wish I could go back to school!* It's everything we were supposed to have, but never did. It's excellence, it's rigor, it's joyful, it's faith-filled, it's purposeful. It is the polar opposite of what kids get in government schools. As soon as I found classical Christian education, I realized how little I knew. I am a graduate of two of the most "prestigious" universities in America—Princeton and Harvard—yet I've never read most of the classics. Homer or Virgil, Plato or Aristotle? I've read next to nothing of them in school. I don't know a word of Latin or Greek, let alone really understanding the histories of Rome and Greece. I never studied Shakespeare, and don't think I ever experienced the Socratic method (except from my *one* conservative professor in college). I never had my faith infused into my education; it was always just an accessory. I can't properly diagram a single sentence, and couldn't tell you the difference between a verb and an adverb. I write like I speak. It just is what it is. We were all failed by our government schools, and we didn't even know it.

The other aspect of classical Christian schools is that it's a *real* community—for students, and parents. The academic term for this is "voluntary association"—another concept that dates back to ancient Greece. English common law describes voluntary association as "two or more persons bound together for one or more common purposes."

Classical Christian schools are the product of intentional voluntary association—they are schools, but they are really a shared mission. The bond between parents, students, administrators, and teachers is real; they don't have to be doing this—they want to. When you walk in the hallways, you can feel it.

Contrast this with government schools, which are associated by students' street addresses. They are mandatory associations. The only thing that binds government schools together is where you happen to live. Parents may have moved to that address, likewise with teachers. But, ultimately, given the progressive agenda driven from the top, their geographic choices are overwhelmed by larger agendas. Government schools are ideological islands, increasingly insulated from communities around them—especially conservative communities. As such, the educational mission is diluted . . . down to the lowest common denominator, and then infused with progressive priorities. Walk any government school, as I have many times during this project, and you will be greeted with their mission: diversity, self-esteem, equity, environmentalism, and inclusion. It's not hard to find. It's painted in the hallways—usually in rainbow colors.

During this project, I've visited many classical Christian schools as well. Some small, some large. Some urban, others rural. All of them are bursting at the seams and full of life. What strikes you when you enter them is how much more simple—or classic—they are aesthetically. The hallways and classrooms are simple, walls adorned with Bible verses, portraits of the founding fathers, cursive writing, and the American flag. If you enter a public school classroom, you are immediately hit with the opposite—bright colors and flowery slogans. At first the contrast seems stark, but it's intentional. The "beauty" in classical Christian schools is the knowledge and love of learning fostered in the classroom. The energy is not on the walls, but instead in the mission and the kids. It's the opposite of government schools, which have colorful walls and fancy technology, but an empty mission.

The same goes for elite private schools, and many Catholic schools. Social justice has become the gospel for most parochial schools in our country. It's no better than government schools; in fact, in some ways it's worse. Government schools are silent on faith, but many religious schools are self-loathing—apologizing for our faith and our history. No matter the school, I know something for certain: two or three hours of "church" each week is not sufficient to counteract forty hours (or more) of social justice indoctrination. Following the crowd = enabling the enemy. Or, as the Left often puts it, status quo = complicit.

More importantly, the state of our country right now requires future citizens who are more than survivors of progressive education. Our Republic cannot survive if future generations blindly follow the progressive pipeline and become ambivalent followers of conventional thinking. In this day and age, in 2022 America, our country needs leaders. We need fighters. We need men and women of wisdom and courage. We need the next generation of founding fathers. It's no wonder our culture and politics is so divisive, negative, and toxic today— it's all a product of the progressive project turned Cultural Marxist Paideia. Most Americans don't know any better. A great example is Congresswoman "Comrade" Alexandria Ocasio-Cortez; you can hardly blame her for her politics; she is a product of a system that worships what she preaches. She is not an outlier; she is the result.

DARE YOU TO MOVE

Perhaps right now for you, moving is not in the cards. Driving farther is not in the cards. Paying tuition, even with a scholarship, is not in the cards. That's still not an excuse to not do something. Just ask my friend "Joe the Plumber." As I was writing this book, my plumber came over to fix a broken toilet in our home. We got to talking, and the topic turned to school. Joe told me that he had pulled his second-grade daughter out of school due to New Jersey mask mandates and a liberal curriculum. He and his wife had joined a "homeschool pod" with other parents in our town who had taken their kids out of the same school.

I'll never forget what he told me: "If you don't play their game, you don't have to play by their rules." Not only was his daughter not wearing a mask all day, but the curriculum had been liberated. Their "pod" was teaching the US Constitution, praying before class, and emphasizing patriotism, as well as cutting-edge technology and business concepts. Joe told me that, prior to making the move, he had attended school board meetings and made his voice heard—but nothing changed. So he took the power into his own hands. His closing comment, while blunt, also struck me: "Most people are sheep, looking for a babysitter for their kids." Unfortunately, he's right—public school is an easy default.

My prayer is that, someday, parents across America won't have to turn to homeschooling or "pods" in order to properly educate their kids. In the meantime, stories like this one give me hope. Joe the Plumber, as a father and a patriot, took the lead. He is living the charge of Ephesians 6:4: "Fathers, do not exasperate your children; instead, bring them up in the training and instruction of the Lord." In order to live up to this change, fathers—and of course mothers—need to take the lead. Get your kids in church. Get them off social media. Get them into "training and instruction of the Lord" every day in school.

As we close, three quick caveats are important. First, in all that we undertake, we should be realistic. Every classical Christian school will have its warts, too. In a young movement of street fighters, you may not see the polish of a well-resourced militia. Most schools will need your help and support to thrive and get better. But they're on your side. And, like Washington's army camped in the snow at Valley Forge, wouldn't we all rather be fighting alongside like-minded friends than in a shiny, climate-controlled building controlled by the enemy?

Second, while this book is about classical Christian schools, it's important to remember that the center of Christian salvation is not education, it's grace. Nobody knows this more than me; my life has been riddled with craters that have required mountains of grace. Without the grace of Jesus Christ, and of many others, I would not be here today. I need Christ. Our kids need Christ. We all need Christ. Without a grace-filled life with conviction, children cannot thrive—something I desperately want for my kids. The church, the school, and the family must be dedicated to the reality of God's grace alone, and each child's faith alone. The call to discipleship begins with faith, but this is where classical Christian education picks up. That faith can be made stronger when wisdom and virtue are cultivated.

Finally, while CCE schools are a huge part of paideia formation, what happens in your home and your local church are just as important to the formation of a child. Parents and pastors need to encourage the WCP in the home and from the pulpit as well. CCE does not replace the role of families and faith; it is meant to reflect and reinforce both. It really does take a village, just not the one Hillary Clinton wrote about.

A DANGEROUS WORLD AWAITS

If you're like me, you have a common refrain these days: *I'm terrified about the world my kids are entering.* We all are, for all the reasons outlined in this book—and splashed across your television every morning and night.

As much as I enjoy the political arena—and have written two books about the importance of fighting there—hoping to take back our country that way is impossible. We can't vote our way out of this problem. The same is true with culture. The only solution as big as the problem is deeper—residing in our hearts, our souls, and our paideia. We have to make big, bold personal choices that will alter the trajectory of our most precious weapon: the affections of our children.

We've heard it before: get married, have lots of kids, and raise them in Christian homes. To that I add this: never let them set foot in progressive government schools. Break the cycle! Instead, join a movement—an insurgency—that contributes to something that will outlast your life. In an upside-down world, classical Christian education is the only comprehensive educational model that can restore our Western Christian Paideia, and give our kids and grandkids at least a fighting chance to save America and Christendom.

Join the insurgency! And then spread the word.

ACKNOWLEDGMENTS

PETE HEGSETH: From the very start, deepest love and gratitude to my amazing wife, Jenny. She shared the vision for this collaboration from the beginning, has been a constant source of encouragement, and championed every aspect of the project—including the creation of our affiliated five-part *FOX Nation* film series, *The MisEducation of America*. There is no film without the book, and a lesser book without the film. Jenny made it all happen; thank you, dearest.

DAVID GOODWIN: This work is a compilation of many who discovered and led the renaissance of classical Christian education in our time. Much of the story in this book came through countless evening conversations, in good books, or as these brothers and sisters quietly labored in some corner of the renewal: David Hicks, Gene Veith, Andrew Kern, George Grant, Susan Wise Bauer, Gregg Strawbridge, Douglas Wilson, Ty Fischer, Tom Garfield, Tom Spencer, Wes Callahan, Evan Wilson, Douglas Jones, Chris Perrin, Sheryl Lowe, Martin Cothran, Marlin Detweiler, Patch Blakey, Daniel Foucachon, N. D. Wilson, Andrew Pudewa, Grant Horner, Louis Markos, David Diener, Daniel

Coupland, Ravi Jain, Kevin Clark, Christian Kopff, Michael Johnson, Andrew Smith, Brian Williams, Bill Stutzman, Jesse Hake, Josh Gibbs, Robyn Burlew, Phillip Donnelly, Chris Hall, Steve Turley, John Mark Reynolds, Matt Whittling, Chris Schlect, Greg Wilbur, Ben Merkle, Bill and Maryellen St. Cyr, Bruce Etter, Michael Van Hecke, and Tom Velasco.

Personally, my journey benefited from my spiritual mentor, John Carnahan; my sister, Debbie Harris, who got me into CCE; classical mentor Andrew Kern; and especially my wonderful wife, Stormy, who, but for her thirty-plus years of walking beside me on this journey, I could not have found my way.

BOTH AUTHORS: Both of us would like to thank FOX Nation producer John Case for his prodigious work on *The MisEducation of America* series, bringing the story of this book to life.

Thank you to the team at HarperCollins—especially Eric Nelson and Hannah Long. You both believed in our project from the beginning, clarified our thinking, and improved our product at every step in the process.

Finally, to our Lord and Savior Jesus Christ, may Your Kingdom be advanced through this humble submission.

NOTES

1. Ross Douthat, "A Crisis Our Universities Deserve," *New York Times*, November 14, 2015.
2. *The Writings of Thomas Paine*, collected and edited by Moncure Daniel Conway (New York: G. P. Putnam's Sons, 1894), vol. 4, https://oll .libertyfund.org/title/conway-the-writings-of-thomas-paine-vol-iv -1791-1804#Paine_0548-04_83.
3. Lawrence A. Cremin, *American Education: The National Experience 1783–1876* (New York: Harper & Row, 1980), 21.
4. Ibid., 35.
5. John Dewey, *The School and Society: Three Lectures by John Dewey* (Chicago: University of Chicago Press, 1900), 41.
6. Editorial Staff, "Religion in Public Schools," *New Republic*, November 14, 1915, 33–34.
7. Editorial Staff, "Father Blakely States the Issue," *New Republic*, July 29, 1916, 319–20.
8. Rod Dreher, *Live Not by Lies: A Manual for Christian Dissidents* (New York: Sentinel/Random House, 2020), 119.
9. "Father Blakely States the Issue," 320.
10. Dallas Lore Sharp, *Education in a Democracy* (Cambridge, MA: Houghton Mifflin, 1922), 10.
11. Woodrow Wilson, "The Meaning of a Liberal Education," *High School Teachers Association of New York*, vol. 3, *1908–1909*, January 9, 1909, 19–31.
12. Charles Potter, *Humanism: A New Religion* (New York: Simon & Schuster, 1930), 128.

13. Lawrence Cremin, *American Education: The Metropolitan Experience 1876–1980* (New York: Harper & Row, 1988), 154–55.

14. As quoted by John Dewey, "American Education and Culture," *New Republic*, July 1, 1916, 215.

15. Francis A. Schaeffer, "On Education," Priorities 1982, https://www.schaefferstudycenter.org/francis-schaeffer-on-education.

16. George W. Carey and James McClellan, eds., *The Federalist: The Gideon Edition*, no. 6 (Indianapolis: Liberty Fund, 2001), 22.

17. Pavlos Papadopoulos, "Liberty and Liberal Education," *Imaginative Conservative*, December 25, 2018, https://theimaginativeconservative.org/2018/12/liberty-liberal-education-pavlos-papadopoulos.html.

18. Werner Jaeger, *Paideia: The Ideals of Greek Culture*, vol. 1, *Archaic Greece: The Mind of Athens*, translated by Gilbert Highet (New York: Oxford University Press, 1939), xiv–xvii.

19. Clement of Alexandria, "Stromateis Book One," in Richard M. Gamble, ed., *The Great Tradition: Classic Readings on What It Means to Be an Educated Human Being* (Wilmington, DE: ISI Books, 2007), 169.

20. Justin Martyr, "Second Apology: Chapter 10," translated by Alexander Roberts and James Donaldson, in Logos Virtual Library, edited by Darren L. Slider, 2008 , https://www.logoslibrary.org/justin/apology2/index.html.

21. Clement of Alexandria, "Stromateis Book One," 169–70.

22. Andrew R. A. Conway, "The University of California and the SAT: Speaking the Truth? Parts 1 and 2," *Psychology Today*, August 9, 2020, https://www.psychologytoday.com/us/blog/channel-g/202008/the-university-california-and-the-sat-speaking-the-truth; https://www.psychologytoday.com/us/blog/channel-g/202008/the-university-california-and-the-sat-speaking-the-truth-0.

23. Ibid.

24. The advantage of the seven liberal arts on reasoning tests can be seen in classical Christian schools, like Hope Academy in Minneapolis, that turn out inner-city kids who perform well on reasoning tests and get into the best colleges on their merits.

25. Kaitlyn Schiess, "What Jerry Falwell Jr. Taught Me at Liberty University," *New York Times*, August 26, 2020, https://www.nytimes.com/2020/08/26/opinion/jerry-falwell-liberty.html?searchResultPosition=2.

26. Vigen Guroian, *Rallying the Really Human Things: The Moral Imagination in Politics, Literature, and Everyday Life* (Wilmington, DE: ISI Books, 2005).

27. "A War, a Teacher, a Lesson, and a Story," *Classical Difference* 2, no. 1 (Spring 2016): 8–13.

28. James K. A. Smith, *Desiring the Kingdom: Worship, Worldview, and Cultural Formation* (Grand Rapids, MI: Baker Academic, 2009), 27–28.

29. Jacques Barzun, *From Dawn to Decadence: 1500 to the Present, 500 Years of Western Cultural Life* (New York: HarperCollins, 2000), 67.

30. David V. Hicks, *Norms & Nobility: A Treatise on Education* (Lanham, MD: University Press of America, 1999).

31. Jackson J. Spielvogel and James T. Baker, *Western Civilization*, 6th ed. (Belmont, CA: Wadsworth, 2005), 66.

32. Herodotus, *The Histories*, translation by George Rawlinson (New York: E.P. Dutton, 1910), https://en.wikisource.org/wiki/The_History_of_Herodotus_(Rawlinson)/Book_7.

INDEX

ABOUT THE AUTHORS

PETE HEGSETH is a *New York Times* bestselling author and the cohost of *FOX & Friends Weekend*—America's number one cable morning show. He is also the host of multiple FOX Nation documentaries, including *The MisEducation of America*. Pete is an army combat veteran and the proud father of seven children.

DAVID GOODWIN grew up on an Idaho farm, spent more than a decade in big tech, and quit to help found The Ambrose School in Boise, Idaho. He is the editor of *The Classical Difference* magazine.